DIGITAL
Photography
and Imaging

Stop Taking Snapshots and Start Taking Photographs

David D. Busch

President and CEO
Roland Elgey

Publisher
Al Valvano

Associate Publisher
Katherine R. Hartlove

Acquisitions Editor
Beth Kohler

Product Marketing Manager
Patricia Davenport

Project Editor
Sean Tape

Technical Reviewer
Jerry W. Olsen

Production Coordinator
Meg E. Turecek

Cover Designer
Jesse Dunn

Layout Designer
April E. Nielsen

Digital Photography and Imaging

The Coriolis Group, LLC
14455 North Hayden Road
Suite 220
Scottsdale, Arizona 85260

(480) 483-0192
FAX (480) 483-0193
www.coriolis.com

Library of Congress Cataloging-in-Publication Data
Busch, David D.
    Digital photography and imaging / by David Busch.
        p.   cm.
        ISBN 1-58880-263-9
        1. Photography--Digital techniques.   2. Image processing--Digital techniques.   I. Title.

TR267 .B872 2001
778.3--dc21

                                                                                    2001053648

Printed in the United States of America
10   9   8   7   6   5   4   3   2   1

A Note from Coriolis

Thank you for choosing this book from The Coriolis Group. Our graphics team strives to meet the needs of creative professionals such as yourself with our three distinctive series: Visual Insight, f/x & Design, and In Depth. We'd love to hear how we're doing in our quest to provide you with information on the latest and most innovative technologies in graphic design, 3D animation, and Web design. Do our books teach you what you want to know? Are the examples illustrative enough? Are there other topics you'd like to see us address?

Please contact us at the address below with your thoughts on this or any of our other books. Should you have any technical questions or concerns about this book, you can contact the Coriolis support team at **techsupport@coriolis.com**; be sure to include this book's title and ISBN, as well as your name, email address, or phone number.

Thank you for your interest in Coriolis books. We look forward to hearing from you.

Coriolis Creative Professionals Press
The Coriolis Group
14455 N. Hayden Road, Suite 220
Scottsdale, AZ 85260

Email: **cpp@coriolis.com**

Phone: (480) 483-0192
Toll free: (800) 410-0192

*Visit our Web site at **creative.coriolis.com** to find the latest information about our current and upcoming graphics books.*

Other Titles for the Creative Professional

Photoshop 6 In Depth
By David Xenakis, Benjamin Levisay

Photoshop Web Graphics f/x & Design
By Laurie Ulrich

Photoshop 6 Visual Insight
By Ramona Pruitt, Joshua Pruitt

Paint Shop Pro 6 Visual Insight
By Ramona Pruitt, Joshua Pruitt

*For my son Jonathan, whose 14th birthday on September 11
was filled with horror rather than celebration. My teenager,
like the rest of us, grew up a lot on that day. Also, in memory of
Father Mychal Judge, a friend of a friend, an inspiring symbol of
the brave souls and innocent victims of that terrible tragedy.*
—*David Busch*

About the Author

Two-time Computer Press Association winner **David D. Busch** has been demystifying arcane computer and imaging technology for Linux, Unix, Windows, and Mac OS users since the early 1980s. As a writer, photographer, and contributing editor for ten leading computer magazines, he has more than 70 books and 2,500 articles to his credit, including *Photoshop 6! I Didn't Know You Could Do That...* (2001, Sybex); *Digital Photography for Dummies Quick Reference* (2000, IDG Books); *PC's For Dummies: All In One Desk Reference* (2001, IDG Books); *Photoshop 6 Complete* (2001, Sybex);*GNOME for Linux for Dummies* (1999, IDG Books); *Mastering StarOffice 5.2 for Linux* (2000, Sybex); *Guerilla Guide to Great Graphics with the GIMP* (2000, Prima); and *The Scanner Handbook, Second Edition* (2000, Hewlett-Packard Press/IDG).

In the computer and imaging field, he's been a contributing editor, columnist, or writer for magazines as diverse as *Home PC, Macworld, Internet World, NetGuide, Windows Magazine, Windows Sources, Computer Shopper*, as well as online resources such as ZDNet and the Internet World Web site.

A PR consultant for Eastman Kodak Company for nearly 20 years, Busch has published photography articles under his by-line in *Petersen's PhotoGraphic, The Rangefinder, The Professional Photographer* and other photo magazines. His photos have appeared on the covers of magazines, and in both print and television advertising.

A regular in many of the early computer magazines, such as *Interface Age, Creative Computing*, and *Microcomputing*, David launched his book-writing career in 1983 with pioneering programming books aimed at owners of Commodore, Apple, Tandy, and IBM PC computers. His initial book was one of the first ever bundled with magnetic media—a cassette tape of his own software.

Busch earned top category honors in the Computer Press Awards the first two years they were given (for *Sorry About The Explosion*, Prentice-Hall; and *Secrets of MacWrite, MacPaint and MacDraw*, Little, Brown), and was asked to serve as Master of Ceremonies for the awards in 1987.

His work now centers around advanced guidebooks to the most popular business and graphics applications, especially Photoshop, as well as digital photography, scanning, and other imaging topics.

Acknowledgments

Most of all, thanks to Beth Kohler, senior acquisitions editor and her colleagues at Coriolis, who let me write a digital *photography* book while all the other publishers seem to be scurrying to produce digital *camera* books; Sean Tape, managing editor, who kept things moving smoothly on parallel paths so I was able concentrate on writing the very best book I could; J. W. Olsen, technical editor, who scrutinized my text through a photographer's eye; and copyeditors Margaret M. Berson and Cheryl Duksta, who helped a mildly dyslexic author remain grammatically correct and consistent. Other contributors included Meg Turecek, production coordinator; and Jesse Dunn, April Nielsen, and Laura Wellander, book/cover designers.

Thanks also to my family and the country of Spain, without whom there would have been a lot of blank spaces in this book where the illustrations were supposed to be; and to historian/photographer Candace Wellman for her gorgeous photos of Ireland. Who says research has to be tedious?
—*David Busch*

Contents at a Glance

Table of Contents

Preface

You've taken your last snapshot. Minutes after cracking the covers of *Digital Photography and Imaging,* you'll be able to grab action pictures that capture the decisive moment at a sports event; create portraits of adults, teens, and children that you'll be proud of; or venture into the digital darkroom to transform shoebox rejects into triumphant prizewinners. At work, you'll amaze your colleagues with tightly composed images for the company newsletter or Web site, professional-looking PR photos, and compelling presentations. This is the book that will show you how to explore the far corners of the fascinating world of digital photography and imaging. Whether you're a snapshooting tyro, or an experienced photographer moving into the digital realm, you'll find the knowledge you need here.

Introduction

Predicting that there is a digital camera or scanner in your future is about as risky as forecasting a laser in your living room or a hologram in your wallet. A leading research group prophesizes 38 million digital cameras in North America *alone* by 2003, and more than one-third of U.S. households already have scanners. The laser in your DVD player and the hologram on your credit card will certainly join the solid-state sensor in your camera as another high-tech tool that's become commonplace.

If you're like millions of others, you're probably wondering, now that you've got that digital image-grabber of your dreams, how do you make the most of it? How do you freeze action to preserve a critical moment at an exciting sports event? How can you make your family portraits look professional? What's the best way to create a last-minute product shot in time to upload it to your company Web site? You'll find the answers within these pages.

Digital Photography and Imaging isn't a digital camera or scanner book. It's a book about digital photography, with an emphasis on photography. My goal is to show you how to take great pictures and make great images that leverage the strengths of computer technology, while taking into account the special needs of digital cameras and scanners. I've tried to limit most of the heavy hardware discussion to the first few chapters, giving you the basic information you need to choose and use a digital camera or scanner. You don't need to understand internal combustion to drive a car, but, even so, it's a good idea to know that your SUV may roll over during hairpin turns. The nuts-and-bolts portions of this book won't teach you about internal combustion, but will help you negotiate those photographic hairpins.

This isn't just a photography book, either. It's a *digital* photography book. The focus is on the special capabilities and needs of computer imaging. You'll learn how to take close-up photographs with cameras that have optical viewfinders, and techniques for producing professional-looking portraits with cameras that aren't designed to work with multiple light sources. No fast shutter speeds? No problem! You'll learn a professional sports photographer's secret for stopping action with any camera.

How to Use This Book

There are a lot of books out there with 300 pages of solid information. Unfortunately, they are too often 800-page books! I've tried to relegate most of the background information and boring parts to the bit-bin long before this book hit the printing press, giving you *only* the 300-odd pages of good stuff. Nor am I going to weigh you down with sage advice about reading this book from front to back, reviewing portions until you understand what I'm trying to say, or remembering to hunt for dozens of marginal icons that point out the only portions actually worth reading. I don't care if you flip through the book and read just the chapters that interest you or skim only the odd-numbered pages, as long as you get busy having fun with your digital camera and scanner.

How This Book Is Organized

This book is divided into three parts, which lead you through the basics of digital photography, scanners, and specific techniques for getting great pictures, and then show you ways to apply what you've learned to improve the professional look and presentation of your work.

Part I: The Basics

This part explains everything you need to know to get started making great digital images with your camera and scanner. You'll learn how to choose your equipment, operate the basic controls, and grab some eye-catching graphics.

Chapter 1: Getting Started

This short chapter tells you more about what you'll be learning in the book, explains the key parts of a digital camera and scanner, and lists the recommended equipment you'll want to have to get the most from the techniques described in Parts II and III.

Chapter 2: Selecting a Digital Camera

This basic introduction to digital cameras includes information on how to narrow down the features you really need for digital photography, so you can purchase a model that's easy to operate, but has features that can keep pace with your growing skills.

Chapter 3: Choosing a Scanner

Here you'll learn about scanners, while building a wish list of features for that perfect image-grabber for home and professional applications. Find out when a scanner is faster and better than a digital camera, discover the differences between different types of scanners, and learn how to choose the best scanner for your needs.

Chapter 4: Basic Camera Controls

Even basic point-and-shoot models have lots of buttons and controls to master. You'll want to learn them so you can spend less time pointing, and more time shooting. You'll learn how to use lens controls and lighting, and get the best exposure.

Chapter 5: Composition

This chapter introduces composition, with tips for planning a picture, finding a center of interest, basic posing, and choosing subject distance for that perfect shot. Learn how to conceptualize and plan your photos, choose your subjects, find out where to stand, and how to position people and things in your pictures.

Part II: Making Great Images

This part focuses on photography, rather than hardware, offering professional photographer tricks that even the newest neophyte can put right to work for personal and business pictures.

Chapter 6: Small Objects Up Close

You'll learn to make your hobby collections or business products look their best whether on location or in a "studio" that the photographer can set up and take down quickly. Learn how to set up a quick-and-dirty "studio" with effective backgrounds and lighting, and use close-up techniques. Find out how to create product "photos" with your scanner, too.

Chapter 7: Photographing People

This chapter includes tips and tricks for photographing people in both consumer and business/corporate environments, including family group photos, head shots, and more formal portraits. Learn how to arrange and photograph groups, full-length portraits, head shots, and other people pictures.

Chapter 8: Shooting for Publication

Learn how to create pictures for publication, whether your destination is the conventional printing press, desktop publishing software, or some other layout and publishing option. You'll discover how to choose the right subject matter, apply lighting and composition techniques, and perfect your architectural and interior photography.

Chapter 9: Sports and Action Photography

Whether it's your kids' Little League or soccer teams, or the company picnic, bowling tournament, or company products in action, you'll need these tips on grabbing fast-moving subjects. You'll learn how to stop action, choose your spots, and use flash.

Part III: Achieving a Professional Look

Knowing what to do with your images after you've taken them is the real key to looking professional. You may need to compile a slide show, do some image manipulation and retouching, or simply print out hard copies for everyone to admire. You'll learn how in this part.

Chapter 10: Digital Presentations

Family vacations or sales presentations can all be highlighted in a well-designed digital slide show. This chapter covers special requirements for digital photographs that will be used in presentations, with tips on creating digital slide shows for home or business. You'll learn how requirements for presentations differ, and ways to create digital slide shows.

Chapter 11: Editing and Retouching Images

Learn how to improve digital images after they've been shot, using common image editing techniques, with image sizing, cropping, and orientation, along with basic retouching techniques for removing defects like red-eye or spots.

Chapter 12: Special Effects

Here you'll learn how to spice up your images with eye-catching special effects, using your image editor's built-in filters and other features.

Chapter 13: Digital Images for the Web

Digital cameras and scanners are perfect tools for creating Web images. This chapter explains some of the things you must keep in mind when working for the Web. You'll discover the special requirements for Web graphics, how to size and crop a photo for a Web page, the best way to create compressed JPEGs and GIFs, floating graphics, and how to send your digital images through e-mail.

Chapter 14: Printing Your Digital Images

This chapter explains everything you need to know to output sparkling hard copies of your most vivid images. You'll learn what kind of printer to use, the differences between laser and inkjet printers, and special requirements for printing digital images.

Appendix: Image Editing Software

In the Appendix , you'll learn about the popular image editing packages, and find out why they are popular.

Glossary

Here you'll find all the key terms used in this book, plus a bonus selection of definitions of other words that you'll encounter while exploring the world of digital photography, scanning, and image editing.

Stalking the Author

Although I'm not your one-stop source for toll-free technical support, I'm always glad to answer reader questions that relate to this book through non-threatening e-mail channels. Sometimes I can get you pointed in the right direction to resolve peripheral queries I can't answer. You can write to me at **photoguru@dbusch.com**. You'll also find more information at my Web site at **http://www.dbusch.com**. If you discover the one or two typos I've planted in this book to test your reading comprehension, you can find an errata page on the Web site, as well, along with an offer of a free copy of the next edition to the first reader to report anything that, on first glance, might appear to be a goof.

Buyer Be Wary

A final warning: I first came to national attention for a book called *Sorry About the Explosion!* This book earned the first (and only) Computer Press Association award presented to a book of computer humor. Since then, my rise from oblivion to obscurity has been truly meteoric—a big flash, followed by a fiery swan dive into the horizon. So, each of my books also includes a sprinkling of flippancy scattered among all the dry, factual stuff. You aren't required to actually be amused, and you can consider yourself duly cautioned.

The Basics

Chapter 1

Getting Started

The first step to gearing your photography up a notch is to know where you're going, and to understand the tools you'll use along the way. This chapter summarizes the thrust of this book, and introduces you to the basic parts of the digital camera and scanner.

Why This Book?

Truman Capote once dismissed the efforts of a lesser author by observing, "That's not writing—that's typing." In the same vein, pointing your camera and pushing the button isn't photography—it's snapshooting. Whether you're capturing an image that will help you recall a treasured vacation years later, or just grabbing a shot of your DVD player for a photographic insurance inventory, you'll enjoy your digital camera a lot more if you put some thought into what you're doing. Although the snapshot is a time-honored American institution, consistently producing images at the next level, and beyond, is a great deal more satisfying.

I wrote this, my third digital photography book, because I felt that too many of the books on the shelves concentrated on the gee-whiz aspects of the technology and stuff that's only peripherally related to picture-taking. I examined several dozen existing books before sitting down to write this one. They averaged about 16 chapters each, which broke down into, unfortunately, perhaps only 3 or 4 chapters actually dealing with digital photography. These were prefaced by chatty chapters explaining the history of digital photography, the pros and cons of digital cameras, and acronym-hobbled discussions of charge-coupled devices (CCD), complementary metal oxide semiconductors (CMOS), and contact image sensors (CIS). There were thick sections on selecting storage media, and each had perhaps half a dozen chapters on image editing.

I'm going to dispense with most of the background "historical" stuff with a few paragraphs later in this chapter. I suspect you don't need any convincing that digital imaging is cool, and you probably have little interest in ancient history. I figure that you don't really want to know anything about amorphous semiconductors, wouldn't bother to read separate chapters on digital camera peripheral devices, and if you want a Photoshop book, you'll buy a Photoshop book.

Further, the manual that came with your camera probably has lots of great tips on how to turn it on, focus, and snap off a picture. There are plenty of general-purpose photography guides that apply equally to point-and-shoot film cameras as to the average digital model.

This book instead concentrates on creative techniques for the digital photographer. There's a bit of nuts-and-bolts information in these first three chapters, and I've included an absolute minimum number of those mandatory chapters on image editing at the end. But everything in between emphasizes getting those shots you really want. If you have a Windows PC or Macintosh and a digital camera, you'll find what you need here. You'll learn:

- Creative posing for group and individual portraits
- How to capture close-up scenes on your desktop using the digital camera's special capabilities
- Using a scanner for close-ups of 3D objects
- How to get great sports and action photos
- Why you need to think fast in spot news situations, and how digital cameras can help
- Tips for taking pictures that will get published
- Professional tips for removing defects
- When a scanner can and *should* be used instead of a digital camera
- Easy special effects that can transform any photograph

Who Are You?

This book is aimed squarely at digital camera buffs and business people who want to go beyond point-and-click snapshooting and explore the world of photography to enrich their lives or do their jobs better. If you've learned most of your digital camera's basic features and now wonder what you can do with them, this is your dream guide to pixel proficiency. If you fall into one of the following categories, you need this book:

- Individuals who want to get better pictures, or perhaps transform their growing interest in photography into a full-fledged hobby or artistic outlet
- Those who want to produce more professional-looking images for their personal or business Web sites
- Small business owners with more advanced graphics capabilities who want to use photography to document or promote their businesses
- Corporate workers who may or may not have photographic skills in their job descriptions, but who work regularly with graphics and need to learn how to use digital images for reports, presentations, or other applications

- Professional Webmasters with strong skills in programming (including Java, JavaScript, HTML, Perl, and so on) but little background in photography

- Graphic artists and others who may be adept in image editing with Photoshop or another program, but who need to learn more about digital photography

- Trainers who need an introductory textbook for digital photography classes

Who Am I?

Before I was seduced by the dark side of technology, I was a professional photographer. I've made my living as a sports photographer for an Ohio newspaper and an upstate New York college; I've operated my own commercial studio and photo lab; and I've served as photo-posing instructor for a modeling agency. People have actually paid me to shoot their weddings and immortalize them with portraits. I even wrote several thousand articles on photography as a PR consultant for a large Rochester, N.Y., company, which shall remain nameless. My trials and travails with imaging and computer technology have made their way into print in book form an alarming number of times, including eight tomes on scanners and three on digital photography.

So, what does that mean? In practice, it means that, like you, I love photography for its own merits and view technology as just another tool to help me get the images I see in my mind's eye. It also means that, like you, when I peer through the viewfinder, I sometimes forget everything I know and take a real clunker of a picture. Unlike most, however, once I see the result, I can offer detailed technical reasons that explain exactly what I did wrong, although I usually keep this information to myself. (The flip side is that when a potential disaster actually looks good, I can say "I meant to do that!" and come up with some convincing, but bogus, explanation of how I accomplished the "miracle.")

This combination of experience—both good and bad—and expertise lets me help you avoid making the same mistakes I sometimes do, so that your picture-taking can get better with a minimum of trial-and-error pain.

I hope this book will teach anyone with an interest in computers and/or photography how to spread their wings and move to the next level. This book will reveal the essentials of photography and only the *important* aspects of digital technology without getting bogged down in complicated details. It's for those who would rather learn the difference between a digital and optical zoom, and how it affects their picture-taking than find out how charge-coupled devices operate.

What You Need

A few of you will be reading this book to satisfy your curiosity about digital photography before actually taking the plunge and buying a camera or scanner. The information here may help you decide just how much camera or scanner you need.

However, most of you already own a digital camera and want to know, "Is this book for me?" That's an excellent question, because books that try to do everything invariably provide too little information for each of its audiences. I'm going to target information for a broad range of the digital picture-taking public, but if you can satisfy a few prerequisites, you'll find this book will be much more useful to you.

Your Digital Camera

I'm going to assume that your digital camera has certain minimal features common to the most widely used digital models, in terms of resolution, an LCD viewing screen, removable storage, and automated features. If you have a camera that exceeds the minimum specs (which I'll list shortly), each chapter will offer additional suggestions of things you can do with your premium capabilities. If you happen to own a camera that doesn't quite meet the recommendations, I'll have suggestions on how to work around your limitations.

I'm not going to name specific models, for the simple reason that model names are irrelevant. One of the cameras I use regularly is an old Epson PhotoPC 600, which will reach a ripe old age of three or four years sometime during the life of this book. Many of you will be using much newer basic cameras with similar features and capabilities, so the exact model you or I use doesn't matter. I also used a Nikon CoolPix 995, which, at the time I wrote this introduction, had been out only a month. The fact that a year from now many of you will be using better cameras that cost half what I paid isn't important, either.

So, when I talk about 4-, 3.3-, 2-, or 1-megapixel cameras with particular features, I mean to refer to those kinds of cameras generically, not a specific model. The techniques in this book apply to all digital cameras within the rough groupings I'll outline in Chapter 2.

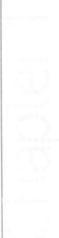

The Specs

For most of the techniques in this book, I'll assume you have a digital camera with at least 2 megapixels of resolution. (If you don't understand resolution right now, don't panic; I'll explain what all these terms mean in Chapter 2.) A camera with a 2-megapixel sensor corresponds to about 1600×1200 pixels, which is enough detail to give you decent 6×8-inch prints at 200-dpi printer resolution. A 2-megapixel camera also can capture enough information to allow some cropping, especially if the image will be used on a Web page, where high resolution isn't necessary.

If you have a 1.0- to 1.2-megapixel camera, that's still cool. I'll show you how to get the most from your resolution, which is plenty for Web pages and 4×5-inch prints. As I mentioned earlier, my trusty old 1024×768-max-resolution Epson camera still gets plenty of use, particularly at its lowest 640×480 setting for eBay auction pictures that must be kept slim and trim for efficient downloading.

Should your digital camera have a 3- to 6-megapixel sensor (or more!), you'll have even more flexibility. You'll be able to make larger prints (full-size 8×10-inch prints are possible at 2048×1536, 3-megapixel resolution), crop small sections out of the center of your pictures, and create more subtle effects. I'll have some suggestions for those of you who have these more advanced cameras, too.

The other most important basic specification will be your lens. To get the most from the techniques in this book, you should have a zoom lens with a 2:1 or 3:1 (or better) zoom ratio and, preferably, a close-up focus setting. Some of the most interesting effects call for a wide-angle or telephoto look and a close viewpoint. However, even if you have a low-cost digital camera without a zoom or close-up ("macro") capability, I'll show you how to use what you have to get similar effects.

Most of the other components, such as amount and type of memory storage, manual/automatic exposure and focusing options, built-in flash capability, and so forth can vary widely. You'll learn how to make the most of each of these features.

Your Digital Scanner

It's not necessary to have a scanner to use this book, but if you do, you'll find some additional techniques that let your scanner complement or substitute for your digital camera. The exact kind of scanner you have isn't important, as long as it's a flatbed model (the kind that look like little photocopiers). I'll explain the differences between the major types of flatbeds, and how their capabilities diverge (that is, some scanners can be used to scan three-dimensional objects, whereas others can't).

Do You Really Need a History of Digital Photography?

I promised to dispense with the history and pros/cons of digital photography in a few paragraphs. Don't blink, or you'll miss this background entirely. In practice, history has no value unless it provides useful perspective. The chronology of digital camera development isn't important; the role of digital photography in the centuries-long struggle to reproduce images *is*.

Digital cameras and scanners are a technological miracle that we've needed for more than 500 years. For millennia, text and pictures were more or less equals: scribes illuminated or illustrated a manuscript at the same time the text was drawn. It took a little longer to draw an illustration, but, as they say, a sketch is worth a thousand words.

However, for much of the last half of the previous millennium, the distribution of text became several orders of magnitude easier than the reproduction of images. Movable type allowed text to reach the masses, but pictures still had to be laboriously carved as woodcuts, engraved in steel, or converted to halftone dots before they could be printed. The transmission of words by telegraph predated wirephotos and fax machines by roughly a century, and the first 35 years of the Computer Age were dominated by text and numbers. Newspaper advertisements in the 1860s were better illustrated than accounts of the Civil War, and computer artists a century later sometimes created portraits by assembling ASCII characters into crude mosaics. (If you've seen these, you'll know why they were considered crude.)

It's only been the past few years that digital cameras and scanners have provided the technology we need to meld text and pictures seamlessly with our documents, computer presentations, Web pages, and other electronic media.

The advantages of digital imaging are simple: If you have a digital camera, computer, and printer, you can capture images, refine, or retouch them, and distribute them through printouts, e-mail, or Web pages. You can accomplish all these things in the span of a few minutes or hours without relying on film manufacturers, photofinishers, professional retouchers, or, in most cases, the postal system.

The disadvantages? Digital cameras still cost more than point-and-shoot film cameras of equivalent features and quality. Digital "film," while almost infinitely reusable, is expensive to buy. Computer-generated prints are still more costly than the drugstore kind. But, to be fair, you buy your camera and "film" once, and then forget about it, and you print only the images you really want—not whole rolls of pictures that end up in a shoebox.

To wind up the historical perspective/pros-and-cons discussion, I'll leave you with a thought. Two centuries ago, unless you had met a relative personally or came from a family wealthy enough to have commissioned a portrait, you probably didn't even know what your ancestors looked like. Your own grandfather might be a stranger to you. Today, you can snap a picture of the old geezer with your digital camera and e-mail it to a long-lost relative who may never be able to drop by for a visit. The average computer owner today can do useful things with images that were beyond the imagination of the wealthiest royalty in the past.

Parts of a Digital Camera

Digital cameras vary widely in appearance, but all of them share certain common components. Although the location for individual components may differ slightly, and the camera body may be square, cubical, or rounded, virtually all digital cameras have a taking lens, an optical viewfinder, a color LCD display panel for previewing an image and showing menus, a shutter release, and a clutch of control buttons. Most also have a slot for removable storage, such as SmartMedia or CompactFlash cards; a built-in electronic flash unit; a top-mounted monochrome LCD panel for displaying the number of exposures left, current camera mode, and other status information; and a serial or USB port for connecting the camera to your computer when you want to download photos. You also may find a tripod socket, or an infrared port for wireless transmission of pictures. Figures 1.1 and 1.2 show the front

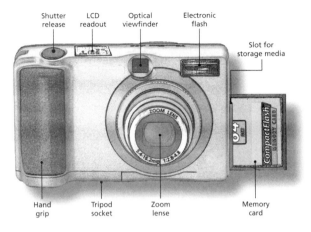

1.1 | Front view of a typical digital camera.

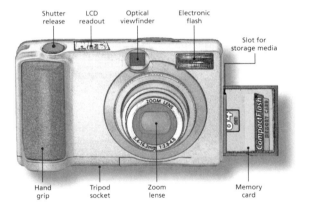

1.2 | Back view of a typical digital camera.

and back of a generic composite camera with the typical placement of components and controls.

I'll explain the functions of each of these components in more detail in Chapter 2.

Parts of a Digital Scanner

The sheet-fed and handheld scanners of the past have all but vanished, leaving us with a burgeoning group of flatbed-style scanners that differ in appearance chiefly by their size. You'll find some that are the size and thickness of an extra-long laptop, and others that more closely resemble desktop photocopiers. There are even a few "all-in-one" scanners that incorporate a printer as well as a scanner.

The typical digital scanner, shown in figure 1.3, is a squat rectangular box a few inches larger on each side than the maximum document size it can accommodate on its glass platen. The most common configuration is for 8.5×11.7-inch originals, but businesses may favor those with 8.5×14 or even 11×14 beds. All flatbed scanners have a lid that closes over the original artwork. Some may have a light source built into the lid so you can scan color slides and transparencies. It's becoming very common for scanners to include one or more front-panel buttons you can use to initiate a scan, or to make a copy. Scanners also have an interface port for linking the unit to your computer through a USB, parallel, or SCSI connection. I'll explain these distinctions more thoroughly in Chapter 3.

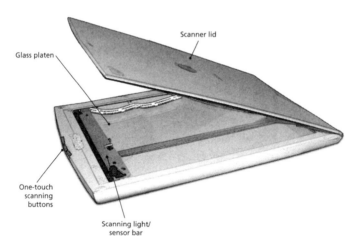

Scanner lid

Glass platen

One-touch
scanning
buttons

Scanning light/
sensor bar

1.3 | Parts of a digital scanner.

Next Up

Now that you have some basic information about the cameras and scanners we'll be using as we explore the digital realm, it's time to make some choices about exactly which devices will best suit our needs. In Chapter 2, I'll describe the various digital camera categories and options you should consider, and then we'll move on to scanners in Chapter 3.

Chapter 2

Selecting a
Digital Camera

This basic introduction to digital cameras includes information on how to narrow down the features you really need for digital photography, so you can purchase a model that's easy to operate, but has features that can keep pace with your growing skills.

Which Camera to Buy

You may have purchased your first digital camera before you ever bought this book. That's great; you already have everything you need to get started taking dazzling pictures. Or, perhaps you're the type who likes to learn everything you can before making a purchase. You may be reading this chapter to make sure that the digital camera selection you make is a wise one, and that your camera will suit your needs for a very long time.

In either case, if you're interested enough in photography to buy this book, it's also very likely that the digital camera you now own or plan to buy in the near future will not be the last one you ever purchase. No matter how feature-laden your current camera is, or how lengthy the feature list of the camera you have your eye on, there will be a better one with more features at a lower price in the future, whether it's a year from now or two years from now.

But that's cool. For most of us, a digital camera isn't a lifetime investment. It's more of a purchase like a computer: a tool we buy now so we can enjoy the advantage of current technology, but with the full expectation of replacing it somewhere down the road with a smaller, better, more powerful, more flexible device—at a lower cost.

No matter what type of digital camera buyer you are—veteran, beginner, or someone who hasn't dipped a toe into the digital waters yet—this chapter will help you. It will assist anyone who is considering the purchase of a digital camera to decide what kind of features are essential, whether the acquisition is likely to be next month or next year. You'll encounter some terms in this chapter that may not be entirely familiar to you, such as *resolution*, *megapixels*, and *zoom*. I'll provide quickie definitions for each of these the first time they are used, but you'll find more complete explanations later in the chapter and in the glossary at the back of this book.

Defining Your Expectations

I managed a camera store for two years, and every Saturday saw an influx of eager photography fans, money in hand (only figuratively, of course), all posing the same question: What's the best camera to buy? I hated to watch their faces fall when I bounced back with a question of my own: What do you plan to do with it? The question "what's the best camera?" is a little like "what's the best car?" Depending on what you plan to do, your needs, like your mileage, may vary. Do you want basic transportation? Do you want an exotic machine that makes your friends drool with envy? Are you looking for a sports utility choice that does everything well once you master its demanding features?

You'll need to ask yourself the "what am I going to do?" question even if you have unlimited funds and could go out and buy the most expensive camera on the market. Photography (digital or otherwise) is one area where the most expensive equipment may not be the best. You can spend a lot, and still end up with a camera that won't do what you want or is so complicated to use that you'll never figure out how to take the pictures you want to take. Unless you put a little thought into your needs, you can easily buy a top-of-the-line camera and end up with a gadget that has features you don't need, is impossible to understand, and makes even simple things difficult to accomplish.

On the other hand, you can't snap up the least expensive model and plan to work around its shortcomings. Unlike a conventional camera that you can sometimes upgrade by buying a better film or a particular add-on accessory, digital cameras don't necessarily "stretch" very well. Rather than make an unfortunate purchase, you'll want to ask yourself the following questions first:

- Is a great deal of image editing in your plans?
- Do you need very high resolution?
- Do you like to experiment, shoot from many different angles and view-points, and take a great many pictures?
- How quickly do you need access to your photos?
- Is your camera likely to be a fairly long-term investment?
- Is size important?
- Is the camera likely to be lost, stolen, or damaged?
- Do you see photography as a creative outlet?
- Do you want to share lenses and accessories with a conventional film camera?

Is a Great Deal of Image Editing in Your Plans?

Many digital photographers plan to do little or no editing of their images. Indeed, they don't even want to *learn* how to fiddle with their pictures. Perhaps you need to take tons of pictures of home exteriors and interiors for a

real estate firm. You want good, sharp pictures, not arty photos. Or, you might be snapping pictures of items for your eBay auctions and will be doing nothing more than cropping your images. Perhaps you require some quickie product shots for an online catalog.

If so, you don't need a high-end camera with extra sharpness and the manual features that will lead to pictures worthy of extensive image editing. An intermediate or basic camera may do the job for you. We'll look at the kinds of features you'll find within various camera categories later in this chapter.

Do You Need Very High Resolution?

Some kinds of photo applications demand higher *resolutions* (the ability of the camera to capture more detail or pixels). Anyone who wants to display large prints (in digital photography, that's 8×10 inches or larger) or crop small sections out of images needs relatively high resolutions, on the order of 3 to 6 *megapixels* or higher (megapixels, or millions of pixels, are the unit used to measure the resolution of digital cameras; the more, the better). If this kind of picture makes up the bulk of your work, you'll need to ask yourself if a conventional film camera might do the job less expensively. When you're thinking of making 11×14-inch or larger prints, or cropping very small portions of images, film still does a better job, less expensively, as you can see in figure 2.1.

However, if big prints and small crops are only part of your overall picture mix, a digital camera can still work for you. Just purchase the highest resolution you can afford and take pictures very, very carefully. I'll explore this aspect more later in this chapter.

Do You Like to Experiment, Shoot from Many Different Angles and Viewpoints, and Take a Great Many Pictures?

If you're a dedicated photo hobbyist, you'll want to make sure your digital camera has the manual features required to produce in-camera effects like those I'll describe in this book. You'll want enough *zoom* (image sizing) capability to provide different perspectives, and enough storage options to keep you from running out of "film" at inopportune times. We'll look at these features more closely, too.

2.1 | An enlarged section of a film image is still sharp (left), but a digital image (right) may look blurry by comparison.

How Quickly Do You Need Access to Your Photos?

The camera you choose can make a difference in how quickly you can download and work with your pictures. Cameras with a USB link or removable storage card and matching card reader in your computer expedite images into your computer at high speed. Cameras that use an old-fashioned serial port can take a minute to download a single picture.

Is Your Camera Likely to Be a Fairly Long-Term Investment?

The president of a major power tool company once remarked, "Most of our customers don't come to us because they want a one-half horsepower 3/8-inch reversible drill. They want *holes*." Similarly, many digital camera buyers aren't looking for a shiny new gadget: They want pictures. Once they acquire a camera that does the job for them, they're not likely to upgrade until they develop an important job their current model can't handle.

In the opposite camp are photo fanatics who always must have the very latest model with the very latest features. They are the equivalent of the car buyers of 20 or 30 years ago who used to trade in their automobile for a new model every year. I loved these folks when I managed the camera store, because we made a little profit on their new camera, then turned around and sold their trade-in for a bit more than we allowed, too.

Such well-heeled photographers are not often disappointed by the constant parade of new hardware in the digital photography realm. New, less expensive, more flexible models are rolled out every month or two. I get dizzy just thinking about how rapidly Nikon has moved from the CoolPix 900 to 950, 990, my own 995, and whatever model made my camera obsolete before this book hit the shelves.

If you don't plan to upgrade, you should get a camera that does the job for you at a price you can afford, and otherwise ignore the cost. If you like to upgrade, on the other hand, you'll want to keep in mind that you'll be duplicating your investment in the near future, and your old camera will be worth more as a hand-me-down to another user than as a trade-in. Don't spend $4,000 for a 4-megapixel digital single lens reflex (SLR; a viewfinder that looks through the actual lens that takes the picture) today if you'll be unhappy and unable to afford the upgrade next year when 6-megapixel models cost $2,000. If your desires are large but your pocketbook is limited, you may want to scale back your purchase to make those inevitable frequent upgrades feasible.

Additional Considerations

Within a particular category, you'll find a surprising number of vendor and model choices. To further narrow down your choices, ask yourself a few more questions.

Is Size Important?

Some intermediate or advanced cameras are small enough to slip into a pocket so you can carry them everywhere. Others with roughly similar features and comparable price tags may be so chunky you'll need a camera bag, perhaps with wheels, to carry them around. On closer inspection, you'll find there are some differences (say, in storage media or zoom lens range), so you'll need to decide if the trade-offs are worth the smaller size.

Is the Camera Likely to Be Lost, Stolen, or Damaged?

Even if you think you need the features, don't buy an expensive digital camera for a child, or for use in dangerous/rigorous conditions, unless you can afford to write the camera off. If you'll be taking most of your pictures at sea during sailboat regattas, you really ought to consider an inexpensive camera or, at least, one designed for underwater photography.

Do You See Photography as a Creative Outlet?

If so, look for cameras with the most convenient manual controls, accurate viewfinders, and other options. If you're serious about photography, you'll probably be happiest with an advanced or prosumer model. Check out the camera in advance. It's not enough to know that the camera offers manual setting of shutter speed and aperture, and manual focus. Do you have to work through three levels of menus to access those features, or can you specify exposure or focus with the press of a button or two?

Do You Want to Share Lenses and Accessories with a Conventional Film Camera?

If you already have a large investment in lenses and accessories, you may be able to justify a digital camera built around a camera body similar to the one used by your film camera. The list of gadgets that can be shared is long, ranging from electronic flash units through filters, close-up attachments, tripods, and so forth. Check compatibility now, before you purchase your digital camera.

Choosing a Camera Category

Most digital cameras can easily be assigned to one of several fairly well-defined categories. Your dream system will fall into one of these.

Basic Point-and-Shoot Models

Anything more sophisticated than a Web cam that costs only a hundred dollars probably falls into this category. Although there are still a few 640×480 resolution models available, most of the point-and-shoot models will have around 1024×768 or 1280×960 (about .8 to 1.0 megapixels) resolution, a built-in flash, and either a fixed focal length (non-zoom) lens or a very modest zoom lens. Focusing may be fixed or limited, and there will be few, if any, manual controls. With basic point-and-shoot models, you press the button and the camera does the rest. Figure 2.2 shows a typical model in this category.

Intermediate Models

Numerically, most digital cameras fall into this category, because these cameras meet the needs of the vast majority of all picture takers. They fall into the 2- to 3-megapixel range (you can probably add a megapixel to these during the life of this

2.2 | Basic digital cameras are compact and affordable.

book), have zoom lenses, and the option of many manual settings for greater control. You'll find these for $400 to $600. These cameras can do most of what you want to do with a digital camera, and, as outlined in Chapter 1, are the standard camera you need for most of the techniques in this book. Figure 2.3 shows a popular intermediate model camera.

2.3 | Intermediate models add more pixels, better lenses, and optional features.

Advanced Models

Spend a little more, and you'll find a growing selection of cameras with a little more resolution (3 to 6 megapixels), a longer zoom range, more manual control options, and other goodies. Generally, though, these cameras are much more complex and potentially confusing to use. You'll find them

2.4 | Features like a hot shoe for attaching an external flash and sensors with 3+ megapixels highlight advanced models.

liberally studded with multifunction buttons and dials, lots of modes, dozens of menus, and thick manuals. If you need the features these cameras boast, prepare to spend some time learning to use them. Figure 2.4 shows an advanced model that's still easy to use.

Prosumer Models

Spend $1,000 to $3,000 and you can add a couple million pixels to your resolution, a few pounds to the weight you'll be lugging around, enough optical glass to detect life on Mars, and virtually every important feature you'll find in a sub-$1,000 SLR film camera. Indeed, in this price range you'll find a few digital cameras that are based on popular Fuji, Canon, or Nikon 35mm SLR camera bodies, with a solid-state sensor replacing the film path. Others, like the model shown in figure 2.5, were designed from the ground up as digital models.

You'll need to spend at least this much for a prosumer model if you want interchangeable lenses and other "real" camera features such as high-speed "motor" drives that simulate the rapid shooting capabilities of professional film cameras, as well as sophisticated multiple flash capabilities.

If you do invest in a "conversion van" of the digital photography world, the downside is that some transformations of 35mm SLRs into the digital realm are clumsy. For example, because the sensors are smaller than the 24×36mm size of

2.5 | Professional photographers and advanced amateurs will find every feature they need in the "prosumer" models.

the standard 35mm film frame, a given lens's field of view (the scope of the image it can encompass) may not be what you expect. Your 55mm normal lens becomes a short telephoto lens, and your 105mm portrait lens becomes a longer telephoto. The price of a prosumer camera is a lot to spend on a device that will certainly be obsolete (from a technological viewpoint; not in practice) alarmingly soon. However, if you've got the bucks and need the features, go for it.

Professional Models

For $5,000 to $30,000 or so, you can get yourself a camera that is in virtually all respects the equal of a professional film camera. You don't need me to outline the features and advantages of these beasts. If you need and can afford one, you already have that information. The rest of us can only drool over the interchangeable lenses, bellows close-up attachments, precise through-the-lens viewing, and other features of these high-end models. I've used various examples in this category off and on since 1995. The scary part is that one $30,000 model loaned to me in the mid-1990s had less resolution than you'll find in an $800 consumer digital camera today.

Fortunately, pros don't see this kind of equipment as an investment as much as an expenditure. What's a $30,000 camera when your client has a multimillion-dollar advertising budget? A full-featured professional digital camera is shown in figure 2.6.

2.6 | Top-of-the-line digital cameras are the equals of their 35mm counter parts (and look like them, too).

Choosing Your Features

Once you've selected the general category of camera that's right for you, you will still need to select the specific features to choose a camera that will take the kind of pictures you want. The chief options to take into account are lens requirements, resolution, storage options, exposure controls, and viewfinders.

Choosing Lens Requirements

The lens is the eye of your camera, which captures and focuses the light from your scene onto your sensor. Your digital camera's lens affects the quality of your images as well as the kinds of pictures you can take. Today it makes little difference whether the lens itself is made of optical glass or plastic: Excellent lenses are available made of either material. What really counts is the quality of the lens, the amount of light it can transmit, its focusing range (how close you can be to your subject), and the amount of magnification (or zooming) that the lens provides. These are some of the things you should consider.

Lens Aperture

The lens aperture is the size of the opening that admits light to the sensor, relative to the magnification or *focal length* of the lens. A wider aperture lets in more light, allowing you to take pictures in dimmer light. A narrower aperture limits the amount of light that can reach your sensor, which may be useful in very bright light. A good lens will have an ample range of lens openings (called "f-stops") to allow for many different picture-taking situations.

F-stops are actually the denominators of fractions rather than actual measurements, so an f2 opening is larger than an f4 opening, which is in turn larger than an f8 aperture, just as 1/2 is larger than 1/4, which is larger than 1/8. You generally don't need to bother with f-stops when taking pictures in automatic mode, but we'll get into apertures from time to time in this book. For now, all you need to know is that for digital photography, a lens with a maximum (largest) aperture of f2 is "fast," whereas a lens with a maximum aperture of f8 is "slow." If you take many pictures in dim light, you'll want a camera that has a "fast" lens. The sensitivity of the sensor, discussed later, is also important for low-light pictures.

Manual Exposure Adjustments

All digital camera lenses with variable apertures (that is, with different f-stops available) adjust themselves for the proper exposure automatically. The only exceptions are the least expensive models with lenses that cannot be adjusted for exposure at all. Serious photo hobbyists and professionals may also want the option found in higher-end cameras of setting the lens manually to provide special effects or more precise exposure. These controls come in several forms:

- *Plus/Minus or Over/Under exposure controls*—With these, you can dial in a little more or a little less exposure than the amount determined by your camera's built-in light-measuring device. Later in this book, you'll learn how to use this sort of control to compensate for unusual shooting situations.

- *Aperture-preferred/Shutter-preferred exposure*—With this option, you can set the lens opening you prefer and the camera will choose the correct shutter speed. Or, you can select the shutter speed you want, and the camera will choose an appropriate lens opening. As you'll learn later in this book, these controls can be used effectively to ensure that the camera will select the aperture/shutter speed combination that works best in low light or, perhaps, to stop action.

- *Full manual control*—With this option, you can set any shutter speed or aperture combination you like, giving you complete control over the exposure of your photo. There are many times when you don't want what the camera considers to be "perfect" exposure. Manual control lets you shoot photos that are "too dark" or "too light" but have the artistic appearance you want.

Zoom Lens

A zoom lens is a convenience for enlarging or reducing an image without the need to get closer or farther away. You'll find it an especially useful tool for sports and scenic photography or other situations where your movement is restricted. Only the least expensive digital cameras lack a zoom lens. Some offer only small enlargement ratios, such as 2:1 or 3:1, in which zooming in closer produces an image that is twice or three times as big as one produced when the camera is zoomed out. More expensive cameras have longer zoom ranges, from 4:1 to 10:1 and beyond.

In addition, there are two ways to zoom a lens. With *optical* zoom, the relationships of the individual elements of the lens are changed to produce the changes in magnification. Because the lens elements can be finely tuned, this produces the sharpest image at each lens magnification. Digital cameras also feature *digital* zoom, in which the apparent magnification is actually produced simply by enlarging part of the center of the image. Digital zoom is less sharp than optical zoom. Indeed, you can often do a better job than most digital zooms by simply taking the picture at your camera's maximum optical zoom setting and enlarging the image in your image editor.

Focus Range

If you'll be doing a lot of table-top or close-up photography, make sure the cameras you're considering have a close-up setting. What's considered close can vary from model to model; anything from 12 inches to less than an inch can be considered "close-up," depending on the vendor. Keep in mind that the closer you get, the more important an easily viewed *LCD display* (that screen on the back of your camera) becomes. You'll also want automatic focusing, if available. Lower-cost cameras with non-zooming lenses may not have focusing abilities at all; they provide sufficiently sharp focus at normal shooting distances (a few feet and farther) and, possibly, at a particular close-up distance (typically 18 to 24 inches). More expensive cameras have automatic focus that adjusts for the best

Zoom Lens Details

The information I've presented so far is all you really need to know about zoom lenses. However, here's a bit more detail for the technically inclined. It's easiest to think of zoom ranges in terms of magnification, but the magnification of an image is actually measured in something called *focal length*. Focal length is the distance from a position in the lens to the plane of the film or sensor, and the magnification is the relationship between the focal length and the size of the film or sensor. Focal length is used to measure whether a lens provides a wide-angle, normal, or telephoto view with a particular size sensor or film.

So, a 6.5mm focal length lens or zoom setting would provide a *wide-angle* picture with a .5-inch sensor, whereas a 12mm focal length lens or zoom setting would provide a *telephoto* effect. Camera vendors often express the focal length of digital camera lenses in terms of how they are equivalent to the common lenses used with 35mm cameras. The reason for that is that most camera buffs already know that a 28mm lens is a wide-angle optic on a 35mm camera, a 50mm lens is a "normal" lens, and a 135mm lens is a particular kind of telephoto. Digital camera sensor size can vary from model to model, so the actual focal length of a digital camera lens means a lot less than its 35mm "equivalent."

setting at any distance. Higher-end cameras may also have manual focusing that can let you "zero" in on a portion of your image by making everything else seem blurry. Figures 2.7 and 2.8 show a pair of close-ups taken with the same Nikon camera, at distances of 4 inches and less than an inch.

Add-on Attachments

Serious photography can often be enhanced with accessories attached to the front of the lens, such as filters, special-effects devices, close-up lenses, or lens hoods. If you need these options look for a digital camera with a lens equipped to accept them. The ability to use add-ons in standard screw-thread sizes (anywhere from 28mm to 52mm or larger) is a plus. Figure 2.9 shows a filter in a standard 28mm screw-thread size.

2.7 | There are close-ups…

2.8 | …And then there are CLOSE-ups.

2.9 | The ability to use standard filters and attachments is a plus.

Selecting Resolution

Image resolution (the number of picture elements, or pixels) your camera can capture, can determine (along with the quality of your lens and sensor) how sharp your images will be. Resolution is measured by the number of pixels wide by the number of pixels high that can be captured by your camera's sensor. The number may not be strictly true because some cameras "manufacture" pixels by a mathematical process called interpolation, but it generally provides a good measure of a camera's relative sharpness. You can establish how much resolution you require by estimating how many of your photos will fall into one of these categories:

- *Low resolution requirements*—Most pictures for Web pages or online auctions; photos that won't be cropped very much; pictures that won't be printed in large sizes. If all your photos are of this type, you may be able to get away with a camera with as little as 640×480, 1024×768, or 1280×960-pixel resolution.

- *Medium resolution requirements*—If you often need to trim out unwanted portions of your pictures or will be making somewhat larger prints, you'll need a higher-resolution camera with resolution on the order of 1600×1200 pixels. Because the actual measurements of the area of the sensor vary greatly, these cameras are most often referred to by the total number of pixels. A sensor with 1600×1200 pixels, or a similar combination that produces two million pixels, is called a *2-megapixel camera*. At the time I write this, a 2-megapixel model has what is considered medium resolution. During the useful life of this book, I expect that medium resolution will expand to 3.3- or even 4-megapixels.

- *High resolution requirements*—If you like to do lots of cropping or make prints that are 5×7 to 8×10-inches or larger, you'll need a high-resolution camera. Today, these are considered models with 3.3 to 5 megapixels or more. In the future, you can expect the number of pixels to increase and the prices to come down, so that 5-, 6-, or 7-megapixel models will be easily affordable by serious digital photographers.

Other Resolution Factors

You'll probably want a choice of resolutions within a given camera, so you can select the best resolution for the job at hand. For example, if you're shooting a large batch of pictures for a Web page or online auction, you'll want to have a relatively low resolution, such as 640×480, available to let you take more pictures, more quickly, with a minimum amount of resizing required in your image editor. You'll also want to be able to quickly switch to maximum resolution to snap a picture you know you'll want to print out.

Your camera's storage format options also can have a bearing on sharpness. Digital cameras usually store photos in a compressed, space-saving format known as JPEG (Joint Photographic Experts Group). JPEG format achieves smaller file sizes by discarding some information that may not be needed in most cases. The JPEG format has various "quality" levels. If sharpness is very important to you, look for a camera that lets you choose the highest quality JPEG mode when you need it, or that has an optional mode for storing in a higher-quality format such as TIFF (tagged image file format).

Some cameras generally label their resolution choices with names like Standard, Fine, Superfine, Ultrafine, and so forth. These terms can vary from vendor to vendor. A typical range in a multi-megapixel model might look like this:

- *Standard*—640×480 pixels
- *Fine*—1024×768 pixels
- *Superfine*—1600×1200 pixels (with medium JPEG compression)
- *Ultrafine*—1600×1200 pixels (with low JPEG compression)
- *Hi-Res*—1894×1488 pixels

Other vendors use more standardized terms like the ones used to define monitor or LCD display resolution: VGA (640×480), XGA (1024×768),

SXGA (1280×960), UXGA (1600×1200), and so forth. To translate these terms into meaningful resolutions, you'll need to check a camera's specifications and see what the terms really stand for.

Storage Options

Some people select a digital camera based on the kind of storage it provides. Virtually all digital cameras have removable storage of some type. Those that don't have storage make you connect your camera to your computer from time to time to download existing pictures to make room for more. In most cases, however, if you need to take more pictures in a session, just buy an additional digital "film" card (usually called CompactFlash, SmartMedia, Sony Memory Stick, or some other trade name). There are still a few things to keep in the back of your mind as you choose a camera.

Number of Photos per Session

The more pictures you take before you can download them to your computer, the more storage you'll need. High-resolution color pictures consume more storage than low-resolution or black-and-white images.

Type of Storage

CompactFlash and SmartMedia cards are the most common. Sony currently offers the most options, with cameras that use its Memory Stick, floppy disks, or even a built-in mini-CD-ROM writer. You may still find some cameras that use other storage devices, such as those from Iomega. Removable storage devices can be inserted directly into a PC Card adapter, floppy disk drive, or other compatible device in your computer. You can also attach an external reader. Your camera also can link to your computer through a serial, IEEE-1394 (FireWire), or Universal Serial Bus (USB) cable. Although I own a CompactFlash reader for my computer, I end up simply linking my camera to the computer directly with a USB cable: it's faster and more automatic. My memory card reader is shown in figure 2.10.

Exposure Controls

Although I mentioned exposure controls under the lens section earlier, exposure involves more than lens settings, of course. Exposure also is deter-mined by the amount of time the sensor is exposed to light (the equivalent of a film camera's shutter speed) and the intensity of the light (which can vary

2.10 | A memory card reader can speed image transfers if your camera doesn't have a fast USB or FireWire connection.

greatly when you're using an external source, such as an electronic flash unit). Digital cameras all have automatic exposure features for both flash and non-flash photography, but some are more flexible than others.

Can your digital camera take low-light pictures without flash? Low-light pictures call for a more sensitive sensor. Camera specs often provide the equivalents to conventional film speeds, measured in ISO (International Standards Organization) ratings such as ISO 100, ISO 200, and ISO 400. The higher the number, the more sensitive the sensor. Many cameras let you vary the ISO rating, making your camera more "sensitive" under particular situations. Later in this book, I'll show you why changing the sensitivity setting is sometimes a good idea, and why it is sometimes not a good idea. As you select a camera, however, look for the stated ISO rating, and see if it can be changed by the user.

Can your camera compensate for backlit or frontlit pictures? Intermediate and advanced cameras may have a simple provision for departing from the "best" exposure determined by the camera's sensor. For example, you may want to adjust the exposure to compensate for subjects that are strongly backlit (that is, an unimportant background is very bright in comparison to your subject matter) or frontlit (the background is very dark), so the exposure is determined by your actual subject, rather than an overall average of the scene. I'll provide some examples of backlit and frontlit pictures later in the book.

Does your camera have various exposure modes fine-tuned for particular kinds of picture-taking sessions, such as sports, portrait, and landscape photography? If so, you can dial in one of these and improve the quality of your pictures effortlessly.

How is the light measured? Digital cameras may have a particular way of measuring light, or may offer several different light-measuring schemes that you can select. For example, your camera may have a "spot" meter that zeroes in on a particular, small area of the image and determines the exposure from that, ignoring the rest of the picture. This feature can be handy when you take many pictures in difficult lighting conditions and would like to specify which area of the picture is used to determine exposure. Or, a camera may measure corners or other specific areas of an image. For the most flexibility, you'll want a camera with several different exposure modes. I'll show you how to use these later in the book.

Can exposure be set manually? I mentioned earlier that cameras that allow setting the lens f-stop manually may also let you choose either shutter priority, or aperture priority (you set one, the camera sets the other, depending on whether a particular fast/slow shutter speed or wide open/closed down aperture is needed for a particular artistic effect), or full manual control over both aperture and shutter speed.

How flexible are the flash features? Some cameras may have a fixed flash range, so that you are limited to shooting only in the range between 2 and 12 feet from your subject. Others have special settings for telephoto pictures (in which you are likely to be much farther from your subject) or for wide-angle shots (in which you are likely to be much closer). You'll also be able to choose whether your flash fires automatically as required, always flashes (useful in some situations), or is always off. With one of my digital cameras, these flash settings apply only when the flash has been popped up from the camera body; you must remember to flip up the flash when it's needed.

It's also useful to be able to use an external flash unit not built into your camera, particularly when you want to use multiple flash for sophisticated lighting, as with portraits. Some digital cameras have a special connector for an auxiliary flash. Keep in mind that those cameras may require that you use only a particular brand of flash, too. (If you don't, the electronic triggering mechanisms may not match and you can "fry" your camera's flash circuitry!)

Viewfinders

You won't have many options for viewfinders. Virtually all digital cameras today have both an optical viewfinder, which can be used to quickly frame an image, and an LCD display screen on the back of the camera for more precise composition and picture review. (Single lens reflex cameras that let you view through the same lens used to take the picture may not have an LCD monitor.)

The only things you need to check in selecting a camera are to see how visible your camera's LCD display is in bright daylight, whether it is large enough to view easily (most digital cameras use a standardized 1.8-inch LCD component), and the amount of power it consumes. The LCDs on some cameras consume so much power that, if the camera is left on all the time, you may find yourself with dead batteries after only a dozen or so shots. Active matrix displays are among the brightest and most power-efficient. Some cameras let you turn on the LCD display only when it is required to compose a picture.

Most of the time, you'll be using your digital camera's optical viewfinder. The location can be important. A window-type viewfinder provides a slightly different view from what the lens sees, which means that part of the image you see may be clipped off when you're taking a close-up. Placing the viewfinder as near as possible to the taking lens reduces the tendency to chop off the tops or sides of heads or other subject matter. Many optical viewfinders have compensation (called *parallax compensation*) that clearly shows the limits of your image. Remember that you also can use the LCD display when framing. We'll look at these factors more in later chapters.

As I noted, if you have a high-end SLR digital camera, you will view your subject through the same lens used by the sensor, giving you a much more accurate preview.

If you wear glasses, you'll want to make sure your optical viewfinder has built-in diopter correction (like that found in binoculars) that you can use to adjust the view for near- and far-sightedness. With such an adjustment, you won't need your glasses at all to see the viewfinder image clearly. If you must wear your glasses while you shoot, make sure you can see the entire field of view. Sometimes a ridge or bezel around the viewfinder may prevent someone wearing glasses from seeing the entire subject area.

Other Features

Once you've chosen your "must have" features for your digital camera, you also can work on those bonus features that are nice to have, but not essential. For example, some digital cameras let you add a voice message to annotate your images with a few seconds of sound. Others may let you record short video clips at low resolution (say, 320×200 pixels). Many have video outputs so you can view your pictures on a TV screen without transferring them to a computer. This is great for previews, and can turn your camera into a portable slide projector! If you shoot many pictures, the ability to choose from cheap alkaline batteries, which you can pick up anywhere in a pinch, to more economical high-capacity rechargeable batteries will be important. Bonus features like these are seldom factors in choosing a camera, but all other things being equal, they are frosting on the cake.

You should, however, consider *ease of use* to be a feature. Some digital cameras have logical layouts, a minimum of buttons and modes, and are very easy to learn. Place a premium on being able to access the most commonly used features without wading through a series of menus. The most frequently accessed features vary from person to person: You may use manual focus or exposure compensation frequently. Someone else may live or die by their ability to adjust shutter speed on a whim.

For that reason, I recommend that you try out any digital camera you are considering buying *before* you purchase it. You may have bought your DVD drive over the Web, but a device like a digital camera, with so many controls and features, is not something to buy through mail order, unless you've had a chance, say, to borrow the same or similar camera from a friend or colleague. Give it a real test drive, using the typical features that you will need. No matter how ideal the specifications may be, until a camera has passed your own ease-of-use test, don't consider purchasing it.

Next Up

By now, you know everything you need to choose the best digital camera for the kind of photography you want to do. You'll find that a scanner complements the abilities of a digital camera quite well, giving you the capability to do some things better, faster, or more conveniently. The next chapter provides the information you need to choose a scanner. They may all look pretty much the same, but scanners can be deceptively different under the hood, where it counts.

Chapter 3
Choosing a Scanner

This chapter will familiarize you with scanners and their features, and help you decide which scanner to buy.

Why a Scanner?

Scanners and digital cameras complement each other perfectly. A digital camera is a self-contained portable device you can take anywhere to capture images of three-dimensional objects of virtually any size. A scanner, when tethered to your desktop computer, excels at grabbing high-resolution images of small objects, especially two-dimensional originals that measure 8.5 by 11 inches or smaller.

Digital cameras lend themselves to the careful composition and thoughtful lighting that foster artistic expression. Scanners, in contrast, are fast-working devices that can be used in a production environment to crank out image after image in a few seconds each. Because scanners are so inexpensive—some very fine models are available for less than $300—they make a low-cost "accessory" for any digital camera. If you're serious about digital imaging, you'll want a digital camera and a scanner. I didn't waste a lot of time in the first two chapters telling you the advantages of using a digital camera. You bought this book—so I figure you're convinced—and the applications for digital cameras are fairly obvious. Virtually everyone has owned a film camera or two, and knows what they can do.

However, scanners are a first-time purchase for many, and there are applications for scanners that you might not have even dreamed of. Here's a quick list of the most popular uses for these digital image-grabbers:

- Convert printed text to an editable document using optical character recognition (OCR) applications. These documents may include letters, brochures, newspaper articles, or other printed material.
- Make copies without a copier using your scanner and printer in tandem.
- Send faxes using your computer's fax modem. A scanner offers two-way faxing at home and can help preserve confidentiality at work by giving you private outgoing fax capabilities without the need to use the departmental fax machine. (Sending out résumés, are we?)
- Capture images of still photos and other objects for presentations. Scanners are great for producing digital images on a tight deadline.
- Create images for Web pages. Put your family photos on your personal Web page, or scan your company's product shots for an online catalog.
- Grab line art—such as logos, decorative alphabets, cartoons, or charts—as well as photographs, for personal newsletters and company publications.

- Produce low-resolution images for screen display or "for position only" (FPO) placement in publications. If your publication is destined for conventional printing and scanning, you can still use your own scans to visualize your layout in your desktop publishing program.

- Create a computerized image database for your real estate firm, hobby collection, family tree, or other application.

- Capture images of three-dimensional objects. If you have a product package or even a small product to include in a presentation, but no photograph, some scanners can capture an image directly. You'll find this route faster than setting up a digital camera.

- Add photos to your email. What better way to convey your message than with an image?

- Capture a photograph or drawing to use as a foundation for original artwork.

- Capture documents such as letters, faxes, memos, and reports for a document management system. These sophisticated systems include optical character recognition to translate the documents into editable text and incorporate search ability so that you can find the information easily.

Did you know all of these? Can you think of any others? Spend a few weeks with a scanner, and I think your list will be even longer than mine.

Kinds of Scanners

I'm not going to spend a lot of time telling you how scanners work, although there are a few paragraphs later in this chapter on resolution where I attempt once more to dispel the Great Resolution Myth. You probably don't care about a scanner's innards and might be perfectly happy if I told you there are tiny invisible elves with little digital cameras inside your scanner, busily snapping away. However, there is one important bit of background you should absorb, to keep from getting confused by all the different types of scanners you may encounter.

In theory, all scanners use very similar components: a light source; a sensor that captures an image line by line; some sort of moving mirror or carriage to allow the sensor to view, or scan, only one line of the original at a time (hence the name "scanner"); and magical circuitry that converts the captured information to digital form. In practice, the chief differences between the various kinds of scanners have to do with the way these components are physically and electrically arranged and the quality of the components themselves.

For example, at the high end you'll find *drum scanners*, the high-priced, high-resolution color separation scanners typically found in the graphic arts industry. The artwork is wrapped around a drum and rotated at high speeds, and illuminated by a laser to produce highly detailed images for electronic retouching and color separating.

We mere humans are more likely to use *flatbed scanners*, which look and work something like a photocopier: You lift the cover, place the original to be scanned face down on the glass, and press a physical button on the scanner or click a button in your software to start the scan. Figure 3.1 shows a flatbed scanner.

3.1 | Flatbed scanners all have the same basic layout.

These scanners can be used with any nontransparent original that will fit on the glass platen. Even thick originals can be scanned with the cover up, and some very large artwork can be scanned in pieces and stitched together within image editing software. Some flatbed scanners can scan relatively flat three-dimensional objects, such as keys, watches, human hands (or other body parts; please don't put your full weight down on the glass!). With a special light source that can be placed above the glass, some flatbed scanners also can capture transparencies or color negatives.

From time to time, you may see a specialized device called a *sheetfed scanner*. These function much like a fax machine, rolling flat originals through the scanner one sheet at a time. You'll find sheetfed scanners as part of fax machines or "all-in-one" devices. The latter, also called *multifunction devices*, combine scanning, printing, copying, and faxing capabilities in one unit. They're useful for small offices, student dorms, or home offices with tight budgets and little space for standalone devices. If you need a photocopier, do a little scanning, send a few faxes, and want a printer included, these units may do the job for you. Because they often contain their own memory, multifunction devices may be able to make copies or send/receive faxes when your computer is turned off.

There are a few other types of scanners, such as the *photo scanner*, aimed at consumers who want to grab images of their snapshots and convert them into images for manipulation or printout with a photo-quality inkjet printer. *Slide scanners* are designed to scan 35mm slides, usually for professional applications, whereas *transparency scanners* can grab images from 6 cm by 6 cm and larger negatives or transparencies. There are attachments for many flatbed scanners that allow capturing images from transparency originals. You also may encounter handheld scanners, video scanners, and overhead scanners that look like a photographic enlarger.

Categories of Flatbed Scanners

This book deals exclusively with the popular flatbed style scanner, available in a sometimes bewildering array of types, even if they all share the flat, photocopier-style layout. This section will help you sort them out. You can't classify scanners using the most popular specifications, bit-depth (number of colors reproduced) and resolution (I'll explain why in excruciating detail shortly), because vendors tend to max out or even inflate those specs as a marketing tool. A 48-bit, 600×1200 dpi scanner can be a sub-$100 entry-level model or a considerably more advanced $400 business scanner. Other features are more reliable indicators.

Entry-Level Scanners

Entry-level scanners offer basic scanning capabilities, sometimes with small sacrifices in speed and quality. They are aimed at new scanner users who want to capture some images, but may not have much experience working with graphics. Entry-level scanners make it easy to slap an original down on the glass, push a button, and end up with a captured image or hard-copy printout. However, you may not be able to add some popular accessories, such as transparency adapters or automatic document feeders.

These models are a good choice if you plan to rely on your digital camera for most of your imaging, and don't know exactly how much scanning you'll be doing. An entry-level scanner's low cost provides a risk-free introduction to scanning and is simple enough to use that you don't need any experience with scanning to get it to work right away. After you've accumulated some experience, you may move up to a better, more fully featured scanner, passing your first scanner along to a family member or needy colleague, or keep it as a backup. Figure 3.2 shows a typical entry-level scanner.

3.2 | Entry-level scanners offer the most-needed features at a bargain price.

Intermediate Scanners

Intermediate scanners are the best option for anyone who needs additional features and more flexibility for just a little more money. A typical buyer may be someone who's creating Web graphics, perhaps capturing images for online auctions, or converting photographic prints to digital files. These scanners typically provide a few extra features, such as multiple front-panel buttons for several different functions, such as scan, copy, and email. They may come with more sophisticated software that allows more advanced image editing. The quality of the scans may be better, too, because of upgraded sensors or optics.

You'll usually be able to purchase an adapter to scan slides and transparencies, as well as an automatic document feeder for scanners in this category. Figure 3.3 shows an intermediate scanner.

3.3 | Intermediate scanners offer better scan quality and more options.

Advanced/Business Scanners

The next step upward is a series of scanners intended for advanced personal or business use. These units tend to be faster, cost a little more, and include a rich bundle of software that provides everything you need to scan, manipulate images, make copies, attach images to email, and send faxes. You'll find optical character recognition (OCR) capabilities and, often, special document management software that can organize a collection of letters, memos, reports, and other documents into a searchable database.

If you use a scanner throughout the day for business applications, one of these scanners will save you time and help you do your work faster. Even so, this class of scanner is still easy enough to use that you'll be able to jump right in even if you have little or no experience in image capture.

Business scanners usually have optional adapters for scanning transparencies (some provide them built into the scanner lid, or include them in the purchase price). Also available are automatic document feeders, often called ADFs. The ADF lets you drop a stack of originals in a hopper and lets the scanner process them one at a time automatically. This feature is especially useful when you're translating an entire document using OCR software, or sending a stack of pages by fax. The only drawback to these add-ons is that with many scanners, you'll only be able to use one at a time. To scan transparencies, you may have to remove the ADF, and vice versa.

Transparency scanning is one application where higher resolution can be important. I'll discuss scanner resolution later in this chapter.

Prosumer Scanners

Only a few years ago, what I call "prosumer" scanners were the only ones available for the desktop computing market. From the late 1980s through the mid-1990s, scanners cost $1,000-$1,500 or more. I once paid $2,400 for a grayscale scanner that could capture a whopping 16 different tones... and I *liked* it. Scanners were considered tools for graphics professionals, and competed chiefly on the basis of image quality, speed, and resolution, with more of any of those three specifications being considered better in all cases. There was a tendency for each vendor to offer only one or two models, all closely clustered in price and features. That was because only a few computer owners were interested in scanners or could afford to buy them, so it didn't make a lot of sense to cut prices or features to offer less expensive models or more types.

Today, technology has made it possible to manufacture good scanners for $100 to $400, so everyone can afford one, especially those who don't use a scanner enough to require the ultimate in speed and quality. At those low prices, it makes sense to cut out a few features to get the price even lower or reduce the quality of the components if you don't need the precision or ruggedness that everyday scanner users demand. Those of us who do need the best performance can still buy the advanced models, which now fall into the new prosumer category, at prices from $500 to $1,500 or more.

Prosumer scanners often have a group of front-panel buttons so that busy workers can still automate tasks when in a hurry. You can scan, copy, email, fax, or capture as a file any original you put on the scanning bed at the press of a button, without fussing with intermediate steps. These scanners use the best sensors and optical systems, and have advanced on-board image processing hardware that optimizes scans before they are sent onward to the computer, providing exceptional image quality. Figure 3.4 shows an affordable prosumer scanner.

3.4 | Prosumer scanners have the resolution and features required for professional graphics applications.

Choosing Scanner Features

Within each scanner category, you'll find sets of features to choose from. Some of these are important (such as how large an area a scanner can capture), but others are effectively meaningless (such as the number of colors a scanner can capture, and its resolution). Unfortunately, the most emphasis seems to be placed on the specifications that don't mean a lot and have little impact on the quality of your scans anyway. In this section, I'll try to sort out some of the key features for you. I'll rank them in terms of *real* importance rather than importance as seen by the typical scanner vendor's marketing department. (I love marketing departments; they are constantly sending me scanners to play with. But their job is to sell you their scanner; my job is to sell you the *best* scanner for your needs.)

Scan Quality

As I'll explain later in this section, the reported resolution of a scanner doesn't have a lot to do with the final quality of the scan. For most flatbed scanners, the type of sensor used and the optical system incorporated in the scanner account for the bulk of the image quality. In the real world, a scanner with 600×600 dpi (dots per inch) resolution (actually, this is a misnomer: the correct term would be *samples per inch*, or *spi*, but everyone uses *dpi* anyway) could easily outperform one that claims 1200×1200 dpi. The former might have a high-quality CCD (charge-coupled device) sensor, true 600×600 dpi optical resolution, and a precision optical system, whereas the latter might feature a relatively fuzzy CIS (contact image sensor) component and fudged resolution claims.

Unless you want to wade through the technical specifications, the only real way to judge scanner quality is by looking at comparable scans. You can find actual sample scans of the devices you're considering on the Web at **www.zdnet.com.** That organization tests scanners in a real laboratory using scientific methods that ignore resolution claims in favor of provable performance.

Scanner Speed

This factor varies in importance from user to user. If you make many scans or produce high-resolution scans of large originals, scanner speed can be vital. It's one thing to have to wait an extra 20 seconds to complete a scan once or twice a day. It's another thing to have to sit there staring impatiently at your display all day long, every day.

CCD vs. CIS

CCD scanners use a highly sensitive solid state sensor measuring about 1.5 to 2 inches in width, a relatively bright light (often a fluorescent tube), and precision optics and mirrors to capture an image. A CIS scanner has no such optical path at all: The sensor itself, which is the actual width of the scanned area, moves underneath the glass a few millimeters away from the original, which is illuminated by relatively dim red, green, and blue LEDs (light-emitting diodes). Because of this configuration, CIS scanners have limited depth of focus and depth of illumination, so the scanned object must be very flat and very close to the glass surface. This precludes scanning 3D objects, or, often, even pages with creases. In the past, CIS scanners have been cheaper to build and have produced significantly lower-quality images, but both the cost advantages and the quality differences relative to CCD scanners have been reduced in recent years. Win some, lose some. You needn't dismiss CIS scanners as an option, but keep their limitations in mind when making a choice, and compare the quality you get before buying.

However, if all you do is grab an occasional image of a much simpler original, such as a snapshot, any scanner will capture the image in 10 to 15 seconds. But you'll be counting those seconds if you're feeding dozens of 8.5×11-inch documents through a scanner. Most vendors supply idealized typical scanning speeds in their specifications, but you're still better off doing your own testing with some actual scans using a computer with approximately the same speed and RAM as your own.

Scanning Size

Flatbed scanners have a physical limitation on the size of the originals you can scan in one operation. The most common size is 8.5 by 11.7 inches, which accommodates both U.S. letter size and European A4 documents. If you scan larger documents, or want to gang a bunch of originals on a scan bed, you'll want a scanner with 8.5×14-inch capabilities. More expensive prosumer or professional models can sometimes handle 11×14- or 11×17-inch originals. Don't forget to check out your future scanner's exact scanning dimensions if a particular size document is important to you.

Physical Size

A scanner won't save you time if you have to travel across the room or office to use it. Make sure your scanner will nestle in a convenient spot on or near your desktop. Most flatbed scanners are only a little larger than the largest area they can scan these days because heftier models have fallen by the wayside. Canon, in particular, specializes in tiny scanners that may be portable enough to carry between your home and office. (If you really want to transport a scanner, look for one that requires only a USB connection and derives its power from that; you won't have to lug a clumsy power brick with you.) There are even a few flatbed scanners that can be tipped on their edge to scan in a vertical position (I'm not making this up) and others with a lid that opens to the side (long edge) of the scanner rather than at the end (short dimension). If your desk space is limited, examine the size and amount of space you'll need to allocate to a scanner before making a purchase.

Software Bundle

Some scanners are furnished with a huge amount of software, including OCR programs like OmniPage, image editors from Photoshop to Photo Deluxe, document management programs, copy utilities, and other goodies. Although the cost of these is disguised within the price of the scanner, the bundles are not free. An expensive scanner may include a full version of Photoshop; an inexpensive scanner may include little more than the software you need to capture images. You'll want to compare prices and make sure you're not paying for software you don't need, or aren't getting the software you really do need.

Color Depth

Color depth is the number of different colors a scanner can capture, usually measured in bits for technical reasons that you don't need to know to use a scanner successfully. The short answer is that the more bits, the more colors a scanner can (theoretically) handle. So, a 24-bit scanner can capture 16.7 million colors, 30- or 36-bit scanners can capture billions of colors, and 42- to 48-bit scanners can grab a Saganesque billions and billions of colors.

On the surface, all those colors may be superfluous. After all, a 1024×768 color image has only 768,432 different pixels. If each and every one of those pixels were a different color (an unlikely event), you'd need only 768,432 different colors to represent them. However, in practice, all those colors are useful. First of all, most scanners lose a lot of information (and potential colors) due to what techies call *signal-to-noise ratios*. Suffice it to say that a 24-bit scanner may end up with only 20 bits of useful information, and a great many fewer colors than required to reproduce an image faithfully. Higher bit-depths like those supposedly generated by 48-bit scanners allow for a great deal of information loss while retaining enough to produce the 24-bit image your computer works with.

In addition, higher bit depths theoretically allow for a greater range of colors, called *dynamic range*. That means that the scanner can preserve detail in very dark areas (such as shadows) while preserving detail in the very bright areas we call highlights. Some photographic prints can test the capabilities of scanners, but you're more likely to need a lengthy dynamic range when scanning transparencies.

The bad news is that scanner vendors lie to you. The specifications they quote often don't have any relation to the real world, because they don't take into account how much information the scanner loses in its complicated electronic innards. One 48-bit scanner may actually be barely capable of producing a 24- or 30-bit scan. Another may offer superior results with "only" 36-bit capabilities.

If you value image quality highly or scan a lot of transparencies, color depth may be especially important to you, so you'll want to check out actual samples (again, using a neutral third party like ZDNet) before making a decision.

> To avoid conflict of interest issues, I probably should mention that when you get to ZDNet, you may find my byline on quite a few of those scanner and digital camera reviews in the Scanner and Digital Camera SuperCenters. I swear I don't get a single penny from any click-throughs you might make while visiting the site. I only do those evaluations as a public service so I can get my hands on the latest and best scanners and cameras.

Scanner Interface

In days past, the interface used to connect your scanner with your computer was important. There were proprietary interface cards that had to be plugged into your computer, and which worked only with a particular scanner. There were SCSI cards that also could be used with hard disks and other peripherals, but were expensive and complicated to install and use. Some scanners used the same slow serial port connections used for modems and mice. A few even tried to link to your computer using the parallel printer port, which was a technological idea whose time was destined to never come.

Happily, today you have fewer choices. Most scanners connect through a universal serial bus (USB) connection. At the time I write this, USB 1.0 and USB 1.1 are the most common; in 2002, the faster USB 2.0 will become more widely used. A few scanners use the IEEE 1394 (FireWire) connection, which is a lot faster than USB 1.x, and about as fast as USB 2.0.

These connections let you attach many more peripherals to your computer and, with scanners that can be powered from the bus, let you dispense with a separate power supply. Figure 3.5 shows the connection panel for a scanner that has a plethora of ports.

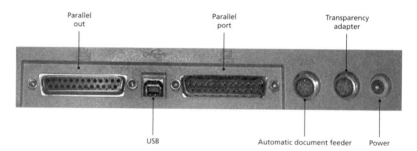

3.5 | Some scanners have even more ports than shown in this illustration, adding SCSI and FireWire connectors to the mix.

Scanner Resolution

All the consumer-oriented articles (and sometimes the books) that deal with scanners harp a lot about resolution. The advertisements boast about how much resolution a scanner has. The boxes the scanners come in print the resolution in large numbers on the front. I used to believe all the myths about resolution, too, until I spent time with some of the scientists who invented the technology we use today. If you've never had a Ph.D. whacking you on the head with a rubber mallet saying, "No! No! No!" until a faulty idea finally left your head, you've missed one of life's rare epiphanies. A true convert, I'm here today to tell you that all the hoopla about resolution, for most users, is *meaningless*. There are two reasons for that.

- *Reason Number One*—Unless you're scanning very small, very detailed objects like postage stamps, currency (if you are, I'll never tell), or transparencies, or are enlarging images a great deal, you'll never, ever need 1200×1200 dpi resolution. You'll rarely need 600×600 dpi resolution. For scanning photographs, grabbing faxes, doing optical character recognition, building document databases—virtually all the work most of us ever do—higher resolutions are not only unnecessary, but actually can be detrimental. They lead to bigger file sizes that occupy needless hard disk space, are impossible to put on a Web page, and are difficult to send as email. Figure 3.6 is an enlargement of a small section of currency scanned at 600 dpi (top) and 1200 dpi (bottom).

3.6 | Highly detailed originals, especially those that include engravings or line art, do benefit from high scanner resolutions.

- *Reason Number Two*—The resolution figures you see quoted by the vendors are often wrong, usually misleading, and don't let you compare the resolution of one scanner to another, anyway. The absolute worst figure to use is maximum *interpolated resolution*, which is the resolution a scanner simulates by creating pixels through a mathematical process. Interpolated resolution isn't entirely fake; the algorithms used to produce the new pixels can be quite sophisticated. However, if you can't reliably compare actual optical resolution between two scanners, how can you expect to get any useful information comparing interpolated figures? A high-quality 600×600 dpi scanner can produce better interpolated 9600×9600 resolution than a ho-hum 1200×1200 dpi scanner in many cases.

In practice, the real limit to the resolution of a scanner—how small a detail it can resolve—is the lens used in a CCD scanner, not the sensor resolution. As I

Where Do They Get Those Figures?

A scanner's sensor is a strip with one element for each pixel captured in the horizontal direction. The sensor moves past each line of the original (or the original is moved past the sensor) to capture in the vertical direction. The vertical resolution is determined by the distance the array is moved between lines. If the carriage is moved 1/600th of an inch between lines, the scanner has a vertical resolution of 600 samples per inch. Some scanners capture the same line twice, slightly overlapping each. That's why you'll see scanners with specifications listing 300×600 or 400×800 optical resolution. In practice, however, these specifications do not reflect a higher resolution in the vertical direction. Because of blurring introduced by the motion of the scanner, the actual resolution in this direction can be *lower* than the horizontal resolution.

said earlier, resolution doesn't measure the quality of an image, anyway, so why pay any attention to this specification? It's a difficult concept to accept, but the real bottom line is that most scanners today have more resolution than you need, so if you like the quality of your scans, don't fret about it.

Other Features

Additional features you'll find in scanners derive from one of two sources. A feature may be something useful that you actually need, or it may be something added just to make the scanner seem to have more capabilities and, by implication, more value. You'll have to weigh these yourself to see if you really want or need these features.

For example, some scanners have lift-off or trick lids that make it easier to scan books and thick documents. There have been a couple of recent scanners with built-in memory card readers so that you can insert a CompactFlash or SmartMedia card directly into the scanner, as shown in figure 3.7. I swear I am not making this feature up (the photo proves that). The rationale is that you can scan directly to a memory card, and then transport the card to a compatible imaging kiosk like those that are popping up in retail stores. There, you can crop and print your scan. Or, you can use the scanner's card reader to transfer images from your digital camera even faster than a direct USB link or dedicated card reader.

3.7 | **Some scanners have high speed CompactFlash and SmartMedia card readers to transfer your scans or digital camera images.**

You may find a scanner with a built-in automatic document feeder, or one with transparency illumination built into the lid. Some have five or six front-panel buttons with one-touch scanning for functions you never knew you needed (such as scanning directly to the Internet). One scanner may be light enough to carry, while another may have what we used to call "road-hugging weight" that minimizes the effects of external vibrations during a scan. Most of these features may be nice to have, but are rarely essential. The choice is yours.

Next Up

We're almost done with the heavy hardware portion of our program. The next chapter explains the basic controls of digital cameras in a generic sort of way, chiefly as a way of ensuring that we're all talking about the same thing when we get started with specific photographic techniques in Part II. You'll learn the relationship between lens aperture settings, focus, lighting, and exposure controls. Then we'll be ready to jump right into creating some immortal photographs with our digital pixel grabbers.

Chapter 4

Basic Camera Controls

Even if you always use your camera in fully automatic mode, you'll want to learn how settings such as lens opening and shutter speed affect your pictures.

Mastering Your Camera Controls

Even basic point-and-shoot models have lots of buttons and controls to master. You'll want to learn them so you can spend less time pointing and more time shooting. By understanding these parameters, you'll know when it is important for you to hold the camera extra steady, or when you should be careful to focus precisely.

If you have a camera with optional manual controls, you'll learn when to override your camera's decisions to improve your picture or achieve interesting special effects. Some cameras have more manual controls than others, so not everything in this chapter will apply to you. Don't be alarmed, however, if not every control is available with your particular camera. In each section where I describe a particular photographic technique, I'll also supply workarounds if your camera doesn't have the setting you might think you need.

This chapter consists largely of implied homework assignments. I'm going to describe the basic controls of digital cameras and explain how they affect your photographs. Your assignment will be to learn how that particular control works with your camera, so you'll know how to make the correct adjustment during some of the practical exercises later in the book.

I know many of you would prefer to skip even the lightweight discussions of camera innards included in this chapter. If you fall into that category, you'll need to read only the sections titled "Essentials" to glean the bare-bones information you must have. You always can come back to this chapter as you work with your camera if you become curious about f-stops and shutter speeds.

Lens Controls: Essentials

The lens is your camera's eye and offers controls over several individual aspects of a picture. These include:

- The amount of light that is admitted to the camera's sensor, which is determined by the width of the lens opening. The exposure also is determined in part by the shutter speed, which I'll cover later in this chapter.

- The sharpness of the image focused on the sensor. The quality of the lens, the size of the lens opening, and whether or not a particular area is in focus all affect the sharpness (in addition to the quality of the sensor itself).

- The size of the image on the sensor. Depending on how far in or out you have zoomed the lens, the relative size of an object in your image can vary from small to large.

- Special attachments used with the lens. Although they are not part of the lens itself, accessories such as filters, close-up attachments, and other add-ons can have a dramatic effect on your pictures.

To work most effectively with your camera, you need to know how to use the zoom lens to make the image look larger or smaller. In addition, you'll want to learn any manual controls your camera provides for setting the lens opening, shutter speed, or focus manually. If you plan to use filters or other lens attachments, learn what size and kind your camera can accept, and how to fasten them to your lens.

That's it for the essentials of lens controls. You'll find more details in the next section.

Lens Controls in Depth

It's good to know exactly what lens controls can do for you, because you can use these settings to improve and enhance your photographs. For example, you can adjust the focus of an image to emphasize or de-emphasize various parts of the picture. You can step back from your subject and zoom in to isolate the subject from the background. Or, you might want to put a special filter on your lens to darken the sky dramatically.

This section explains exactly how lens controls work; Part II offers examples of how to put them to work. If you're a veteran 35mm photographer who uses a single-lens reflex camera (or perhaps a sophisticated rangefinder model), you probably already know much of the information on f-stops and depth of field that follows. However, digital cameras and their lenses differ sharply from 35mm models in ways you might not have considered. I'll outline some of these differences in the sidebar that follows. Skip the sidebar if you're not a 35mm photographer who already has a basic understanding of things like focal lengths and apertures.

Digital Lenses for 35mm Photographers

The frame size of 35mm film is nearly always 24×36mm, so lenses of a particular focal length produce images with size relationships that are well known and familiar. Lenses with focal lengths of 18mm or less produce ultrawide views; focal lengths of 20mm to 35mm are considered wide angles; normal lenses are usually 50mm to 58mm; short telephotos range from 85mm to 135mm; and true long lenses start at about 180mm.

Similarly, a lens with an f1.2 to f1.8 maximum lens opening is considered fast (although longer lenses need a bit less of a maximum aperture to qualify); f2.0 to f2.8 is considered a fairly slow lens; and maximum f-stops from f3.5 to f5.6 are considered acceptable only for specialty optics, zoom lenses, and longer telephotos.

All that conventional wisdom goes out the window when you're talking about lenses for digital cameras. First, the size of the sensor in a digital camera is smaller than the 35mm frame size. One high-end digital model based on a 35mm SLR camera body uses a sensor that measures 15.1mm by 22.7mm, so the effective focal length of lenses used with that camera must be multiplied by 1.6, converting a 50mm normal lens into an 80mm telephoto. Sensor sizes vary, so you'll see models with 8mm-32mm zoom lenses described as having the equivalent focal lengths of a 38mm-152mm zoom for a 35mm camera, whereas a seemingly similar camera with a smaller sensor will claim the same effective range using a 5.6mm-22.4mm lens. The actual focal length of a digital camera lens tells you nothing about its magnification; you'll need the 35mm equivalent for that.

The other invalidated rules of thumb involve depth of field. Your digital camera lens at a real focal length of 32mm may provide the same magnification as a 152mm conventional telephoto, but its depth of field at a particular lens opening will be more akin to that of a 35mm film camera lens with a much wider angle. Accordingly, using selective focus is a bit more challenging with digital cameras.

Aperture Settings

The *aperture* is the size of the lens opening that admits light to your camera's sensor. Apertures are expressed in f-stops, which, as I mentioned in Chapter 2, can be thought of as the denominator of fractions, so the larger the number the smaller the f-stop, just as 1/8 is smaller than 1/4, which is smaller than 1/2. Because an f-stop is a fractional kind of relationship, that also means that the value is relative to the diameter of the lens itself. A setting of f4 on a very small lens will have a much smaller absolute size than a setting of f4 on a lens with a larger diameter. This is all techie stuff that you don't really need to understand to take good pictures. All you really need to know is that the larger the number, the smaller the f-stop; the smaller the number the larger the f-stop, as you can see in figure 4.1.

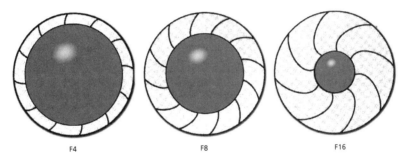

F4   F8   F16

4.1 | Doubling the f-stop number from f4 to f8 to f16 cuts the amount of light reaching the sensor 4× each time.

Usually, your camera will set the f-stop for you automatically when you're using one of its auto-exposure modes for *existing light* (non-flash) or flash photography. Because the f-stop affects the range of your image that's in sharp focus, you may want to monitor what aperture is being used as you take pictures. Digital cameras usually have a display that shows the current f-stop. You may have to press down the shutter release partway to lock the exposure to view this information. If your camera allows you to set aperture manually, you should learn how to do this; some of the techniques described in later chapters work best when you have full manual control.

Relationship between f-stops

It is often useful to understand the relationship between f-stops, especially if you happen to be calculating or adjusting exposure manually. For example, f4 is not twice as large as f8. (It's *four* times as large.) The relationship actually is derived from the square root of 2 (1.4), with each whole-number f-stop corresponding roughly to a power of the square root of 2. So, each of the following numbers in the series represents a halving of the amount of light admitted to the sensor (as you move from left to right), or a doubling of the amount of light (as you move from right to left):

f1.4 f2 f2.8 f4 f5.6 f8 f11 f16 f22

On a film camera, an f-stop is an actual notched "stop" on the lens barrel, with half-stops sometimes marked or given their own detent. That's why you'll see values roughly halfway between the full stops, such as f4.5 between F4 and f5.6. With a digital camera, you won't need these approximations; your camera's electronic exposure meter will set the exact f-stop required or let you set the exact stop manually, whether it's f5.1, f5.2, or f5.6995. It's still sometimes useful to keep the original f-stop designations and their relationships in mind when taking pictures.

One final aspect to keep in mind is that with some zoom lenses the effective f-stop can change depending on how much zoom you're using. A lens' largest aperture might be f2.8 at its normal or wide-angle setting but effectively f4.8 at its longest, telephoto setting. (I'll describe wide-angle, normal, and telephoto zoom settings later in this chapter.) This idiosyncrasy is normally important only when you're taking pictures at the widest aperture (for example, in dim light). In such cases, you'll want to keep in mind that your lens admits somewhat less light at its telephoto position than at its normal or wide-angle setting.

Before we move on, make sure that you understand the following tidbits:

- The aperture is used to control how much light is admitted to the sensor through the camera's lens.
- The larger the number, the more light is admitted.
- Each full stop admits half/twice as much light as the next in the series.

I'll show you how lens aperture affects focus and exposure in later sections of this chapter.

Focus and Depth of Field

As you work with digital photography, you'll find that focus (the area of the subject that is sharpest) and depth of field (the range of your subject matter that is in sharp focus) are two of your most valuable artistic tools. You can choose to narrow your focus so that only a shallow plane is sharp, concentrating all attention on that portion of your subject. Or, you can choose to have everything in your picture sharp and use other means to create a center of interest. (We'll look at these techniques in the next chapter, which introduces composition.) Digital cameras usually make using focus and depth of field as an artistic tool a bit challenging, because under most conditions nearly everything in your picture will be fairly sharp, when compared to the same picture taken with a 35mm camera that, for technical reasons, has less of a sharpness range at a given magnification and f-stop. But don't let that stop you.

It's easiest to think of focus as a plane that's parallel to the back of your digital camera (and its sensor). Everything that lies in that plane will be sharp; anything in front of or behind the plane will be less sharp. The farther an object is from the plane of focus, the less sharp it will be, so something in the far background may be very blurry, while an object very close to the camera in the near foreground also will be blurry.

Although only the plane of focus will be extra-sharp, objects relatively close to that plane will still be acceptably sharp. This range of acceptable sharpness is called the *depth of field* of an image. Luckily for us, depth of field is not distributed 50/50 in front of and behind the plane of focus. In practice, two-thirds of the acceptably sharp area will be in front of the main focus, while one-third will be located behind that plane, as shown in figure 4.2. This usually works very well, because for most pictures the area of interest is around the plane of focus and slightly in front of it.

The amount of depth of field is affected by three things: the f-stop, the focal length (zoom setting) of the lens, and the distance of the object from the lens. The smaller the f-stop, the more depth of field provided in front of and behind the main point of focus (but still adhering to that 1/3-2/3 ratio mentioned earlier). Wider zoom settings provide more apparent depth of field, whereas

4.2 | The kitten's face is sharpest, but some of the depth of field extends to the brick wall in front of it, and less to the other kitten behind it.

telephoto zoom settings provide less apparent depth of field. The farther a focused object is from the camera, the more likely that the "bonus" depth of field (which, remember, is greater in front of the object) is likely to encompass subject matter we're interested in. With a digital camera, this means that depth-of-field considerations are likely to be most important for close-up photographs; anything farther than five or six feet away is likely to be sharp regardless of the f-stop or zoom setting.

A lens set at its widest aperture of, say, f2.8, zoomed to the maximum setting and focused on an object very close to the camera will have the shallowest depth of field. You can use this attribute when shooting portraits to focus all interest on your subject's face. A lens set at its narrowest aperture of, perhaps, f22, set at the wide-angle position, and photographing a subject far from the camera will have the greatest depth of field. That can be important when taking fast-moving sports pictures where you don't know precisely where your subject will be at the time the picture is taken.

Why Not Use Small Apertures Always?

If the smallest apertures produce the most depth of field, why not use them as often as possible? Ignoring the artistic aspects (having everything in focus may not always produce the best-looking pictures), it's important to know that the extra depth of field provided by small apertures comes at a price. An effect known as *diffraction* reduces the overall sharpness of an image at a lens' smallest apertures. So, although more of an image will be acceptably sharp, the overall sharpness of the image will be slightly reduced. A lens is usually sharpest at one or two f-stops smaller than its largest opening. A lens with an f2.8 maximum aperture will usually provide the sharpest overall image (and a good compromise in depth of field) at f4 or f5.6. Smaller apertures are useful when you want even more depth of field and don't mind losing a very small amount of sharpness.

You'll notice that as you zoom in, say to zero in on a face for a portrait, the background goes blurry and objects in the foreground become less sharp. That's because depth of field decreases as the focal length, or zoom setting, of the lens increases. Wide-angle lenses provide a great deal of depth of field; telephoto lenses offer very little.

Ordinarily, your digital camera will focus your images automatically as you shoot, unless you have a so-called fixed-focus camera (which usually means you have a non-zoomable lens, as well). Fixed-focus cameras can produce acceptable sharpness for a typical range of shooting distances (and they sometimes have close-up settings that expand this distance slightly), but you're better off having automatic focus, especially because you can usually override your camera's setting by holding down the shutter release button part way when the part of the image you want to emphasize is sharply focused. Optional full manual focus control is even better. Advanced cameras often have several automatic focus modes and focus areas. For example, you may be able to choose between having your camera collect its focusing information from several areas within the subject area, or to work only with a "spot" focus area (usually in the center of the viewfinder), as shown in figure 4.3.

4.3 | Your autofocus system may select from one of several zones, or concentrate on the center of your subject area.

In Part II, I'll show you ways to use depth of field and focus as creative tools. You'll want to learn to use your camera's aperture and focus controls before then.

Zooming In and Out

The final lens control that you'll need to familiarize yourself with is the zoom control, which adjusts the size of the image. This is the easy one to master. Zooming is familiar to anyone who has seen a kung-fu movie with a shot that zooms in on the alarmed face of the beleaguered hero (or has done the same thing at a family wedding with a camcorder to emphasize the terror on the groom's visage). Zooming enlarges and reduces the size of the image by varying the focal length of the lens from wide angle to telephoto, and back again.

Digital camera owners are lucky. It's much easier to design a sharp zoom lens with the modest focal lengths required by a digital camera sensor, so you can usually count on your lens having more sharpness than your sensor can absorb regardless of the zoom setting. However, there are some aspects of digital zoom lenses you should be aware of:

- Digital camera zooms generally don't provide quite the wide-angle view that a good short zoom lens for a 35mm camera provides. That's a function of the short focal lengths built into digital zoom design; if your 5.6mm lens provides the equivalent of a 38mm lens on a 35mm camera, there's not a lot of engineering room to create a lens much shorter than that with a wider angle of view (there simply aren't too many lenses with focal lengths less than about 5 mm, period). However, you can work around this limitation by purchasing a wide-angle attachment for your zoom, described later.

- The most common zoom ranges for digital cameras are in the 3:1 to 4:1 magnification range. That doesn't give you much in the way of a serious telephoto effect, either. You may end up with only the equivalent of a 105mm to 150mm tele with the average digital camera. Some higher-end models zoom up to 10:1 or more (equivalent to 35mm to 350mm on a 35mm camera), but these cameras are expensive.

- Many digital cameras have both optical (true) zoom and digital (simulated) zoom. The latter imitates a longer zoom effect than the same camera provides optically by enlarging the pixels in the center of the sensor to fill the entire image area. The results can be good, but you'll lose some sharpness when you zoom digitally, as you can see in figure 4.4.

- Like many zoom lenses for film cameras, digital camera zooms often change their maximum aperture as you zoom in and out. Your camera's exposure meter will take care of the change automatically. The important thing to know is that the maximum amount of light-gathering ability provided by your lens will decrease as you zoom in. The amount of the loss may be slight, or it may be more substantial, depending on the design of the lens. One 3:1 zoom may change its maximum aperture from f2.8 to f4.8 as you zoom in (more than a stop and a half difference), while another may change only from f2 to f2.5 (roughly half an f-stop). More expensive lenses generally display less light loss; that pricey 10:1 lens I mentioned early changes only from f2.8 to f3.5 as it zooms.

Learn how to operate the zoom lens of your camera smoothly. Generally there will be a rocker-type switch that zooms out when you press its left side, and zooms in when you press its right side. Your camera's optical viewfinder will zoom as well to compensate for the change in focal length. If you're lucky enough to own a digital single-lens-reflex, you will, of course, be enjoying the same view the sensor will see.

Lens Accessories

Lens accessories let you attach add-ons to the front of your lens to provide additional creative tools, or to improve the quality of your pictures. Typical accessories include the items described in the following sections.

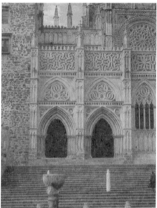

4.4 | Top, a normal shot; center, 3× optical zoom; bottom, 5× digital zoom.

Lens Hoods

Lens hoods prevent extraneous light that isn't needed to make an exposure from striking the lens. A bright light source, such as the sun or a strong lamp located off to either side of your subject, can hit the lens at an angle, causing flare and reducing contrast. Good camera design includes a bit of built-in shading, so you might not need a hood at all. In any case, a lens hood is most important when you're using your lens at its maximum magnification. When zoomed to the telephoto position, the lens has a much narrower field of view, so there is a much larger area for an intrusive light source to occupy. Lens hoods are less needed at wide-angle settings. Longer zoom lenses (over 5:1) tend to benefit from a lens hood, too, because they are generally more complex lenses with many elements that are more prone to degradation when extra, unwanted light starts bouncing around inside the lens.

Filters

Filters are useful add-ons that provide additional effects and capabilities. For example, a *neutral-density* (ND) filter is a dark gray filter that reduces the amount of light reaching the sensor. A *polarizing* filter reduces certain reflections from glass and shiny objects and can darken the sky dramatically. A *fluorescent* (FD) filter adjusts for the incorrect color balance you can get from fluorescent lights. There are many other useful filters that we'll explore later in the book.

Close-up Lenses

Close-up lenses are filter-like devices that allow focusing at a closer distance so you can take pictures of very small objects (or normal-sized objects at indecently close range). These are most useful with cameras that lack very close focusing capabilities, but such lenses are available for one of my digital cameras that already focuses down to .8 inches (2 cm).

Wide-angle/Telephoto Attachments

Wide-angle and telephoto add-ons create a wider view and better telephoto effects by decreasing and increasing the built-in magnification of your lens. Although such attachments do degrade image quality slightly, they let you get pictures you'd never otherwise be able to produce. Tiffen, for example, makes a .56× wide angle (which converts a 38mm lens into a 21mm wide-angle) and a 2× telephoto attachment (which converts a 150mm lens into a super 300mm telephoto), as you can see in figure 4.5.

Special Effect Attachments

Special effect attachments are filter-like accessories that produce special effects, such as multiple images, star effects, or other interesting looks.

Attaching lens accessories can be easy if you have an intermediate- or advanced-level digital camera. These models are usually furnished with a standard screw-thread or bayonet mount that accepts a variety of lens add-ons. If you're very lucky, your lens mount will be compatible with inexpensive third-party accessories, which is great if you need that special filter or accessory. Otherwise, you may be stuck with a more limited range offered by your camera vendor.

Because many digital camera lenses are relatively small in diameter, you may not be able to share lens add-ons with your 35mm camera. For example, my Nikon digital camera takes 28mm screw-in accessories, whereas most of my lenses for my Nikon SLRs require 52mm accessories. If the size differential isn't too great, you may be able to adapt larger lens add-ons for use with smaller lenses through the use of one or more *step-up* rings.

For example, if your digital camera uses 43mm filters and you already have a supply of 55mm accessories for your film camera, you may be able to find a 43mm-55mm step-up ring adapter or, more likely combine, let's say, a 49mm-55mm step-up ring with a 43mm-49mm step-up ring. Make sure that the resulting conglomeration doesn't obscure your viewfinder or flash (or be prepared to live with the consequences). Rings also can function as an unintentional lens hood and clip off the corners of your image, adding an effect called *vignetting*.

You're not sunk if your camera doesn't have screw threads. Tiffen makes a lens mount adapter that snaps onto many common digital cameras and provides 37mm screw threads to accept that company's accessories. In a pinch, you also can simply hold a filter in front of your lens, or tape it to the camera body.

4.5 | Add-on wide-angle/telephoto attachments can give you extra-close views (center) and extra-wide angles (bottom).

Lens Care

Preventive maintenance is the best approach when caring for your lens. If you're vigilant, you can avoid most potential problems entirely. Because of the small front diameter of many digital camera lenses, you'll want to avoid fingerprints, dust, scratches, and other things that can degrade your image. Even a tiny scratch looms large on a lens with a small surface area. Lenses can be a little softer than other types of glass or plastic, so you must treat them with extra care.

Some digital camera owners mount a plain glass filter or a skylight filter (which filters out some of the ultraviolet light that can give photos a bluish cast) permanently on the front of their lens. Such filters are cheap (usually $10 or less) and can be cleaned a little more carelessly than the lens itself. If such a filter becomes scratched, throw it away (or apply a little petroleum jelly and use it as a custom-made "glamour-blur" filter) and replace it with a new one.

Personally, I don't buy the "skylight-filter-as-protection" argument. I want the maximum sharpness my lens can provide, and an extra layer of glass, however carefully cleaned, can only degrade the image a little. I'll accept the use of a filter when I want to take advantage of the filter's effects, but if a permanent filter were so advantageous, camera vendors would include them with their products.

A good compromise is to use a plain glass filter in place of your *lens cap*. Remove the filter to take serious pictures (and remember to be extra careful of your lens while you shoot). However, if you should happen to run across a once-in-a-lifetime fast-breaking picture-taking opportunity, your camera will be ready to fire up and shoot *without* removing the filter. After all, if you happen to spot Elvis pumping gas at a convenience store, are the tabloids really going to care if your pictures are tack sharp?

Here are some additional tips for avoiding lens problems:

- Turn off your camera when it's not being used, particularly if your camera has a retractable cover that closes over the lens. Although digital cameras may turn off their electronics after a few minutes, they may not close the cover automatically.

- Watch your fingers! Even the cleanest hands have oily fingerprints that can blur your image.

- Keep rain or snow from falling on your camera lens. Even the cleanest precipitation contains atmospheric dust and grime.

- Take care when shooting in smoky environments. Smoke can besmirch your lens' pristine surface after even a few minutes' exposure.

- When it does come time to clean your lens, avoid rubbing it with tissue paper. Even the softest tissue, when combined with hard dust grains that have settled on your lens, can be as rough as sandpaper. Instead, blow off dust with a syringe or canned air (be careful not to tilt the can and spray propellant all over your lens!) and brush the lens surface lightly. Use a lens brush or a makeshift brush made by rolling up a piece of lens-cleaning tissue and tearing off one end, as shown in figure 4.6. If a little moisture is needed to remove an oily fingerprint, breathe on the lens or use special lens cleaning fluid.

4.6 | **Sometimes lens cleaning tissue is best used as a brush.**

Lighting Controls: Essentials

The basic lighting controls you need to learn involve using your electronic flash unit. You'll want to master:

- Changing the flash mode. Your options may include always on, always off, automatic mode (flash only when necessary), fill-in flash (to provide extra illumination to light up inky shadows), and red-eye reduction mode (a special flash option that helps reduce those awful red reflections in the eyes).

- How to use external flash units, if they're available for your camera.

- How to use multiple flash units for special lighting effects.

Light Controls in Depth

In Part II, I'll be showing you how to use lighting effectively in a variety of situations. For now, you'll just want to learn what the different types of lighting are, and how your digital camera's controls provide you with different options.

Existing Light Indoors

Indoor existing light is sometimes called *available light*, but the term has met with some contention. Strictly speaking, if you have an electronic flash or a million watts worth of floodlights that you can turn on your subject, that light is just as available as the illumination that's already there. But most of the time when we say available light, we mean the light that exists in an indoor location without any augmentation by the photographer.

Existing light photos usually mean pictures taken without flash, but, as you'll learn later in this book, that doesn't mean you can't craft the light that's there to suit your needs. Indoor lighting may come from windows, overhead illumination, lamps, a fireplace, light bubbling up from an illuminated whirlpool bath, a flashlight placed under your chin while you're hiding in a tent, or any number of sources. To shoot effectively with existing light, you'll need to learn how to switch your flash unit off and use the exposure and focus controls (discussed elsewhere in this chapter) that are built into your camera.

Existing Light Outdoors

Outdoor existing light can be bright daylight, the extra-bright glare found on sandy beaches or snowy ski slopes, moody lighting at dusk or dawn, overcast illumination on a dismal day, or any of countless other outdoor situations you'll encounter. This type of flash-free picture also requires skillful use of your camera's exposure and focus controls.

Time Exposures

Time exposures are a special kind of indoor or outdoor existing light exposure, produced by leaving the shutter open for a long period of time (usually one second to a minute or two). You can get some very interesting effects with time exposures, and I'll show you more than a few of these in Part II. To work with time exposures, you'll need to learn to use your camera's Time or Bulb exposure control. It may also be useful to learn to use your camera's self-timer and master using a tripod to hold the camera steady.

Flash Indoors

You can use flash indoors to stop action at a basketball game, light up a group shot, create a sensitive portrait, or simply grab a picture at your child's birthday party. To use flash effectively, you'll want to learn about your camera's various flash modes. Pay special attention to any red-eye reduction mode your camera may offer. This mode may use a pre-exposure blast from the electronic flash to close down the irises of your subjects eyes prior to the actual exposure, thus reducing the chance of getting those terrible red reflections.

Your camera may have a connector for an external flash or a "hot" shoe you can clip an auxiliary flash onto. You can use the external flash to provide extra illumination, or as a second flash to provide more sophisticated portrait lighting. The important thing to learn is how your camera maker recommends connecting these additional flash units to your digital camera. You may have to use only flash units built specifically for your camera, because some third-party devices use triggering voltages high enough to fry the circuitry of your camera. (I'll provide some tips on how to avoid this disaster later.)

Flash Outdoors

Flash may be useful outdoors, too, when you want to take pictures at night, need to brighten up an overcast day, or simply want to fill in the shadows on a bright day. Your camera probably has a flash mode that allows using the flash even when there is plenty of light, as shown in figure 4.7. It may be an "always on" mode that fires the flash at all times, or, if you're lucky, a more advanced fill flash mode that lets you balance the flash with the existing illumination easily.

4.7 | Outdoors, fill flash can be used to lighten dark shadows.

No matter how you're using your flash, you'll want to check your camera's manual to see what the recommended *flash range* is for your unit. No electronic flash unit has unlimited power, and the farther away your subject is from the flash, the less light it will receive. In fact, flash illumination dissipates with the inverse square of the distance: Relocate an object that's four feet from the camera to a point eight feet away, and it will receive one-quarter as much light (not one-half). The flash range, then, will be a recommended distance, such as 6 to 15 feet, over which the electronic flash can effectively illuminate a subject. There are some subtle ramifications to flash limitations that we'll explore later in the practical chapters. For now, learn about your own camera's flash range, and don't try to take pictures from the 100th row at your next concert!

Exposure Controls: Essentials

The final key camera control you'll need to master are the adjustments that determine how well-exposed your picture is. Your digital camera probably has automatic exposure controls, but these are likely to be more flexible and offer more options than you might think. You'll want to learn some basic techniques.

- Learn about your camera's automatic exposure modes. You may be able to choose from various picture-taking situations, such as sports photography, landscapes, portraits, and so forth, with an exposure mode fine-tuned for the kinds of subject matter encountered under those conditions.

- Find out whether your camera has an aperture-preferred setting (in which you choose the lens aperture and the camera's exposure meter will select the correct shutter speed to match) or a shutter-preferred setting (in which you choose the shutter speed, and the camera selects the aperture). As you'll learn, each of these modes has advantages in specific types of situations.

- See if your camera allows overriding its exposure settings to add a little extra light, or subtract a bit of exposure to produce special effects or to compensate for unusual lighting situations.

- Learn how to lock in a particular exposure that's been calculated automatically, so you can expose for a particular subject, then step back and take the picture from a different position.

Exposure Controls in Depth

Digital cameras do a good job of examining a scene, deciding which parts are important, and then exposing to emphasize those subjects. However, as you exercise your artistic talents, you'll want more control over the exact exposure. Perhaps you want to force a slow shutter speed to produce an arty blurring effect in a fast-moving object. Conversely, you might want to use the highest possible shutter speed to freeze action. Other times, you might want to use a particular f-stop to maximize or minimize depth of field. Or, you may want to add a little extra light to wash out a picture, or subtract some light to provide a subdued, moody look.

You don't need to use full manual control over your camera's exposure to be in command of your exposures. Indeed, you can often let the camera do most of the work, then tweak the image a bit with a plus/minus exposure compensation button. As we plug away through the practical exercises in Part II, you'll learn a little more about how exposure works, and how to make it work for you.

However, you'll want to understand that there is no such thing as perfect exposure. Even if the camera could reproduce every color and every shade exactly, that might not be what you'd want. Instead, a digital camera's exposure meter does as well as it can. If you think about it, calculating an exposure is a tricky proposition, even with a photo that's seemingly as simple as a portrait. If your subject happened to be a Kabuki performer or mime, their pale white makeup would reflect much more light than if your subject were someone with a deep tan or dark complexion. What if there were other light sources or bright objects within the frame? Wouldn't that throw off the exposure meter? Or, how about a black velvet background?

In practice, an exposure meter may average all the light in the frame, select only what its programming indicates may be important areas, or concentrate on a specific portion of the picture (usually the center). On average, exposure programs assume that important subject areas reflect about 18 percent of the light. (This figure was determined by photographic scientists who presumably gave it a great deal of thought.) You may even have seen one of the professional photographer's 18% gray cards, which are sometimes used as an exposure standard, or as a neutral color reference for a photographic colorist. In practice, a digital camera's exposure circuitry will assume that the light it is reading represents 18% of the illumination falling on a subject and adjust the exposure to match. If your subject is more or less reflective (for example, there is a lot of sky in the photo), you may want to make an adjustment to compensate.

Understanding Shutter Speeds

Your chief tools for controlling the exposure are the aperture (amount of light reaching the sensor), discussed earlier in this chapter, and the shutter speed, which controls the length of time the light is allowed to expose the sensor.

Shutter speeds are typically measured in whole seconds and fractions of a second, and, in a typical camera, may range from 1 second to more typical speeds like 1/60th and 1/125th of a second to incredibly brief exposures on the order of 1/2000th of a second. Digital cameras may use signals to the CCD to simulate an electronic shutter, or may have a built-in mechanical shutter that actually opens and closes for the requisite amount of time. Some cameras use a combination of both.

Shutter speed affects not only exposure, but also the action-stopping capabilities of your camera. At slow shutter speeds, your subject has plenty of time to move during an exposure, creating a blurry effect. At higher shutter speeds, action can be frozen in time, as you can see in figure 4.8. Subject motion isn't the only potential cause of smudgy pictures, either: If your hand shakes during an exposure, you'll find that everything in the scene looks blurry. Learning to select the right shutter speed for a particular picture-taking situation can be an important step on the road to photographic artistry.

4.8 | A high shutter speed freezes action.

You don't need to worry about the finer points of exposure now. I'll offer suggestions for getting the best exposure when we tackle each of the projects in the book. All you need to learn is how to manage your camera's exposure modes.

Other Controls: Essentials

Depending on your digital camera model, you may have several dozen other controls to master before you'll have complete dominance over your image grabber. You don't need to learn all of them immediately. As you work with your camera, you'll discover that a particular control can enhance your picture-taking experience, sending you scurrying to your camera's instruction manual for enlightenment. Here's a quick checklist of some of the more common controls you'll encounter.

- *Image size/resolution*—You don't have to take every picture at the maximum resolution possible with your camera. You'll find that you can squeeze more shots onto your storage media at lower resolutions, and may end up with images that better suit your intended application for them. That is, if you're snapping off a large group of snapshots for a Web page, you probably don't need a bunch of super-high-res images when a set taken at 640×480 or 1024×768 resolution will do.

- *Image compression*—Your camera may offer a choice of how much each image is compressed before it is stored on your removable media. The higher the compression ratio, the more images you can store. But on the flip side, you'll lose some picture information (forever) if you squash your pictures down. If highest quality is important to you, learn how to select minimal (or no) compression.

- *White balance*—Every light source has its own color "temperature," which can range from comparatively bluish (at high noon) to quite reddish (at dusk or indoors under incandescent illumination). Your camera may adjust its white balance automatically, or allow you to do it manually. If you find that the color of your pictures is unintentionally balanced incorrectly, learn to use the white balance facility.

- *Image adjustment controls*—Your camera may have built-in image fine-tuning controls that improve the saturation (color richness), sharpen pictures by increasing the contrast, eliminate non-picture artifacts that appear in your images as electronic "noise," or perform other magic.

- *Capture modes*—Some cameras allow taking single shots, continuous streams of pictures (as with a 35mm camera motor drive, multiple shots, or even 30 to 40 second movie clips). You may find these useful for sports photography, grabbing motion for your Web pages, or analyzing your golf swing.

- *Sensitivity*—Digital camera sensors usually default to the same sensitivity or speed as an ISO (International Standards Organization) 100 film. You may be able to set this value to ISO 200, 400, or 800 when you need extra sensitivity, or let the camera choose the setting itself. Keep in mind that boosting sensitivity in a digital camera has the same effect as choosing a faster conventional film: You'll often end up with extra grain or noise in your picture, even though you can capture pictures in lower light, with faster shutter speeds, or smaller lens openings than you could with a lower setting.

- *Monitor controls*—The color LCD display on the back of your camera uses a lot of juice. To prolong battery life, you'll want to learn how to turn the monitor on and off. Most cameras let you specify how long the LCD display or, indeed, the entire camera remains active when you haven't taken a picture for a few minutes. You also should be able to control what information is displayed on your monitor screen. Choices may range from date/time to focus indicators, a battery life indicator, picture thumbnails, or zoomed views of the photos you've already taken.

- *Viewing and deleting frames*—Among the things you can do with digital cameras that you can't do with film cameras is delete images from your electronic "film" before they ever get to your computer. Your camera may have a quick delete feature that lets you erase an image immediately after you've taken it. Or, you may want to browse through your shots and delete selected frames. The ability to edit images in your camera can save time later on, and stretch your picture-taking sessions by removing bad images from the memory card.

Next Up

The last chapter in Part I introduces the basics of composition. You'll need to know a little of how to arrange objects in your image to produce the most pleasing view. Everything you'll learn about building good pictures can be applied to the practical chapters in Part II. Get ready to dig in, because your basic photographic education is nearly complete.

Chapter 5

Composition

Good composition is music to the eyes. Just as the ear prefers to hear sounds arranged in certain ways, our eyes are engaged and entertained by shapes displayed not in random order but, rather, in specific arrangements. This chapter will show you how to compose your pictures in the pleasing ways that turn good photographs into great ones.

The Tools and Techniques of Composition

Good composition is not a concept that was discovered by accident. Cave dwellers knew that painting an image of a predator on a wall adjacent to a picture representing a human hunter symbolized danger, challenge, or excitement. Early Greeks incorporated proportion and scale into their buildings and sculptures, making them seem alive and vibrant, rather than still and static. Works of art dating many hundreds of years before the invention of photography are treasured today not simply because they are representations of people or scenes from the past or mythology. The very best artwork is admired, in part, because its composition is harmonious and pleasing, like a royal family portrait by Velásquez, or perhaps edgy and disturbing like Picasso's famous war protest painting of the bombing of Guernica. You'll learn that the way objects are arranged in your pictures can be as important as the subject matter itself.

The Tools

Once you move beyond the point-and-shoot stage of photography, you'll discover that you have a whole set of versatile tools—and strategies—that you can use to create your compositions. You can use these singly, or in combination, applying any or all of them to your pictures to create the exact arrangement you want. Here are the most commonly used tools and strategies in your repertoire.

Moving the Figures or Objects

Who hasn't tried to make a group photo more interesting by asking everyone to squeeze a little closer together, or by moving the taller folk to the end of the line or the back of the group? Or perhaps you've photographed still lifes, flowers, or your train collection, and you moved an object to produce a more interesting arrangement.

You'll discover there are many picture-taking situations in which it's entirely practical to move things around to better suit your image or, even, as an experiment to see what might look better, such as in figure 5.1. Posing, which involves arranging body parts—such as arms, legs, and faces—in interesting ways is a related tool. If you're working with inanimate objects or very patient people—and have the time to spare—you'll be able to create interesting compositions with ease.

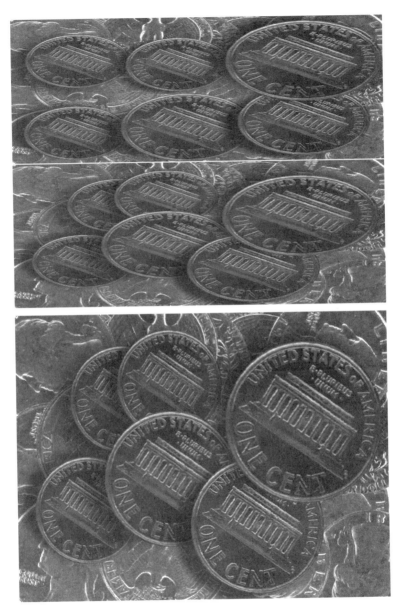

5.1 | Arrange objects carefully so they form pleasing compositions.

Changing Your Point of View

The Great Pyramid of Khufu has squatted stolidly on the same 14 acres of Egyptian sand for roughly 4,600 years, and it isn't likely to move a bit to the right or left to better suit your photographic composition. Whether you're shooting monuments, buildings, scenery, or stubborn humans, you'll encounter situations where your viewpoint must be changed to get an arrangement you like. You may want to stoop to get a lower angle, climb up a bluff or mount a ladder to achieve an aerial view, or step back, forward, or to one side. Often, you'll find that even if you could move a figure or object in your picture, the better choice is to leave your subject matter unmolested and adjust your point of view instead (see figure 5.2).

5.2 | Sometimes simply changing your point of view can improve a composition.

Zooming/Cropping

A composition can be changed dramatically by adjusting the framing of your image, either by zooming in or out, by switching lenses (if you're using an interchangeable lens camera), or by cropping the picture within your image editing program. This kind of framing (as distinguished from arranging your subject matter within a frame, which is discussed in the next section) often can be done most effectively after the picture is taken, through judicious cropping. However, because digital images can't be enlarged infinitely without

5.3 | Zooming in on a subject can provide extra emphasis.

the pixels becoming intrusive, you'll want to keep the zoom setting in mind when composing the original shot, to minimize the amount of cropping that has to be done, as with the close-up photo shown in figure 5.3.

As you'll learn in Part II, zooming also can become a compositional tool when you use it to increase or decrease the amount of an image that is in focus. A telephoto picture in which only your subject is sharp, or a wide-angle image in which everything is in focus, each makes use of this effect.

Digital Retouching

National Geographic magazine actually did find a way to relocate the Great Pyramid from its traditional home on the Giza plateau, kicking off a famous controversy in the process. The magazine's artists used digital retouching techniques to squeeze two pyramids together to create a tighter vertical composition that better suited the magazine's February 1982 cover. Those who held the magazine in esteem for its highly detailed and accurate photography were outraged. If nearly perfect digital composites could be made (ordinary photo retouching is relatively easy to detect by an expert), could we really say that "seeing is believing?" Would it ever again be possible to trust our "unbiased" press? A strict code of conduct for photojournalism has since been adopted, and the public (except for conspiracy theorists and *X-Files* fans) seems less concerned about photo manipulation today, which you might surmise from the true-to-life picture shown in figure 5.4.

5.4 | It's a beautiful day in the neighborhood.

So, unless you're a photojournalist working for a news publication or an advertiser attempting to deceive customers, digital retouching is an entirely appropriate and useful tool for creating pleasing compositions.

The Techniques

Some snapshots may turn out to have good composition by happenstance, but most good pictures are created. How do you create a picture? First, learn the guidelines for good composition. I refuse to call them rules, because one of the best ways to use guidelines is to know when to step outside them, which you should be willing to do without hesitation. Rules, in contrast, are something that we have qualms about breaking, and constraining you to rigid tenets of composition is not my intent. After you've learned the guidelines, you'll realize that well-composed pictures often take careful planning and sometimes patient waiting.

You might want to think of these guidelines as techniques that you can choose to apply, or not apply, to any particular picture-taking situation. There are six universal techniques that you'll find detailed in every book, article, or course on composition, although not always under precisely the same names. I'll describe them briefly here, then spend some time showing you how each operates.

Simplicity

Simplicity is the art of reducing your picture only to the elements that are needed to illustrate your idea. By avoiding extraneous subject matter, you can eliminate confusion and draw attention to the most important part of your picture.

The Concept of Thirds

Placing interesting objects at a position located about one third from the top, bottom, or either side of your picture make your images more interesting than ones that place the center of attention dead-center, which most amateurs tend to do.

Lines

Objects in your pictures can be arranged in straight or curving lines that lead the eye to the center of interest, often in appealing ways.

Balance

We enjoy looking at photographs that are evenly balanced with interesting objects on both sides, rather than everything located on one side or another and nothing at all on the other side.

Framing

In this sense, framing is not the boundaries of your picture but, rather, elements in a photograph that tend to create a frame within the frame to highlight the center of interest.

Fusion/Separation

When creating photographs, it's important to ensure that two unrelated objects don't merge in a way you didn't intend, such as in the classic example of a tree growing out of the top of someone's head.

Simplify, Simplify

When Thoreau told us to "simplify, simplify," many wondered why he just didn't say "simplify." My own theory is that the 19th century American author, poet, and philosopher wanted to emphasize just how important simplification is. It's that simple. Let nothing intrude into your photograph that doesn't belong there, and your viewer will automatically focus on the information you intended to convey.

Start with a Concept

The first step in simplification is to conceptualize your photo by planning the kind of picture you intend to take. By that, I don't mean you need to sit down and map out an outline of your intent before every snap. But you should have a good idea of the kind of picture you're looking for (a portrait, sports action shot, or lush scenic); know how it will be used (on a Web page, in print, displayed on the wall); who will be viewing it (family, clients); and whether you want to convey a message (poverty, a fun vacation). Having a plan will help you with the other decisions you need to make.

Select a Single Center of Interest

Next, you should decide on a single center of interest. A viewer's eye shouldn't have to wander through your picture trying to locate something to focus on. You can have several centers of interest to add richness and encourage exploration of your image, but you should create only one main center that immediately attracts the eye. Think of Da Vinci's *Last Supper*. Four groups of Apostles each form their own little tableaux, but the main focus is always on the gentleman seated at the center of the table. You may enjoy visiting Versailles or the Riviera when you travel to France, but Paris will always be your starting point.

The center of interest should be the most eye-catching object in the photograph; it may be the largest, the brightest, or most unusual item within your frame. Pose your spouse next to a pink elephant, and the pachyderm is likely to get all of the attention. Replace your mate with, say, a bright green space alien and the elephant may become secondary. Gaudy colors, bright objects, large masses, and unusual or unique subjects all fight for our attention, even if they are located in the background in a presumably secondary position. Your desired center of attention should have one of these eye-catching attributes or, at least, shouldn't be competing with subject matter that does.

Avoid having more than one main center of attention. You can certainly include other interesting things in your photograph, but they should be subordinate to the main subject. A child can be seated on the floor playing with a kitten, but if the kitten is instead dangling from a branch somewhere in the background, you'll end up with competition for the viewer's interest.

In most cases, the center of interest should not be placed in the exact center of the photograph. Instead place it to one side of the center. We'll look at subject placement in a little more depth later in this chapter. In figure 5.5, at left, the main subject is exactly centered in the frame; she looks like she's been cemented to the floor, in fact. At right, she's been moved off center to a more natural and comfortable position.

5.5 | **Don't place your center of interest in the exact center of the photograph. Move it off center to create a less static look.**

Eliminate Unimportant Material

Choose plain, uncomplicated backgrounds (this goes hand in hand with eliminating competing centers of interest). A small change in the background can make a dramatic difference in simplifying your picture.

Crop out unimportant objects by moving closer; change your perspective by stepping back or by using your zoom lens. Remember that a wide-angle look emphasizes the foreground, adds sky area in outdoor pictures, and increases the feeling of depth and space. Moving closer adds a feeling of intimacy while emphasizing the texture and details of your subject, as shown in figure 5.6. A step back might be a good move for a scenic photo; a step forward, a good move for a portrait.

5.6 | Moving in adds intimacy and better shows texture and details.

Remember that with a digital camera, careful cropping when you take the picture means less trimming in your photo editor, and less resolution lost to unnecessary enlargement. Finally, when eliminating unimportant aspects of a subject, make sure you don't need the portion you're cropping. For example, if you're cropping part of a car, make sure the part that remains is recognizable as a car and not a lumpy glob that viewers will waste time trying to identify. And don't cut off people's heads!

Choose an Orientation

One way to eliminate extraneous objects is to choose the correct orientation for your picture. Beginners often shoot everything with the camera held horizontally. If you shoot a tall building in that mode, you'll end up with a lot of wasted image area. Trees, many portraits, and tall creatures, such as giraffes or NBA players, all look best in vertical mode. On the other hand, landscapes, team sports photos, groups playing Twister, and snakes are logically pictured in horizontal mode. And a few subjects are best portrayed in a square format (in which case you'll probably shoot a horizontal picture and crop the sides). Figures 5.7, 5.8, and 5.9 show subjects that are best portrayed in horizontal, vertical, and square orientations.

5.7 | Landscapes lend themselves to horizontal compositions.

5.8 | Figures, whether alive or not, often look best in vertical compositions.

5.9 | Some subjects have no strong horizontal or vertical lines and may look best in a square composition.

The Concept of Thirds

You'll see the idea of dividing your images into thirds referred to as the rule of thirds quite a bit, and this is one case where I'm not obsessive about avoiding hard-and-fast rules. It's a good idea to arrange your pictures using this guideline much of the time, and when you depart from it, it's a great idea to know exactly why.

Earlier, I mentioned that placing subject matter off center is usually a good idea. Things that are centered in the frame tend to look fixed and static, whereas objects located to one side or the other imply movement, because they have somewhere in the frame to go, so to speak.

The rule of thirds works like this: Use your imagination to divide your picture area with two horizontal lines and two vertical lines, each placed one third of the distance from the borders of the image, as shown in figure 5.10. The intersections of these imaginary lines represent four different points where you might want to place your center of interest. The point you choose depends on your subject matter and how you want it portrayed. Secondary objects placed at any of the other three points will also be arranged in a pleasing way.

5.10 | To use the rule of thirds, divide your image with imaginary lines placed one third of the way from each border. The intersections mark logical positions for your centers of interest.

Horizons, for example, are often best located at the upper third of the picture, unless you want to emphasize the sky by having it occupy the entire upper two thirds of the image. Tall buildings may look best if they are assigned to the right or left thirds of a vertical composition. Figure 5.11 shows a scene arranged into thirds. Notice how the horizon is roughly a third of the way from the top, and the important structures of the castle all fall at the intersections of the imaginary lines.

5.11 | Locate the horizon and other important elements at the points where your imaginary lines intersect.

One important thing to consider is that if your subject is a person, an animal, a vehicle, or anything else with a definable front end, it should be arranged in a horizontal composition so that the front is facing into the picture. If not, your viewer will wonder what your subject is looking at, or where the animal is going, and may not give your subject the attention you intended. Add some extra space in front of potentially fast-moving objects, so it doesn't appear as if the thing is just about to dash from view. The burro shown in figure 5.12 isn't known for its speed, so only a little space is needed at the left side of the frame.

5.12 | This fellow won't be going anywhere soon, but it is still a good idea to include a little extra space to his left, so he'll be seen as facing into the frame.

Oddly enough, it's not important to include this extra space in vertical compositions for anything that doesn't move. A tree or building can butt right up to the top of an image with no problems. We don't expect the object to be moving, so we don't feel the need for a lot of space above it. A Saturn V rocket, on the other hand, would be best positioned a bit lower in the frame.

Using Lines

Viewers find an image more enjoyable if there is an easy path for their eyes to follow to the center of interest. Strong vertical lines lead the eye up and down through an image. Robust horizontal lines cast our eyes from side to side. Repetitive lines form interesting patterns. Diagonal lines conduct our gaze along a more gentle path, and curved lines are the most pleasing of all. Lines in your photograph can be obvious, such as fences or the horizon, or more subtle, such as a skyline or the curve of a flamingo's neck. Lines might even be implied, such as a collection of windmills that retreat into the distance, like those in figure 5.13.

5.13 | The curved road draws your eye to the windmills as they recede into the distance, whereas the closer windmills attract your gaze back to the foreground.

As you compose your images, you'll want to look for natural lines in your subject matter and take advantage of them. You can move around, change your viewpoint, or even relocate cooperative subjects somewhat to create the lines that will enhance your photos.

Lines can be arranged into simple geometric shapes to create better compositions. Notice the imaginary triangle created by the subjects posing at a Roman ruin outside the Spanish city of Avila in figure 5.14 and the other lines in the image that further concentrate interest on the upper portion of the photo. The lines join the subjects together and create a unity that wouldn't be there if they were all standing in random positions. As a quick grab shot with impatient young subjects, it's not the best group photo possible (I'll show you some better posing techniques later in this book), but the picture does show how lines can work together.

Balance

Balance is achieved by arranging shapes, colors, brightness, and darkness in such a way that they complement each other, giving the photograph an even, rather than lopsided, look. Balance can be equal or symmetrical, with

5.14 | These four students arranged themselves into a pyramid composition that avoids the standard line-up look.

equivalent subject matter on each side of the image, or it can be asymmetrical, with a larger, brighter, or more colorful object on one side balanced by a smaller, less bright, or less colorful object on the other.

Figure 5.15 shows an image that on first glance has a balance of sorts. The light castle image at the far right is more or less offset by the darker foliage on the left side. However, because the castle is clearly intended to be the center of interest for this photo, the more you look at it, the more you get the feeling the picture is a bit lopsided.

By taking a step back, we can include more of the road and wall leading to the castle and a bit more of the structure on the right side, as shown in figure 5.16. This cropping does several things. It balances the picture and moves the center of interest closer to one of the "golden" intersections defined by the rule of thirds. The walls and road provide converging lines that attract our eye to the castle.

5.15 | The large light and dark masses on the right and left sides of the picture don't really balance each other as they should. The picture appears to be lopsided.

5.16 | Cropping less tightly provides a more balanced picture with converging lines that draw our eyes to the castle.

There's still something wrong with this picture. The tree branches at the right side aren't connected to anything. They appear to be growing out of the side of the picture frame. We can crop most of them out and improve the balance of the image even further, as you can see in figure 5.17.

Framing

Framing is a technique of using objects in the foreground to create an imaginary picture frame around the subject. A frame concentrates our gaze on the center of interest that it contains, plus framing adds a three-dimensional feeling. A frame also can be used to give you additional information about the subject, such as its surroundings or environment.

Composition

5.17 | Removing the tree branches improves the picture even further.

5.18 | Trees are a classic prop used to construct frames for outdoor portraits.

You'll need to be creative and look around your subject to find areas that can be used to frame it. Windows, doorways, trees, surrounding buildings, and arches are obvious frames. Figure 5.18 shows a classic environmental frame with converging tree trunks used to form a frame around the model.

5.19 | This archway forms a partial frame around the image.

Frames don't have to be perfect or complete geometric shapes. Figure 5.19 shows how a bit of archway can be used to frame a plaza.

Generally, your frame should be in the foreground, but with a bit of ingenuity you can get away with using a background object as a framing device. In figure 5.20, the archway actually frames the hanging bell, but it also serves as a border of sorts around our seated, weary traveler. Because the human figure is relatively close to the frame, the juxtaposition works. If a large archway were 20 or 30 feet behind the subject, the frame wouldn't add the appearance of depth that we'd like to have.

Fusion/Separation

Our vision is three-dimensional, but photographs are inherently flat, even though we do our best to give them a semblance of depth. So, although that pole holding up the volleyball net at your company picnic didn't appear to be obtrusive to the eye, it appeared to be growing directly out of the head of

5.20 | Background objects can sometimes be used as frames if you plan your picture carefully.

your boss in the final picture. Or perhaps you cut off the top of his head on purpose to minimize that bald pate. But now it appears as though his head is attached directly to the top of the picture.

You always need to examine your subject through the viewfinder to make sure that you haven't fused two objects that shouldn't be merged and that you have provided a comfortable amount of separation between them. When you encounter this problem, correct it by changing your viewpoint, moving your subject, or by using selective focus to blur that objectionable background.

Figure 5.21 shows Rodin's *The Thinker* with, at left, an unfortunate structure growing out of the top of his head. Changing camera position slightly produces the more reasonable image at right.

5.21 | Rodin probably wasn't picturing a thinking cap when he conceived of his famous sculpture (at left). Moving slightly to the right relocated the rooftop so that it helps define the garden in which the artwork is located.

Indeed, choosing a good background is an important part of composing any photograph. Avoid busy, gaudy, or bright backgrounds that will draw attention from your subject. Indoors, you might want to use a plain wall or a seamless background for a portrait or, perhaps, position your subject in front of a wall of books that lend a dignified air to the picture. Outdoors, take advantage of trees, grass, skies rich with fluffy clouds, or textured walls. Remember how strong lines can lead the eye and look for them in your backgrounds to avoid distracting the viewer from your intended center of interest. Figure 5.22 shows a picture with a plain background.

5.22 | A plain background puts the emphasis where it belongs: on your subject matter.

Composition

Next Up

Congratulations! You've finished the introductory section and are now armed with all the weapons you need to create great pictures of your own. In Part II, we'll explore typical picture-taking situations and discover ways to make the most of them. Next up is a chapter on close-up photography.

Making Great Images

Chapter 6

Small Objects Up Close

If you want to explore your digital camera's capabilities methodically, close-up photography can let you use your image grabber to capture a whole new world that exists right under our noses. Whether you're shooting pictures outdoors or in a ministudio, macro photography is fun.

Why Macro Photography?

Of all the various categories of photography that you can explore with a digital camera, close-up photography of small objects (including tiny living creatures) is one of the best matches for an electronic camera's capabilities. This is one arena in which digital cameras better the average film camera in several respects. Consider these advantages of digital cameras in close-up (or macro) photography:

- Virtually all digital cameras have a liquid crystal display (LCD) that shows (more or less) exactly what you're going to get. If you know a few secrets, you can avoid all the framing and lighting problems that plague most point-and-shoot film cameras.

- You won't burn up film bracketing exposures "just in case." You can examine each shot immediately after you take it and stop only when you've got the exact photo you need.

- A corollary to the "what you see is what you get" nature of digital photography is that you can avoid the inconvenience of reconstructing a close-up setup, which can be tedious to tear down and reassemble later.

Most digital cameras focus a lot closer than their non-SLR (single lens reflex) film camera counterparts, making them much more suitable for close-ups. Digital camera lenses are more compact, which means that engineering close-focus capabilities is easier for the designer. Moreover, it doesn't make much sense to have macro capabilities in a point-and-shoot camera that doesn't accurately frame the image at close range.

If you haven't explored the world of close-up photography, you're in for a treat. Macro photography is a lot of fun. Most digital cameras have all the capabilities you need built right in, unlike microphotography, which requires add-on equipment, such as a microscope and adapters to couple your camera to an eyepiece. As you'll see later in this chapter, scanners can be used for close-ups, too. Some of the things you can look forward to in the realm of small object photography include the following:

- *It's inexpensive*—You don't have to travel to Europe to find exotic locations. You'll discover a whole new world of images in your backyard or attic.

- *It's perfect for taking your time and exercising your creativity thoughtfully*— Most close-up subjects (other than insects or small animals) are inanimate, so you can explore various angles, adjust lighting, or think about special effects without worrying about a squirming victim that's eager to get back to their TV show, knitting, or anything other than your photo session.

- *Close-up photography can be a perfect complement for many other hobbies*—Collect coins or stamps? Capture your collection for a photographic inventory. Are you something of a nature or science buff? Use your digital camera for macro shots of flowers, insects, pond scum, or whatever fascinates you. Feel underappreciated for your skill at Japanese embroidery? Show off your needlework with some stunning close-ups. Figure 6.1 shows a close-up photo of a hand-painted ceramic plate.

6.1 | Show off your craft skills with vivid close-up photos.

On Location or in the Studio?

Before embarking on your close-up photography expedition, you'll need to decide whether you'll be photographing your subjects in your studio—which can be a simple, homemade setup on your kitchen table—or on location—that is, in a natural environment, whether it's outdoors or on the shelves showcasing your pewter soldier collection.

You may or may not have any choice about venue. Convincing a tree frog to sit in one place on your kitchen table while you snap away may be difficult. But the poor fellow may sit quietly (if terrified) on a tree trunk, doing his level best to blend in by turning browner while you grab some interesting nature shots. Photographing a subject (living or not) in its natural habitat has the added advantage of providing other objects in the photograph that provide a sense of scale. Familiar objects that are dwarfed by the main subject of your picture make the subject seem that much larger by comparison. (You can use this effect as a trick even in the studio by deliberately choosing comparison objects that are larger or smaller than we expect, as shown in figure 6.2.)

6.2 | Even in the studio, you can choose objects to provide a true—or false— sense of scale.

Many inanimate objects may look much better when removed from their habitat and photographed against a plain background. A simple background is less distracting and concentrates interest on your intended subject.

Aside from suitability, there are advantages and disadvantages associated with both location and studio shooting. Keep in mind that by studio I mean any indoor location you set up specifically for photographs on a temporary or permanent basis.

On location, you'll have less control over factors such as lighting or weather. Although you can augment existing lighting to an extent, rainy, snowy, or windy conditions must be worked with as they come up. In the studio, on the other hand, you can adjust your lighting any way you like, and if your roof is in good repair, the weather probably won't be a factor.

Conversely, studio photography typically requires more setup time and effort. You'll need to arrange lights, the background, perhaps set up a tripod, and perform other chores depending on how elaborate your studio is. In the field, setup may be nothing more complicated than rearranging some loose rocks or twigs. On the other hand, even though set-up may be a breeze, you can find yourself spending hours getting exactly the right shot. Ansel Adams was renowned for meticulous planning of every element of his scenic photographs, including the placement of the moon!

To play devil's advocate for a moment, it's also possible for studio photography to be a huge time-saver, even if it's from not needing to jump in your car (or venture out into your backyard) to your location. I photograph many small objects for sale on eBay and have set up a permanent little nook with a seamless backdrop and standard lighting. I can grab an item, plop it down in the ministudio, snap off a picture with my digital camera, and be viewing the photograph on my computer 3 minutes later.

Studio photography is excellent if you want consistency. I photograph my wife's collection of Lladró porcelain on the same backdrop using similar lighting every time, so the resulting pictures look like they were photographed at the same time even though months may have elapsed, as you can see in figure 6.3. It can be difficult to achieve the same consistency on location, where lighting and backgrounds can vary much more.

6.3 | **A ministudio can provide consistency when photographing the same kinds of subjects over time.**

Setting Up a Close-Up Studio

A studio setting, especially for close-up photography, needn't be elaborate. You can gather a few components and use them around your kitchen or dining room table, if you like. If you can set aside a portion of your home for a semi-permanent studio setup, so much the better. This section will outline some of the elements you need to collect.

Background

For close-up photography in a studio, backgrounds generally should be plain, so they won't detract from the object being photographed. One popular type of background is the so-called seamless backdrop, which combines the surface that the subject rests on and the vertical background behind it, with a smooth, often invisible transition between them. Seamless backgrounds are extremely flexible because you can go for the seamless look or use lighting to provide different amounts of illumination on the foreground and background, producing a degree of separation that is still smooth and nondistracting.

Cloth

For some types of photography, I like to use a large piece of cloth as a seamless background. A good choice is a piece of velour in an appropriate size. I have several examples in different colors, measuring about 54 inches wide and 8 or 9 feet long, so I can use them for objects in a variety of sizes (or even for portraits). Even at $5 or so a yard, these cloths are a bargain.

Velour cloths are doubly useful because they have a different texture on each side: the fuzzy velour side and the smooth reverse that has a bit of shine to it. Use either side, depending on the look you're trying to get. You can stretch the cloth out to give a seamless effect or add folds and wrinkles to make it look like a drape. If your cloth becomes soiled, just toss it in the wash.

Purchase several different colors in muted pastels as well as brighter hues. Blues and browns are good shades to start with, and you might want to consider a black drape as well. These really soak up the light, isolating your subject. When you take a picture against a black background, you can easily select your subject in your image editor if you'd like to extract it to drop into another photo. Figure 6.4 shows how cloth can be used as a background.

6.4 | **A few yards of cloth can become a versatile background for close-up photography.**

Seamless Paper

Professional photographers find rolls of seamless paper indispensable. I've photographed everything from rock groups to truck clutches on a seamless paper backdrop, and you'll find this kind of background useful for close-up photography as well.

You can buy them at most camera stores that cater to professional photographers. The big problem is that the most easily obtainable paper rolls are a bit large for close-up work. Although some narrower rolls may be available, the standard sizes are 9 feet and 12 feet wide. Even a 9-foot by 36-foot roll, which costs about $40, is a little unwieldy for a ministudio.

If you don't mind hacking away with a saw, you can cut one of these rolls into more manageable 4.5-foot widths. The paper eventually gets soiled or torn (it will last longer when used for close-up photography because you won't have people walking all over it), so getting two narrower rolls for the price of one is good economy. If you're not planning to use the paper for portraits or other types of photography, a better choice may be to split the cost with a friend who also needs narrower seamless rolls. That way, you can each have a roll of a particular color and double the number of colors you have in stock.

Another option is to use poster board for your seamless background. Poster board is not quite as good because the standard sheets aren't really large enough if your close-ups will involve anything that's more than a few inches on a side. (You can often purchase poster board in larger sizes from art supply houses.) You'll find that with standard poster board, the background or foreground (or both) aren't large enough to let you choose different angles (nothing beats a long roll of paper that's 4 feet wide or more in such cases). Poster board is also more difficult to manage: It's rigid and may not stay where you want it without taping it or propping it up.

However, poster board is cheap, cheap, cheap, so you can have many colors. Whether you're using poster board or seamless paper, in addition to a few colors, you'll want some white for shots that call for a pristine neutral background. If your funds are limited, go for some blues and browns in medium shades. You can pump on some extra light to make them appear lighter in tone, or you can tone down the lighting on the background to make them appear darker, as shown in figure 6.5.

6.5 | Imaginative lighting can produce professional results, even with a simple paper or poster board background.

Supports

Another key component for a home studio is supports for your background, lighting, and camera. Professionals buy this kind of hardware and don't mind paying big bucks for it because good quality supports can be a lifetime investment. For example, I paid approximately $100 for a Bogen Husky IV tripod when I was in college and have used it ever since with everything from 4x5 view cameras to digital cameras to 8mm camcorders. I've used the same light stands for more than 20 years.

However, you don't have to pay big bucks. Inexpensive equipment can do the job for you, and you can even make some of it yourself. This section will tell you everything you need to know about assembling your supporting cast for your studio.

Background Supports

Cloth backgrounds are light in weight and can be supported by just about anything you care to set up, including duct tape applied to nearby furniture. (I've taped backgrounds to the bookcases and fireplaces from time to time.)

If you're tearing down your studio often, you might want to invest in a couple professional light stands, which are telescoping aluminum affairs with tripod-like bases, available in heights from 7 feet to 9 feet and taller. You can set one stand on either side of your shooting area, place a wood dowel between them as a horizontal support, and drape your cloth over that.

Paper rolls are a bit more problematic because they can weigh 20 to 30 pounds each. Professional light stands can support them (use a piece of metal pipe or thick wood closet pole as your horizontal support) or you can build something out of 2×4 lumber if you're handy. When I've had a permanent studio, I usually nailed multiple homemade supports to the ceiling rafters, or used simple eye-hook bolts like those shown in figure 6.6, so I could have five or six rolls of paper all hung at the same time.

6.6 | Homemade supports can hold your rolls of paper.

Lighting Supports

The kind of supports you need for your lighting will depend on the kind of lighting you are using. (We'll look at lighting options later in this chapter.) Light stands are great if you're going to use electronic flash or photo-type incandescent lights, and they will really come in handy if you plan to shoot portraits in an expanded studio like the one I'll describe in the next chapter.

However, if you're using ordinary household lamps, particularly those of the high-intensity variety, the lamp's own support mechanism will do just fine.

Camera Supports

You really ought to have a tripod if you're serious about close-up photography. A tripod holds the camera steady and makes it easier to frame a picture through a digital camera's LCD display screen. You'll also find it easier to focus manually if the camera is mounted on a tripod. Finally, a tripod provides consistency from shot to shot, so all the pictures of, say, your pewter soldiers are taken from the same distance and camera angle.

Tripods come in many varieties, from single-leg unipods to tiny tabletop tripods to full-sized studio units. Smaller tripods can be useful if size alone makes the difference between whether you'll carry the tripod with you or not, so you may need a small one for location use. However, I'm spoiled by a big, sturdy tripod and recommend the best quality unit you can afford for studio use.

A good tripod will be heavy enough that it will stay put as you use it and will not slide around on the floor. The legs will be rigid and won't flex. The tripod won't sway and wiggle (especially important if you're making a long exposure). Some tripods are built large to accommodate heavy cameras, but digital models rarely weigh more than a few ounces. You'll be looking for ruggedness and what carmakers euphemized as "road-hugging weight" in your tripod. Figure 6.7 shows a well-used tripod.

Key components to look for in a tripod include the following:

- Legs that adjust easily, so you can change the height of the tripod quickly.
- An adjustable center column that's long enough to let you move the camera up or down by a few feet without the need to adjust the legs.
- A center column that's reversible so you can point the camera down to the floor for some close-ups.
- A tilt and swing head that flips in horizontal and vertical directions, so you can quickly change the camera angle. (Note that with some professional tripods, the tilt head is a component that's purchased separately.)
- Locks that let you tightly fix the legs, center column, and tilt head at precisely the position you want.

If your close-ups consist of flat objects, such as stamps, coins, photographs, needlepoint, and so forth, you might want to consider a special kind of camera support called a copystand. These are simple stands with a flat

6.7 | A good tripod should be the foundation of your digital close-ups.

copyboard and a vertical column on which you fasten the camera. The camera can be slid up or down the column to adjust the camera-subject distance. Copystands provide a much more convenient working angle for this type of photography, particularly if your digital camera allows swiveling the lens and viewfinder in different directions.

Lighting Equipment

The lighting you'll use to illuminate your close-up pictures falls into three (maybe three and a half) categories.

- Existing light (that is, the light that's already there, whether you're indoors or outdoors). You can manipulate this light using reflectors or other gadgets, so you're not strictly limited to what's at hand.

- Electronic flash, either the flash unit built into your digital camera alone or that unit augmented by additional and "slave" flash units, if you're getting fancy.

- Incandescent illumination, which can be photoflood lights, high intensity lamps, or any similar lamps you choose to set up, such as in the setup shown in figure 6.8.

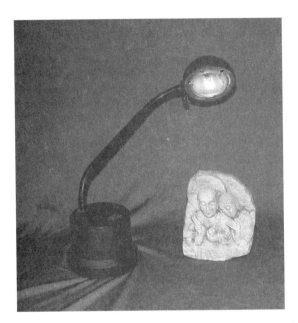

6.8 | Close-up lighting equipment doesn't have to be elaborate.

Strictly speaking, you also could use light emitted by the subject itself, but unless you're photographing a candle or a lightning bug, that's not the usual situation. Later in this chapter I'll show you how to use these different types of lighting. This section is concerned only with the equipment itself.

Existing Light

Reflectors and light blockers of various types are invaluable for modifying the light falling on your subject, whether you're using existing light, incandescent illumination, or electronic flash. However, with existing light, these gadgets may be the only tool you have, so they become all the more valuable. You should have some of these available in your close-up arsenal at all times.

Reflectors and light blockers can be simple and are easy to make. The following include some different kinds of reflectors and light blockers:

- *White cardboard*—A piece of poster board makes a great reflector. You can actually fold a piece into quarters and unfold only as much as you need for your photograph. You'll want white because it is neutral in color, although other shades can be useful for special effects.

- *Foamboard*—Those ultralight boards of plastic foam sandwiched between paper or plastic sheets are commonly used to mount photos or to construct exhibits. They make great reflectors, too, especially if you need larger sizes that are rigid but also light in weight. They don't fold easily and are probably more useful for portraits and group pictures, but if you have a small hunk of foamboard, keep it handy.

- *Aluminum foil*—Tape aluminum foil to a piece of white cardboard (you can use the reverse side of your white cardboard) to produce a reflector that generates less soft illumination with more snap. Crinkle the aluminum foil so it will reflect light evenly.

- *Mylar sheets*—Get yourself a "space blanket" from the camping department of your favorite retailer and use the sheet as a handy high-contrast reflector that can be folded up and carried in a pocket.

- *Tents*—If you're photographing a very shiny object, a light tent may be the best tool to even out your lighting. Photographic tents are usually made of a translucent material and placed right over the object you're photographing.

- *Black cardboard or cloth*—Sometimes you need to block light from a glaring source to produce softer illumination. A sheet of black poster board can help, although even black board reflects some light. For extra light absorption, consider a small piece of black velour. If you're trying to take photos of seashells in their natural habitat (actually, the seashore is more of an afterlife for dead shells), a black cloth will help.

Electronic Flash

You can use the electronic flash unit built into your digital camera for quick shots, but most of the time you'll find that direct flash of that sort isn't the best illumination for close-ups. In fact, if your subject matter is inanimate, electronic flash probably isn't the best choice at all. The chief advantage of electronic flash is that its short duration can help freeze the image of moving objects, such as people or frogs. However, it's much more difficult to visualize how electronic flash will look in the finished picture. Some kinds of electronic flash units you can use for close-ups include the following:

- *Built-in flash*—This is the flash unit built into your digital camera. You'll find that in extreme close-ups, the light it produces will look unnatural and may not illuminate your subject evenly.

- *External flash units*—Many digital cameras have a connector for attaching an external flash unit. These can be inexpensive flash units designed for conventional film cameras or more elaborate (and more costly) devices with modeling lights, which are extra incandescent lamps that mimic the light that will be emitted by the flash.

- *Slave flash*—These are electronic flash units with light-detecting circuitry that automatically triggers them when another flash goes off. You can also purchase add-on slave detectors that set off any flash. Slaves are useful when you want to use two or more electronic flash units to provide sophisticated lighting effects.

- *Ringlights*—These are circular electronic flash units that fit around the outside of a camera lens, providing very even lighting for close-ups. Ringlights are generally a professional tool used by those who take many close-ups, particularly with interchangeable lens cameras. If you can afford an SLR digital camera, and you do enough close-up work to justify a ringlight, they make a great tool.

Incandescent Lights

Good old-fashioned incandescent lights are usually your best tool for lighting close-ups of things that don't hop around or wiggle. Although not as intense as electronic flash, that's not usually a problem with your camera locked down on a tripod and with longer exposures. Incandescent lights are cheap, too. The most important thing to remember when using them is to set your white balance manually or make sure your camera's automatic white balance control is turned on. These lights are much more reddish than daylight or electronic flash.

Any gooseneck high intensity lamp or table lamp that you can twist and turn to adjust its angle will work great as illumination for close-up pictures. Other types of lamps also can be used but will be less flexible, so to speak, when it comes to positioning. High intensity bulbs may have too much contrast, especially for shiny objects. You can use reflectors to soften their light or investigate adjustable neck lamps that can use conventional soft white light bulbs.

Additional Close-Up Equipment

In many cases, you won't need any more gear than what I've listed so far. However, you might want to consider a few more accessories.

Close-Up Lenses

Many digital cameras focus very closely indeed, in some cases down to an inch or less. That's usually as close as you'll want to go because if you get much closer than that, a three-dimensional object will be very difficult to light. There simply wouldn't be enough room between the lens and subject to allow decent lighting. An exception would be if you were photographing a transparent or translucent item, such as a transparency, but in most cases being able to focus a few inches away is close enough.

However, some vendors have a looser definition of close focusing, so you may happen to own a digital camera that allows getting no closer than a foot or two. Or perhaps you own a fixed-focus digital camera that offers acceptable sharpness for everything from a few feet to infinity. You, too, can take close-up pictures if you know the secret.

First of all, your fixed-focus camera may still have a macro setting. This may be in the form of a lever or dial that can be used to set the focus distance manually. All you do is measure the distance to your subject and dial in the right focus on a scale.

Tip from the pros: Is your lens cap tethered to your camera by a chain or strap to keep it from getting lost? Consider putting markings on the strap so you can use it as an impromptu measuring tape when you need to gauge distance manually.

The other secret is the close-up lens, actually an add-on filter-like device that adjusts the focus of your camera's built-in lens to allow narrowing the gap between you and your subject matter. Just fasten one of these gadgets using your camera's filter mount and start shooting.

6.9 | Close-up lenses are classified by their diopter values.

Close-up lenses, such as the one shown in figure 6.9, are generally labeled with their relative strength or magnification using a measure of optical strength called diopter. A lens labeled "No. 1" would be a relatively mild close-up attachment; those labeled "No. 2" or "No. 3" would be relatively stronger. Close-up lenses are commonly available in magnifications from +1 diopter to +10 diopters.

The actual way close-up magnification is calculated is entirely too complicated for the average photographer—unless formulas such as Magnification at Infinity=Camera Focal Length/(1000/diopter strength) are your cup of tea—and not particularly useful. That's because the close-focusing distance varies with the focal length of the lens and its unenhanced close-focusing capabilities. However, as a rule of thumb, if your lens normally focuses to 1 meter (39.37 inches), which is a little more than 3 feet, a +1 diopter will let you focus down to 1/2 meter (about 20 inches); a +2 diopter to 1/3 meter (around 13 inches); a +3 diopter to 1/4 meter (about 9.8 inches); and so forth. A +10 diopter will take you all the way down to about 2 inches—and that's with the lens focused at infinity. If your digital camera's lens normally focuses closer than 1 meter, you'll be able to narrow the gap between you and your subject even more.

In the real world, the practical solution is to purchase several close-up lenses (they cost roughly $20 each and can often be purchased in a set), so you'll have the right one for any particular photographic chore.

> **Tip from the pros:** *You can combine several close-up lenses to get even closer (using, say, a +2 lens with a +3 lens to end up with +5), but avoid using more than two close-up lenses together. The toll on your sharpness will be too great with all those layers of glass. Plus, three lenses can easily be thick enough to vignette the corners of your image.*

Bellows

If you have a digital camera with a removable lens, you can also purchase a bellows attachment, such as the one shown in figure 6.10, that fits between your lens and your camera. When used with a camera lens (that is, a macro lens) designed especially for close-ups, you'll get the sharpest possible close-up pictures. The downside? Bellows attachments are expensive ($100 or more), reduce the light reaching your sensor by 2X to 4X or more, depending on how extended the bellows is, and are probably overkill for most close-up applications.

Slide Copiers

Some vendors (Nikon, for one) offer slide copying attachments for digital cameras. You can use these to convert your favorite color slides to digital images without the need to purchase a special slide scanner. If you take many 35mm transparencies, or have taken them in the past, a slide copier attachment is a good investment. Although you can copy slides with an unadorned digital camera that focuses close enough, a slide copier is faster, more consistent, and should produce better quality.

Taking Your First Close-Up

You've got all your equipment and environmental needs squared away. It's time to take your first close-up picture. The following sections describe a step-by-step approach that allows you to apply what you've learned.

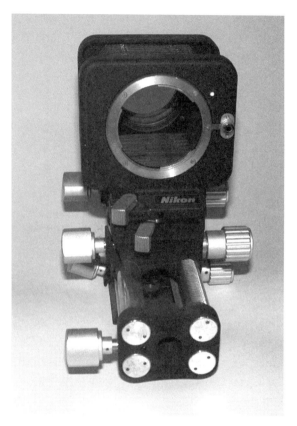

6.10 | **Bellows attachments for interchangeable lens cameras offer very close focusing capabilities.**

Arrange Your Subject and Background

The first step is to arrange your subject and its background. If you're shooting in a ministudio, set up the background on a table or other surface with enough space in front of the setup to let you get close with your camera and tripod (if you're using a tripod). Arrange your subject at the angle you want, making sure it won't tip over or move unexpectedly. Bits of modeling clay can be used to fix many items to the shooting surface. (Remember that some kinds of clay may contain oils that will stain cloth or paper.) Sometimes I prop up items with bits of wood, placed so they won't show up in the photo. Figure 6.11 shows some inexpensive clamps that can be used to hold objects being photographed.

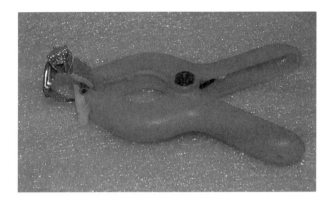

6.11 | These clamps cost 33 cents and work great for holding close-up objects.

If you're shooting on location, police the area and remove any dead branches, leaves, rocks, extraneous fauna, or anything else you don't want to appear in your photo. Now is the time to simplify your background. Look closely for dirt that can be cleaned away to improve your photo.

Set Up Your Camera

If you're using a tripod, adjust the length of the legs so they provide most of the elevation you need. The center pole should be used to fine-tune the height of the camera; if you set the legs too short and have to crank the center column way up, the tripod will be top-heavy and less stable.

> *Tip from the pros: If you do happen to use a fairly light-weight tripod, you can increase its stability by suspending a weight from the legs. Don't bother carrying ballast around with you; tote a lightweight but sturdy bag (those mesh bags that oranges come in are perfect) and fill it with rocks as needed.*

Arrange the tripod and camera so you can use the tripod's swivel head to get the angles you want. If you have trouble getting close enough because the tripod's legs get in the way, don't be afraid to reverse the center pole and shoot down on your subject.

Deploy Your Lights

If you're shooting in a ministudio, you'll probably want to use at least two lights to illuminate your subject from both sides. Shine the lights directly onto your subject or bounce the light off a reflector like those described earlier in this chapter. Make sure there is some light on the background to separate your subject from its surroundings.

You may have to get creative with lighting on location. If you're not using external lights, take advantage of reflectors to bounce additional light into the shadows and light-blocking objects to create softer shadows from direct sunlight or illumination, as shown in figure 6.12. In this photo, a white reflector off to the right side of the photo was used to brighten up the cat's eyes.

6.12 | White reflectors can brighten dark areas of your outdoor photos.

As you light your scene, remember that depth of field is always limited when taking close-ups, so anything you can do to increase the amount of light available will make it possible to shoot at a smaller aperture, which in turn increases depth of field.

If you happen to be using your camera's built-in flash, lack of enough light will rarely be a problem. In fact, you may find yourself with too much light, even at your lens's smallest f-stop, and end up with a washed-out picture. Several possible solutions to this problem include the following:

- *Step back a little and use a tighter zoom setting to produce the same size image*—The flash will be that much farther from your subject and less likely to wash out the picture. Remember that electronic flash obeys the inverse-square law: A light source that is 12 inches away from your subject produces only one quarter as much illumination as it does when it's 6 inches away.

- *Use your camera's exposure value (EV) control to deliberately underexpose the picture*—This fools your image grabber's automatic exposure mechanism.

- *Consider covering your flash with a layer or two of tissue paper or other neutral translucent covering*—You'll cut down on the light and soften it a bit at the same time.

Frame Your Photograph

With everything in place, it's time to actually compose your photo. The following are some of the things you need to consider:

- *Choose an appropriate zoom setting (focal length) for your picture*—Some digital cameras offer close focusing only at particular focal lengths (that is, they focus closely at medium to telephoto settings but not at the wide-angle setting), so your choice may be limited. Remember that wide-angle settings can add apparent distortion to your image, making things that are closer to the lens appear much larger than they normally look. This effect is most pronounced with close-ups. A normal or short telephoto zoom setting may produce a more natural look.

- *Frame your picture to exclude extraneous subject matter*—Get in tight to produce a photo that will require a minimum of enlargement and will be as sharp as possible. Close-up pictures are often an exception to the rule about arranging your subjects off center. Many good macro photos have the main subject smack in the middle of the frame, or only slightly off center, as shown in figure 6.13.

- *Make sure your camera has been set to close-up or macro mode*—This is usually represented by a flower icon on your status LCD display.

6.13 | In this case, placing the subject near the center of the photo provides a showcase for the blooms.

- *Focus very carefully*—Some cameras allow switching autofocus to a center-oriented mode. Use that if your subject matter is indeed in the middle of the picture. Switch to manual focus if your camera offers it. You might want to use aperture-priority mode, if available, and select the smallest f-stop available to increase the depth of field. And keep in mind what you learned about how depth of field is arranged: Two thirds is allocated to the area in front of the plane of sharpest focus and only one third to the area behind it.

- *Check to make sure the back of the camera (where the sensor is located) is parallel to the plane in which your main subject lies*—That's the plane you'll be focusing on—and where the maximum amount of sharpness lies. If the camera is tilted in relation to the plane of the main subject, only part of the subject will be in sharp focus. Unless you're shooting for a special effect, you want as much sharpness as you can get. Figure 6.14 shows a relatively flat subject placed parallel to the back of the camera to produce a sharp plane of focus.

6.14 | Keeping the plane of the object parallel with the back of the camera provides optimum depth of field even at wide apertures.

- *Watch your camera's focus indicator*—This may be an LED (light emitting diode) light near the viewfinder that glows green (or some other color) when the image is in focus.

- *Use your camera's LCD display to evaluate your framing, composition, and focus*—The optical viewfinder of your digital camera won't show you exactly what you are going to get, and may indeed cut off part of the picture area.

Tip from the pros: Many digital cameras have a connector that allows displaying the camera's output on a TV screen. You may even have forgotten you have this capability. Your indoor studio can include a TV or monitor to use in previewing your shot. Even a 20-inch color TV will provide a picture that is larger and easier to view than your camera's 2-inch LCD display. Close-up photography is a perfect application for this feature. You can use the TV to review your pictures as you take them, too.

Take the Photo

The big moment has arrived. It's time to take your first close-up. Here are some last-second tips for you:

- *Your digital camera may have several automatic focus lock methods*—My own camera, for example, can be set to continuous autofocus (changing focus at all times up until the moment of exposure) or to lock at a particular focus when the shutter release is partially depressed. If you're taking photos without a tripod, you may want to use continuous autofocus to compensate for slight movements you make as you frame the photo. Locking focus at a particular point is best when you are confident that the focus you have when you press the shutter release is the focus you want for the final picture.

- *If your subject is inanimate and you're using a tripod, consider using your digital camera's self-timer to trip the shutter after a delay of a few seconds*— Even if you press the shutter release carefully, you may shake the camera a little. Under incandescent illumination with a small f-stop, your camera will probably be using a slow shutter speed that is susceptible to blurring with even a little camera shake. The self-timer will let the camera and tripod come to rest.

- *Some digital cameras also have a socket for a remote shutter release*— These also can let you keep your hands off the camera when taking a picture and have the added advantage of tripping the shutter at the exact moment you want (just before the frog takes off, for example), rather than after a delay of indeterminate length.

- *Wait a few seconds after you hear the camera's shutter click before doing anything*—You want to be sure your camera is not making a lengthy exposure or time exposure. That click might have been the shutter opening, and the camera may still be capturing the picture.

- *Review your photo immediately on your camera's LCD display (or that big TV you set up)*—You want to check for unwanted reflections (especially those produced by flash) and other problems.

Avoiding Parallax Errors

There will be times when you simply must use your camera's optical viewfinder to take a close-up photo. Perhaps you're outdoors and the sunlight washes out your camera's LCD screen. Or maybe you're taking a grab shot on the spur

of the moment: It's either bring the camera to your eye and snap or lose the picture entirely. Some photos don't require deep thought and planning before you take them. Most of the close-ups I take for eBay auctions are of the quick-and-dirty variety, using my camera's optical viewfinder.

In all of these situations, you need to keep possible parallax error in mind. Parallax causes problems because what you see through the optical viewfinder is not the same as what is seen by the camera's sensor through the taking lens. At differences of more than a few feet, this difference is very minor, but as your subject gets closer to the camera, the variance becomes significant. At distances of a foot or less, a quarter to a third or more of what you think you see through the viewfinder isn't shown in the actual picture, as you can see in figure 6.15.

The amount of image area affected is determined by the distance between the taking lens and the viewfinder as well as the distance to your subject. If the viewfinder is directly above the camera's lens, you'll lose a little of what appears at the top of the viewfinder in your actual photo. If the viewfinder is off to the left, some of the left of your image may be cut off. With many digital cameras, the viewfinder window is both above and to the left of the taking lens, affording the opportunity of accidentally cropping your photo in two directions at once. The default danger zones apply only when you're holding the camera horizontally; if you're taking a vertical photo, the area subject to parallax errors migrates along with your viewfinder.

More expensive cameras may have some compensation built into the optical viewfinder; it may tilt slightly to compensate for parallax error. It's more common, though, to simply place guidelines in the viewfinder that show where the safe area is and expect the photographer to keep the subject matter lined up properly. If you keep in mind that the correction marks in the viewfinder are only an approximation of what your camera really sees, you can usually avoid the worst parallax transgressions. Adjust on the safe side by including a little extra area around your main subject and you'll do fine. You can always crop out unwanted elements with your computer software, but you can't add a part of the image that was never captured.

**6.15 | You see the view through the optical viewfinder shown at top
. . . and your camera's sensor sees the image at bottom.**

Also remember that your camera's built-in electronic flash suffers from parallax error, too. At very close distances, the flash will probably not illuminate the lower part of your subject. I am often able to fix this by placing a small white card out of the picture area but located in such a place to allow some of the flash illumination to bounce down onto the subject.

Scanners for Close-Ups

If you own a scanner, you already have one of the best close-up accessories you could ask for. Scanners are designed and built for grabbing images of things that are only a fraction of an inch from the device's sensor. Many scanners work great as capture devices for flat items and some kinds of three-dimensional objects, such as stamps, coins, toy soldiers, small dolls, your butterfly collection, and similar items.

Scanners have considerably more resolution than digital cameras at macro distances, so your results will be crisp and sharp. Snap a picture of a 4×5-inch object with a 3 megapixel camera, and you'll end up with, of course, 3 million pixels of information. Scan the same object at a modest 600 spi (samples per inch) with even the least expensive scanner, and you've got almost 2.5 times as many pixels to work with (if you need to). You can see a comparison in figure 6.16.

6.16 | The same coin, captured with a digital camera (left) and with a scanner (right).

As I cautioned in Chapter 3, however, remember that some kinds of scanners don't have sufficient depth of field to scan three-dimensional objects successfully. If you want to use your scanner regularly as a close-up device, make sure you have one with a CCD (charge-coupled device) sensor rather than a CIS (contact image sensor) scan element.

Next Up

People are more interesting than things, but I elected to kick off Part II with this chapter on close-up photography rather than the people pictures chapter that follows. Why? Because a lot of what you learned in the past few pages can be applied to photographs of people. You can use these studio techniques and lighting tricks, plus a few more tricks that I plan to show you, with humans (and pets).

Chapter 7
Photographing People

Photographing your friends, family, colleagues, and even perfect strangers can be one of the most rewarding channels for your digital camera creativity. People make exciting and fascinating subjects who challenge the skills you'll master in this chapter.

People Photography

Photographing your fellow human beings is a fascinating outlet that has become the lifework of some of our most talented photographers. Who can forget compelling documentary photography, such as Dorothea Lange's *Migrant Mother*, or the lively celebrity photography of Richard Avedon? Perhaps you admire Yousuf Karsh's powerful portrait of Winston Churchill. Closer to home, you may find your wedding photos or baby pictures are the things you treasure most amidst all the cluttered possessions in your home.

Pictures of people are more than simply a way of capturing human nature in still images. Photographs of humans in action or at rest are a way of documenting history and preserving memories. The existence of so many different categories of people-oriented pictures, from fashion photography to portraiture, demonstrates the depth of this particular photographic field.

I'm going to start you on your exploration of people pictures by giving you some tips on how, where, and why to take photos of men, women, and children. You'll find that the organization of this chapter parallels, to a certain extent, the discussion of close-up photography in Chapter 6. Indeed, I used that chapter to introduce some ideas and lay the groundwork for the more detailed information you'll find here.

Because photography of people is such a broad topic, I'm going to concentrate on portrait photography in this chapter. I plan to introduce you to the basic equipment you'll need, plus the fundamentals of lighting and posing. Most of this information also applies to other kinds of photography of humans, such as weddings or Little League team photos. In addition, you'll find more people-picture techniques in Chapters 8 and 9.

On Location or in the Studio?

The very first people pictures, whether painted or captured on daguerreotypes, were often created in the studio because a studio allows the artist or photographer to control easily the lighting, background, props, and other elements. With sittings that could take hours and exposures that could take minutes, it was easier to create the images in a space set aside especially for that purpose. Traveling photographers sometimes carried along tents that could be used as portable darkrooms or studios.

Even after more portable cameras and faster films and lenses freed photographers to capture documentary images and insightful candid pictures anywhere, portraits were still most often confined to studio settings. Things changed quite dramatically in the swinging 70s, when professional portrait photographers became eager to set up lights in a living room to create family portraits in the family's own habitat. The popularity of that trend soon led to what was labeled environmental portraiture: posed photographs taken with scenic backgrounds, such as the one shown in figure 7.1.

7.1 | Portraits don't have to be confined to the studio: You can take them outdoors.

Now, several decades later, you'll find yourself facing the same decision. Should you shoot portraits in your studio or on location? Many of the pros and cons are the same as those I outlined for close-ups in Chapter 6, that is, studio photography gives you greater control over the environment and consistency but may require more time to set up and execute. When your photography turns to people rather than objects, an additional element comes into play.

Studio portraits are usually more formal. With a professional-looking back-drop, or a serious background such as those omnipresent shelves of professional journals you see in so many executive portraits, a studio portrait can have a formal or official appearance. Even the crazy Mylar backgrounds and wacky props they're using for high school portraits these days retain a sense of formality in the finished product.

Location portraits, on the other hand, end up having a casual air no matter how hard you try to formalize them. The most carefully staged photo of the Speaker of the House posed on the steps of the U.S. Capitol will still look less formal than a relaxed portrait of the same legislator seated in a studio with only the American flag in the background.

My feeling is that you should master both studio and location portraiture. You'll want a studio-style picture for a newspaper head shot or for mounting over the mantel, but you'll probably prefer an environmental picture to hang above the couch in the family room or to use for your holiday greeting cards. It's great to have an option.

Setting Up a Portrait Studio

A home portrait studio is a bit more complicated than the little niche for close-ups I described in the last chapter. People pictures take up more room, and you may not have that much space to devote to a studio on a full-time basis. Instead, you'll want to choose the space and gear you need and arrange things so that your portrait studio is as easy to set up and tear down as possible. This section will expand on the studio setup advice laid out in Chapter 6.

Background

Backgrounds are an important consideration for more formal portraits. You can get great casual pictures with the gang posed on the couch in the living room, and, in fact, you should try some of the lighting techniques discussed later in this chapter in that sort of an environment. Good lighting can elevate the family room portrait well above the snapshot category. However, if you want a true studio portrait, you're going to have to arrange for a more formal background. Luckily, that's easy to do.

Cloth

I've had great luck with those velour cloth backdrops I mentioned in the last chapter. The key is to purchase cloth that is wide enough and long enough to allow posing one or more people full-length. This requires finding a bolt that is 54- to 60-inches wide. Purchase a piece that is a lot longer than you think you need. Six yards isn't too much when you want to stretch the cloth up to the ceiling, then drape it down on the floor. Make sure your fabric is easily washable because it will get soiled from people walking on it. Buy as many different colors as you can afford.

Seamless Paper

Seamless paper is available in 9- and 12-foot widths and around 36 feet long. Paper backdrops are easily damaged because they become wrinkled with handling and dirty as people walk on them. When a piece becomes soiled, just rip it off and roll off some more. If you can, avoid using seamless paper on thick carpets. They don't provide enough support for the paper, so it rips more easily. A wood floor may be a better choice.

Make Your Own Backdrop

You've probably admired those abstract backgrounds with, perhaps, a cloud effect, such as the one shown in figure 7.2. Painted backdrop canvases are available for big bucks from professional photography supply houses, but you can easily make your own, as I did.

7.2 | Using a sponge to dab paint on a piece of canvas can create a workable backdrop for portraits.

Tip from the pros: Although professional photographers won't blink an eye at purchasing backdrops they can use repeatedly, most don't hesitate to create their own props and backgrounds to give their photography a customized, personal flavor. When my studio was a going concern, I used the reverse side of 4×8 sheets of paneling to create dozens of backgrounds for individual portraits. Of course, I had a permanent studio to store them in. You're probably better off using sheets of awning canvas. The secret is to use a sponge to paint them with colors. You'll be surprised at the results, even if you're not the artistic type. Start painting, using lighter colors in the center and working your way toward the edges with darker pigments. The sponge will give the surface an arty, splotchy effect that will look great, especially when it's out of focus. Browns and earth colors are recommended for men; brighter colors, especially blues, work well for women and children. Remember, if you make any mistakes or don't like your initial results, you can always paint over them.

Supports

The same kind of supports you may have collected for the close-up photography described in Chapter 6 will serve you in good stead for people pictures. You'll need stands for your background, lighting, and camera, although in many portrait situations you'll want to dispense with a tripod.

Background Supports

Whether you're using cloth backdrops, seamless paper, or another background, you'll need some sort of framework to support it. I prefer sturdy light stands for lightweight backgrounds and ceiling supports for heavier paper rolls. You may not be able or willing to nail anything to your ceiling (this is one instance when having a basement or attic is great), but you can still build some sort of easily disassembled framework to hold your backdrop.

Tip from the pros: You can purchase spring-loaded vertical supports that fit tightly between your floor and ceiling but can be released and stored when not in use. These work well with sturdy ceilings or those with overhead beams. You can try making your own: Cut a 2×4 a few inches shorter than your ceiling height. Pad one end of the 2×4 so it won't damage your ceiling, then put the end that rests on the floor in a coffee can with a spring mechanism of your choice. Press the 2×4 down to get enough slack to slide it in place, then release to allow your spring to hold it firmly in a vertical position. The spring must be strong enough to resist the downward pull of your backdrop material.

Lighting Supports

You can use the same kind of light stands or other supports for your lights that I described in Chapter 6. As I mentioned earlier, light stands, such as the one shown in figure 7.3, are a lifetime investment. Unless you manage to lose one, they'll last forever. You'll need to add clamps or other fasteners to fix your lights, and, perhaps, umbrellas to the stands.

7.3 | Light stands are a lifetime investment.

Camera Supports

A tripod is not essential for people photography, particularly if you're using electronic flash, and in many cases can be detrimental. You'll want to be able to roam around a little to get various angles, move in and out to change from full-length or three-quarters portrait to close-up.

The only times you'll need a tripod for portraits is when you need to lock down the camera to get a precise composition or when you're working with relatively low light levels and need the tripod to steady the camera. For example, you might be shooting a series of head shots for your company and would like each photo to be taken from the exact same distance and angle. Or you may be taking pictures using diffused window light or with household lamps as your illumination. Perhaps you simply want the camera to hold still while your camera's self-timer gives you a short delay to get in the photograph yourself. In all three cases, a tripod can be useful as a camera support.

Lighting Equipment

Lighting is one of the most important tools for creative portraiture. The way you arrange your illumination can have a dramatic effect on the mood of a photo. Lighting can focus interest on your subject. You can even use lighting techniques to improve the looks of a subject with less-than-perfect features.

So, although very good portraits can be taken with just one light source, you'll find that mastering multiple light sources opens new creative avenues. But note that I said multiple light *sources*. You don't have to encumber your home or office studio with dozens of different lights. Often, a skylight, window, or reflector can serve as an effective light source. Outdoors, you may work with the light from the sun, supplemented by reflectors or electronic flash. You'll learn how to use these light sources later in this chapter.

Existing Light

The existing light indoors or outdoors can be perfect for good people pictures. Rembrandt reportedly cut a trapdoor in the ceiling of his studio and used that to illuminate many of his portraits. If you have a room with a skylight, you may find that suitable for portraits at certain times of day. Some memorable pictures have been taken using only the soft light that suffuses from a window. Indeed, you'll find references to north light (that is, a window orientation that produces diffuse light from dawn to dusk) throughout painting and photographic literature.

Electronic Flash

Electronic flash is often the best choice for indoor portraiture. The short duration of flash captures a moment in a fraction of a second, without danger of blur from a slow shutter speed. The high intensity of flash means you can use small f-stops if you want, so all of your subject will be in sharp focus. Flash can be reduced in intensity, as well, giving you the option of using selective focus, too. Flash can be harsh and direct or soft and diffuse.

The chief problem with electronic flash is that it is difficult to preview how flash illumination will appear in the final picture. Fortunately, you can overcome this limitation, and I'll show you how later in this section.

Electronic flash comes in many forms, from the built-in flash on your digital camera to external battery-powered units to studio flash that operate from AC power or large battery packs. Unless you're moving into portraiture in a big way, you don't need studio flash units. However, investigate external battery-powered flash units that are compatible with your digital camera. Many digital cameras cannot use electronic flash intended for film cameras because conventional flash units use a voltage to trigger the flash (through a switch in the camera) that is too high and is likely to fry the electronics of a digital model.

Some add-on flash units have a built-in device called a slave sensor that triggers the flash when the sensor detects another unit firing. These can be safely used with any camera because they have no direct connection to the camera. You also can purchase detectors that attach to any flash unit, turning it into a slave flash.

If you're using an external flash, make sure you turn off your digital camera's internal flash unit. Some digital camera models require you to have the internal flash flipped up, even if disabled, to activate the external flash connector. Check your camera's instruction manual carefully to see exactly what you need to do to use an external flash unit.

If you use your electronic flash on stands, you may be able to rig an incandescent light alongside each to give you some indication of what your lighting looks like. These modeling lights work especially well if your electronic flash is pointed at a reflector, such as an umbrella. That's because the softening effect of the umbrella reduces the variation in illumination that results when the flash and incandescent lamp aren't in precisely the same position.

Incandescent Lights

You'll find that incandescent lights are inexpensive, easy to set up, and make it simple to preview your lighting effects. You never have to worry about what your lighting will look like if you use incandescent lamps.

Unfortunately, lamps are not as intense as flash and may not provide enough illumination for good handheld exposures at short shutter speeds. Or if the lamps are intense enough, they may be too hot to pose under for long periods of time. In addition, incandescent lamps are much redder than the illumination provided by daylight or electronic flash, so you may have to change your camera's white balance control to compensate. (Many digital models have automatic white balance control, but it's not foolproof.)

Although you can use just about any light, you might want to investigate incandescent lamps made especially for photography. They aren't overly expensive, and hardware, such as mounting clamps, umbrella adapters, and so forth, are easier to buy for them.

Lighting Paraphernalia

Dozens of different gadgets and accessories are associated with portrait lighting equipment. You don't need all of them, but it's useful to learn a bit about what's available because much of this paraphernalia can be made or purchased at low cost.

Reflectors

Reflectors bounce some of the illumination from other light sources onto your subject, serving as a low-cost secondary light source in their own right. Large sheets of foamboard, which you can stand up and lean against things at the proper angle, poster board, Mylar sheets, or anything that reflects light can be used.

Gobos

Gobos and cookies are the opposite of a reflector. They can be a black drape or sheet placed between a light source and the subject to block some light, and they are handy when you have an unwanted light source, such as a window, that's spoiling the effect you want. These items are actually more of a tool for video and cinema photographers and for stage productions because they can include cutouts that let some light through to produce an interesting combination of light and shadows, such as window frames, trees, or logos. However, still photographers should know about them and use them when appropriate.

Barndoors and Snoots

These devices limit where the light from a flash or lamp goes, as shown in figure 7.4. A barndoor has two or four hinged flaps that can move into or out of the path of the light. Subtle adjustments can be made to feather the light on your subject. Snoots are conical devices that focus the light down to a narrow spot. They are excellent for creating a light that illuminates a small area, such as the hair of the subject.

7.4 | Barndoors and snoots can be used to direct light with great precision.

You can easily make your own barndoors or snoots out of cardboard or tin. (Tin is a better choice for accessories used near hot incandescent lamps.) Spray paint them with black heat-resistant barbeque grill paint.

Umbrellas

A good set of umbrellas is the best investment you can make for portrait photography. Umbrellas soften the light in ways you can control and use for artistic effect. For example, a soft-white umbrella provides very diffuse illumination, but you also can purchase umbrellas with shiny silver or gold interiors, which provide a broad light source that still has snap and contrast.

Umbrellas produced for professional photographers are compatible with various lighting clamp systems that make them easy to set up and manipulate.

Tip from the pros: Gold umbrellas, in particular, are prized for the warm illumination they provide. They are used extensively for fashion and glamour photography because of the flattering skin tones their light produces. Silver umbrellas have more contrast and snap than soft-white models. The edges of the illumination provided by silver umbrellas is more sharply defined, so you can angle the umbrella to feather the light on your subject (that is, place strong light on some parts and fade to less light on others).

However, you also can use ordinary umbrellas of the type people take out into the rain. I found a source selling white umbrellas that collapse down to less than a foot in length for about $5.00 each. I picked up a dozen, and I use them in photojournalism-type situations (I can hold the umbrella and flash unit in my left hand and shoot with the camera held in my right hand), but you can jury-rig clamps to hold them to light stands or other supports. Collapsible umbrellas usually have small diameters and must be used relatively close to get a soft, wraparound lighting effect. Larger sizes are needed to provide illumination from greater distances (say, 10 to 12 feet). Figure 7.5 shows an inexpensive umbrella that's transportable and versatile.

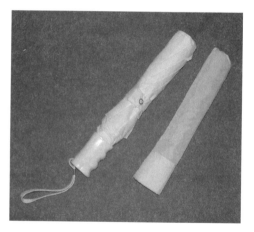

7.5 | If you can find a plain white collapsible umbrella, you can use it for your portrait work.

> *Tip from the pros:* You don't have to point the concave side of an umbrella at your subject. Orient the convex side toward the subject and shine your flash or incandescent light through the umbrella for an even softer, broader, and less-intense lighting effect.

Light Boxes

A light box is a large framework with a translucent front and space to insert a flash or lamp. Light boxes provide very soft, diffuse illumination. If you're ambitious, you can build one 6 feet tall (cover the framework with a white bed sheet or other translucent material) that can illuminate groups or full-length portraits.

Lighting Basics

Entire books have been written about portrait lighting, but I have only part of a chapter, so I'm going to introduce you to the basic techniques of lighting people attractively. Once you've mastered these fundamentals, you'll find ways to expand them as you gain experience. Your first task is to learn about the different types of multiple light sources. This section will provide a brief introduction to lighting techniques (see figure 7.6 for a diagram of a typical portrait lighting setup). There will be some additional nuts and bolts later in the chapter.

Using Multiple Light Sources

You don't need to use all the light sources I describe in this section, but it's good to know about them and know how they are used. Remember that these individual light sources don't have to be flash units or lamps. For example, you can use a reflector placed at the camera to bounce light into shadows as a replacement for a fill light.

Main Light

The main light, or key light, is the primary light source used to illuminate a portrait. It may, in fact, be the only light you use, or you may augment it with other light sources. The main light is most often placed in front of the subject and on one side of the camera. Some kinds of lighting call for the main light to be placed relatively high, above the subject's eye level, or lower, at eye level. You usually won't put a main light lower than that.

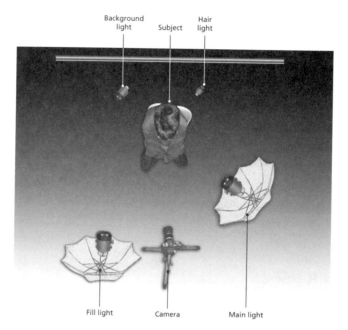

Background
light | Subject | Hair
light

Fill light | Camera | Main light

7.6 | This is a simplified diagram of a typical portrait lighting setup.

Placed to the side, the main light becomes a sidelight that illuminates one side, or the profile, of a subject who is facing the light. Placed behind the subject, the main light can produce a silhouette effect, if no other lights are used, or a backlit effect, if additional lighting is used to illuminate the subject from the front. I'll show you how to create lighting effects using the main light shortly.

Fill Light

The fill light is usually the second most powerful light used to illuminate a portrait. Fill light lightens the shadows cast by the main light. The relationship between the main light and fill light determines, in part, the contrast of a scene. If the main and fill are almost equal, the picture will be relatively low in contrast. If the main light is much more powerful than the fill light, the shadows will be somewhat darker, and the image will have higher contrast.

Fill lights are most often placed at the camera position, so they fill the shadows that the camera sees from the main light.

Tip from the pros: In lighting handbooks, you'll often see references to lighting ratios, which compare the relative strength of the main light to the fill light. Professional photographers can calculate these ratios using a device called a flash meter, which is a light meter that measures the brief illumination dispensed by an electronic flash unit. The goal is not to figure a ratio for some esoteric purpose but, rather, to see whether the main and fill lights complement each other in the desired way to produce a high-key (high-contrast) or low-key (low-contrast) picture. If you're using incandescent lights or electronic flash with modeling lights, you can estimate the relationship visually.

Background Light

A light illuminating the background is another common light source used in portraits. This light is used to determine the degree of separation between the subject and the background and also can provide interesting lighting effects on the background. You can even turn the background light toward the back of the subject, producing a halo or backlight effect.

Hair Light

A hair light is usually a small light directed at the hair of the subject to provide an attractive highlight. Often, a snoot or barndoor is used to keep the hair light from spilling down on the subject's face. A hair light must be controlled carefully so it doesn't form an overexposed hot spot on the subject's head.

Lighting Techniques

Although I'll describe each of the most common lighting techniques, you'll want to set up some lights and see for yourself exactly how they work. Later in this chapter I'll provide a diagram that shows exactly how to achieve a particular effect.

Short Lighting

Short lighting, also called narrow lighting, is produced when the main light illuminates the side of the face that is turned away from the camera, as shown in figure 7.7. This is a very common lighting technique that can be used with men, women, and children.

7.7 | With short lighting, the main light source comes from the side of the face directed away from the camera.

This type of lighting tends to emphasize facial contours, so it's an excellent technique for highlighting those with "interesting" faces. It also tends to make faces look narrower, so those with plump or round faces will look better with short lighting. Use a weak fill light for men to create a masculine look.

Broad Lighting

Broad lighting is the opposite of short lighting. The main light illuminates the side of the face that is turned toward the camera. It de-emphasizes facial textures (teenagers may love this effect) and widens narrow or thin faces. Figure 7.8 shows the same subject pictured in figure 7.7 but with broad lighting instead of short lighting.

Butterfly Lighting

Butterfly lighting was one of the original glamour lighting effects. The main light is placed directly in front of the face above eye level and casts a shadow underneath the nose. This is a great lighting technique to use for women. Butterfly lighting tends to emphasize the ears, making it a bad choice for men and women whose hairstyle features hair pulled back and behind the ears. Figure 7.9 shows a portrait with basic butterfly lighting at left and the final result with a little diffusion added at right. Notice that the ears aren't a problem with this portrait because they are hidden behind the model's hair.

7.8 | **Broad lighting widens narrow or thin faces by emphasizing the side of the face turned towards the camera.**

7.9 | **Butterfly lighting was one of the original glamour lighting effects.**

Rembrandt Lighting

Rembrandt lighting is another flattering lighting technique that is better for men. The main light is placed high and favors the side of the face that is turned away from the camera. The side of the face turned towards the

7.10 | Rembrandt lighting lends an Old Masters' touch to portraiture.

camera will be partially in shadow, typically with a roughly triangular highlight under the eye closest to the camera, as shown in figure 7.10.

Side Lighting

Side lighting is illumination that comes directly from one side and is good for profile photos. You also can achieve some dramatic half-face pictures if your subject is illuminated from one side but is facing the camera. The amount of fill light determines how dramatic this effect is. For figure 7.11, I used no fill or background lights at all, producing this stark profile.

7.11 | Side lighting can create dramatic profile photos.

Backlighting

With a backlit photo, most of the illumination comes from behind the subject and doesn't really light the subject as much as it defines its edges. Use additional fill light to provide for detail in the subject's front. For figure 7.12, I took a portrait of the clown by placing a light behind his head. The existing room light was sufficient to illuminate his face. The camera was placed on a tripod for a relatively long 1/2-second exposure.

7.12 | Backlighting helps define the edges of a portrait subject.

Taking Your First Portraits

It's showtime (again!). This section will lead you through taking your first portrait photos, showing you how to pose and light your subjects successfully. I'll assume you already have your background put up and your lights set up and ready for artistic arrangements.

Posing Your Subjects

The important thing is that your victim or victims must be relaxed and comfortable. The days when portrait subjects had to be immobilized in head braces for their daguerreotypes are long past. Don't make your subjects stand for anything other than a full-length portrait. Stools make a great seat because they discourage slouching. An individual can sit tall in a stool, alert and ready to take your direction. Because they have no backs, stools won't intrude on your picture, either.

But don't be afraid to use other kinds of resting places or to incorporate them into the photo. Figure 7.13 shows a rocking chair that's apparently not as uncomfortable as you might think.

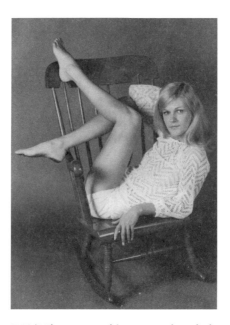

7.13 | When your subjects are relaxed, they are more comfortable being photographed.

If you're photographing an individual, you can try different poses as you work. For group pictures, you'll probably want to try and arrange everyone in a pleasing away and take several sets of pictures of each pose before moving on. Use the compositional rules you learned in Chapter 5 to arrange your group. For example, in figure 7.14, the three gangsters' faces are arranged in the upper third of the frame. Although all three heads are roughly on the same level, they actually form a curving line, pointing to the upper right corner, which is the same direction the tommy gun held by the Big Boss is pointed.

7.14 | Avoid having all the heads in a lineup at exactly the same level.

A better arrangement is the faux-Victorian family in figure 7.15. Note how the figures are all turned slightly toward the center of the photo, the seated matriarch (my mother-in-law, actually). Despite the difference in height between the various family members, their faces all form a tight little trapezoid that could actually form a composition of its own.

This photo also illustrates one of the rules of thumb for positioning a camera for individual and group photos: If you're shooting photos of your subjects from the waist up, position the camera at chest or eye level. For this full-length photo, the camera was placed at waist level (which happened to be eye level for my mom-in-law).

When shooting individuals, you can vary the camera's viewpoint slightly to portray your subject in a more flattering way. For example, raise the camera slightly above eye level if you want to elongate a nose, narrow a chin, broaden a weak forehead, or de-emphasize a prominent jaw line. If your subject has a wide forehead, long nose, or weak chin, lower the camera a little. If you encounter someone with a strong jaw and long nose, however, you're in a heap of trouble.

7.15 | Position the camera at waist level for full-length portraits.

I'd need six or seven chapters to provide detailed instructions on posing humans, and even then I could provide you only with guidelines because you're working with living, breathing people and not statues you can arrange any way you like. Your best bet is to look through magazines or books and find poses you like, and then try them out with your subjects. Even the best-looking poses don't always look great with every subject.

Nobody's perfect, and a portrait is the bad time to discover exactly where an individual's imperfections lie. The following are some general tips to keep in mind to minimize defects:

- *Try to photograph the edges of hands, such as in figure 7.10, because they are more attractive than the backs or palms of hands, as shown in figure 7.15—* The bottoms of feet are downright ugly, but you can sometimes get away with side views, such as in figure 7.13, if the feet are young enough and there are other things to look at in the photo.

- *Bald heads are pretty cool these days, but if your subject is sensitive about a bare pate, elevate your victim's chin and lower your camera slightly.*

- *For long, large, or angular noses, try having your subject face directly into the camera.*

- *To minimize prominent ears, try shooting your subject in profile, or use short lighting so the ear nearest the camera is in shadow.*

- *Use lighting to maximize your subjects' positive attributes—and de-emphasize their flaws—*If you want to minimize wrinkles or facial defects, such as scars or bad complexion, use softer, more diffuse lighting; take a step backwards and photograph your subject from the waist up to reduce the relative size of the face; keep the main light at eye level so it doesn't cast shadows; consider using a diffusing filter or add diffusion later in your image editor.

> **Tip from the pros:** *Diffusion is a great way to add a soft, romantic look to a portrait, even if your subject doesn't suffer from significant facial imperfections. You can purchase diffusion filters or make your own by smearing a little petroleum jelly around the edges of the plain glass skylight filter. Figure 7.16 was taken using a smeared filter, whereas for figure 7.17 I boosted the contrast and added diffusion in Photoshop.*

- *If your subject is wearing glasses, be wary of reflections off the glass—*Have the subject raise or lower his or her chin slightly, and make sure your flash is bouncing off the face at an angle, rather than straight on.

Arrange Your Lighting

Next, you'll want to arrange your lighting. Choose your lighting based on the guidelines I presented earlier in this chapter, but feel free to experiment. The following sections provide some quick instructions for arranging your lights to reproduce each of the key lighting techniques. Keep in mind that each of the techniques can also be reproduced as its own mirror image: If the subject is turned the opposite way from the direction I use in each illustration, just swap the main and fill lights from the right to left side, or vice versa.

7.16 | A little petroleum jelly on a skylight filter can create a soft, blurry edge around a centrally sharp image.

7.17 | You also can add diffusion within an image editor.

Short Lighting

With short lighting, the main light illuminates the side of the face turned away from the camera. In the bird's-eye view shown in figure 7.18, our subject is looking over the photographer's right shoulder. The main light is at the right side of the setup, and the fill light is at the photographer's left.

Because the fill light is about twice as far from the subject as the main light, if both lights are of the same power, the fill light will automatically be only one-quarter as intense as the main light (thanks to the inverse-square law). If the shadows are too dark, move the fill light closer or move the main light back slightly.

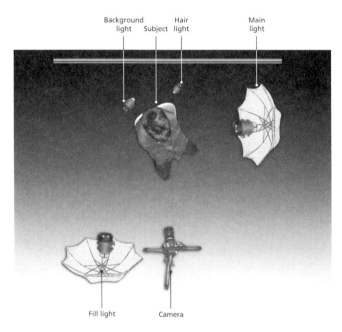

7.18 | With short lighting, the main light source comes from the side of the face directed away from the camera.

Broad Lighting

As you know, broad lighting is the opposite of short lighting. The main light illuminates the side of the face turned toward the camera, as you can see in figure 7.19.

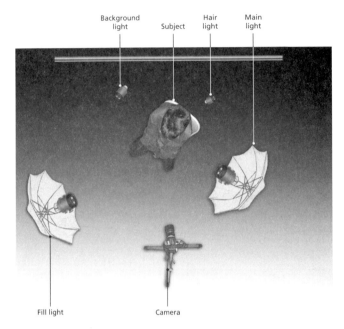

Background light • Subject • Hair light • Main light • Fill light • Camera

7.19 | Broad lighting illuminates the side of the face turned toward the camera.

Butterfly Lighting

Butterfly lighting is easy to achieve. Just place the main light at the camera position and raise it high enough above eye level to produce a shadow under the nose of the subject. Don't raise the light so high that the shadow extends down to their mouth. You can use a fill light if you want to reduce the inkiness of the shadows, as shown in figure 7.20.

Rembrandt Lighting

For Rembrandt lighting, place the light facing the side of the face turned away from the camera, just as you did with short lighting, but move the light up above eye level. Eliminate or reduce the strength of the fill light for a dramatic effect or soften the shadows with fill light. Figure 7.21 shows you how to arrange lights for a Rembrandt effect.

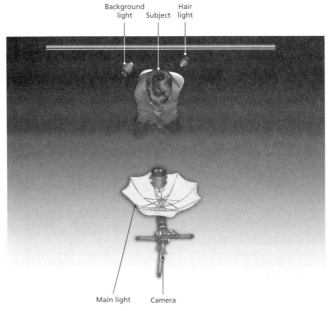

7.20 | **Butterfly lighting is a glamour lighting effect.**

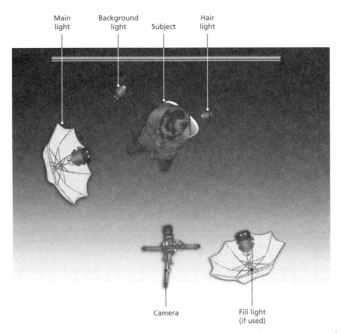

7.21 | **Remember to move the main light above the camera, as if it were a trapdoor in the ceiling of Rembrandt's studio.**

Side Lighting

Side lighting comes primarily directly from one side. You can use it for profiles or for half-face effects, such as of the Fab Four on the much copied/parodied cover of *Meet the Beatles/With the Beatles*. As I mentioned, the amount of fill light determines how dramatic this effect is. Figure 7.22 shows you how to set up lights for side lighting. You can place the main light slightly behind the subject to minimize the amount of light that spills over onto the side of the face that's toward the camera.

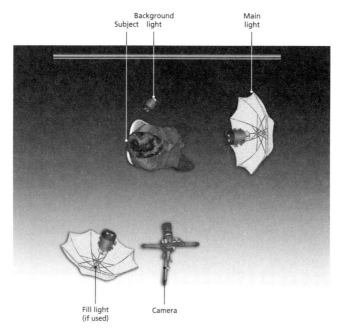

7.22 | Side lighting can create dramatic profile or half-face photos.

Backlighting

With a backlit photo, a strong amount of light comes from behind the subject, enough to illuminate the edges. You can use the background light for backlighting and put your main and fill lights to work in a subordinate role by reducing their intensity. Or you can use the main light as the backlight (place it below or above the camera's field of view) and fill in the shadows with your fill light. One way of producing backlighting is shown in figure 7.23.

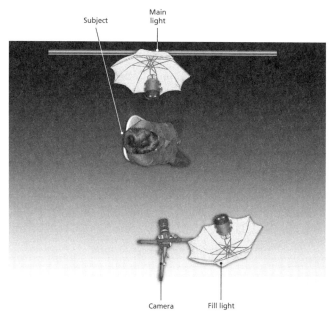

Subject Main light

Camera Fill light

7.23 | Backlighting provides a dramatic effect.

Choosing a Lens for Portraits

The zoom setting you use for portraits can have a significant effect on how flattering the final photograph is. As I've mentioned before, wide-angle lenses tend to introduce apparent distortion, making things closer to the camera (such as noses) look much larger than things farther away (such as ears). Wide angles also narrow faces, sometimes to a ludicrous degree. So, wide-angle settings (the equivalent of 35mm or wider with a 35mm camera) are very bad for portraits. You might be tempted by tight confines to use a wide-angle setting for portraits, but you should resist the temptation.

Telephoto lenses tend to widen faces. A long telephoto setting (say, the equivalent of 150mm to 200mm) is usually a bad choice for portraits. Your best bet is a compromise: a short telephoto setting that provides a flattering rendition of features but does not widen the face unnaturally. For full-length photos, try the equivalent of 50mm to 85mm; for 3/4-length portraits, 85mm to 105mm; for head-and-shoulders portraits, nothing beats a 105mm setting.

Take the Picture!

You'll want to take lots of photos to capture various expressions and angles. Keep talking with your subject, and not just to provide them with instructions on where to place their arms and legs or how to tilt their head. Mention how great they're doing; tell them how much they are going to like these photos.

Tip from the pros: *Over time, you'll develop a breezy line of patter that keeps your models relaxed. When working with amateurs, I use some funny stock phrases, such as, "Oh, I see you've done this before" or "Sorry, but we have to keep doing this until I get it right." You don't have to be that corny, but you'll soon collect a stockpile of jokes and phrases that will put your subjects at ease.*

If you're using electronic flash, make sure you allow enough time for your flash to recycle between pictures. I've been lucky enough to use studio lights with almost instantaneous recycling. In fact, my equipment has a setting that turns off the modeling light briefly as the flash triggers, then turns it back on only when the flash unit is ready to go for the next picture. You may have to watch the LED ready light on the back of your flash units. If you're using nonrechargeable batteries, the time between flashes may increase dramatically as the batteries are depleted. Have plenty of extra batteries on hand. Because rechargeables can die without warning, it's especially important to keep spares available.

Tip from the pros: *People may blink during a flash exposure, and you'll end up with a photo showing their eyelids instead of their eyes. The problem is particularly troublesome when shooting groups: The more people in the picture, the greater the odds one of them will have their eyes closed. Although you can review each shot on your LCD, a faster way is simply to ask your subjects to watch for the flash and then tell you whether it was red or white after the picture was taken. If the flash was red, they viewed it through closed eyelids, and that particular picture, at least, is no good.*

Next Up

You'll find more people-picture situations in the following two chapters, which deal with taking pictures for publication and with sports and action photography. Remember that everything in this chapter, as well as those that follow, apply to photographs of animals, too.

Chapter 8

Shooting for Publication

This chapter will show you how to create
pictures for print publication, whether your
destination is the conventional printing
press, desktop publishing software, or some
other layout and publishing option.

Get Published!

You, too, can be a published photographer. If getting into print is your goal, your digital camera and your photographic skills are exactly what you need. This chapter will cover the photographic techniques you need to perfect, along with some advice on preparing your work for publication.

If your initial sights are not set too high (that is, you're looking to see print in your local newspaper or regional magazine, rather than *National Geographic*), you can easily get published. Some of the most common outlets include the following:

- *Self-publishing*—Print your own newsletter, publish a fanzine about your hobby or favorite TV show, or, if you're ambitious, investigate subsidy publishing, where you pay the publishing costs but receive most or all of the profits. You'll have total control, and if your work is good, you may even find a market to help offset your costs.

- *Company newsletters and publications*—If your company is a small one, your managers might be delighted to find a willing photographer. Even larger organizations may be open to employee-submitted work. If *photographer* isn't in your job description now, it could be in the future, and, at the very least, published photos will look good on your résumé.

- *External company public relations (PR) and advertising*—I once had a photo published in the prestigious publication *Scientific American*, even though I don't possess a scientific mind. I'm not making this up. My picture wasn't published as editorial matter: A PR photo I took for a client was used in a full-page advertisement my client purchased.

- *Trade magazines*—You'll always have the most success photographing what you understand well, and you can translate knowledge of your industry into print at any of the many trade publications that cover it. Photos at conferences or trade shows are a good place to start. The pay may be low or nonexistent to start, but if you become a regular contributor to a magazine, your work can pay off. Of my entire portfolio, my photo of a sludge mixer on the cover of *Waste and Water Management* is still one of the items I'm most proud of.

- *Special interest publications*—Every hobby or special interest, from model trains to whatever it is they do with yachts, has its own clutch of magazines, like the one shown in figure 8.1. If you understand the field, you can get

8.1 | You, too, can be published in a special interest publication.

published, even if you submit nothing more than tips or tricks photos. I once came up with 15 different things you could do with an empty film can (for example, fill it with water and freeze, then use it to cool down hot developer without diluting it) and ended up with a whole series of tips and tricks photo/captions.

- *Local newspapers*—You can submit photos to your local paper on behalf of your school, club, or business. If you're good, you might even be able to convince the paper to hire you as a part-time stringer.

What's Different?

You might ask what's different about shooting for publication, as opposed to taking pictures for your Web site, desktop presentation, or personal photo album. Fortunately, the differences aren't as dramatic as you might think, especially in this electronic age. In the past, newspapers preferred black-and-white glossy prints, and magazines insisted on color transparencies. You'll find that today newspapers are glad to get color prints such as those produced by top-notch ink jet printers and can even work with TIFF (tagged image file format) files saved on CD-R (recordable CD-ROMs). Magazines, too, are amenable to TIFF files if you can provide them in high enough resolution.

Therein lies the chief difference in creating images for publication: the sharper and higher the resolution, the better the images will reproduce. A 3-megapixel camera will create pictures sharp enough for most publication applications, short of a full-page or double-page spread. Even a 2-megapixel camera can provide sufficient resolution if you crop tightly and don't waste a lot of space.

So, you'll want to use the highest resolution setting and lowest JPEG (Joint Photographic Experts Group) compression ratio your camera provides. Some cameras can save as TIFF files without discarding any image information at all, as shown in figure 8.2. The chief drawback of this mode is that you may be able to shoot only one or two pictures per memory card in ultrahigh res mode.

8.2 | The difference between a TIFF image saved by a digital camera (left) and a JPEG image saved by the same camera (right) can be significant.

Colors should be rich and fully saturated, with a full range of tones (unless you're shooting an arty picture that intentionally limits the tones and colors). Try to avoid having important details in shadows or very bright highlights because they may not reproduce well. This is especially true if your target publication is a newspaper. Although production techniques have improved dramatically, newsprint still sucks up a lot of ink, causing the half-tone dots that make up an image to enlarge slightly. Shadows, especially, often are reproduced darker than they appear in your original picture.

You'll also want to compose your picture carefully and eliminate wasted space and unnecessary elements. Your photographs may appear on a page laid out so they are only a few inches wide, so if you want important details such as faces to appear wider than a fingernail, you should make them a prominent portion of your photo. Figure 8.3 shows a typical publicity shot with nice, large faces.

8.3 | If you want your subjects to be recognizable, make their faces large.

Public Relations Photography

Although this section is directed primarily at external publicity, most of the information applies to company publications, or even personal newsletters, you might contribute to. As my old journalism prof always reminded me, one of the publics that public relations targets is the members or employees of the company or organization. You want their support, just as you desire the understanding of the general public through traditional news media. Great photos and good publicity can help.

The following sections include some tips for creating what PR folks call deliverables, in attractive and publishable photographic and caption format.

Arranging a Photo-Worthy Event

As a reformed PR flack, I don't want to reveal any trade secrets (the buzzword *deliverables* may be enough for this chapter), but the key to staging a photo-worthy event is not so much the event itself as it is the interesting story angle. It's the interesting hook that makes readers of your company publication, fanzine, or local newspaper want to look at the photo and read the text that accompanies it. In fact, you may even find that the concept itself creates the justification for the event. Consider these situations: Your company is approaching its 75th anniversary. Your service club is donating used eyeglasses for the benefit of the poor in a developing country. Your school is holding a Book Fair. Your softball team has the most dominant pitcher anyone has seen locally in many years. An overeager classmate is flying 12,000 miles to attend your 20-year class reunion. These all may be interesting items, but they clearly don't have an "event" attached to them. Try some of these on for size (and I'll admit that some of them are overly gimmicky or corny—but they just might work):

- *The company's 75th anniversary*—Is the founder or first customer still alive? Does anyone have a sample of the very first product made by the firm (buggy whips and slide rules make great, picture-worthy anachronisms)? Is the first office/factory/retail site still standing; how is it being used today? Make a presentation or stage a celebration involving any of these and you have a photo opportunity.

- *Service club donation*—Does the developing country or organization have a local representative who can accept your donation? Do you have enough eyeglasses to fill, perhaps, a huge barrel that you can photograph? Can you give an award to the member who collected the most pairs of eyeglasses?

- *Book fair*—I took a photo featuring a huge stack of Harry Potter books at our school's previous book fair, then released the picture to our local newspapers two weeks before the next fair, which happened to take place a few days after the Harry Potter movie opened. Instant newsworthiness, as you can see in figure 8.4.

8.4 | Tying this publicity photo in with a movie premiere made it newsworthy (at the time).

- *Softball pitcher*—Maybe you could stage a stunt where your pitcher strikes out batters blindfolded?

- *Class reunion*—See if your classmates can show up wearing native/festive costumes from the countries where they are now living. Turn the reunion photo into a cultural exchange.

There's nothing inherently wrong with manufacturing an event, too, as long as it isn't done in a cynical or dishonest way. I was the PR guy for a regional group of an international organization that promoted literacy. I asked our 350 local members to nominate local teachers who happened to be outstanding educators. We also distributed nomination forms to each of the schools in our 10-county area. There was no voting; our board simply read through the nominations and selected the teachers who seemed to be doing a great job. We gave them awards and a dinner, and we took pictures. We had at least one good photo for each of the counties in our region. The teachers were thrilled by the appreciation and publicity, and my organization gained recognition and support in our region through its Excellence in Teaching awards.

Staging the Photo Shoot

In setting up the photo, you can follow most of the rules of composition that I outlined for you in Chapter 5. The following sections include some suggestions that relate more directly to this chapter.

Selecting Subjects

You'll want to select your victims from among those who are most relevant to the event, of course. Don't ignore the real hard workers, managers, and movers and shakers simply because they aren't the most photogenic. It's your job as the photographer to put them at ease and make them look good. Nobody likes the resentment that arises when the prettiest are always selected for the photos, least of all the chosen ones themselves. Instead, follow these guidelines:

- *Use only the minimum number of people that you can get away with*—Two are great; three acceptable. If you use more than that, it should be because everyone is equally deserving; that is, they are all receiving the same award, or each represents a different organization that contributed. You'd probably want to include every member of a championship bowling team and, perhaps, their sponsor. You probably wouldn't want to photograph every member of an advertising agency's creative team that just landed a big account.

- *Photograph a variety of people*—If the group has been photographed before, find out who, among those with equal standing, has already been featured. Give someone else a turn, if possible.

- *Consider dividing a large group into several smaller groups, if you do find yourself with a large group to photograph*—Give each group something different to do. You don't want a photo of six people receiving an award, followed by an otherwise identical photo of six different people receiving the award. I'll have some suggestions for handling group photos in a later section.

All else being equal, if you can select subjects with a mixture of seniority, experience, or backgrounds, you'll have a more interesting picture. Include members of both sexes and those from different ethnic groups, without appearing to be condescending. (You wouldn't, for example, want to include a very junior male member of a department in a photograph of its top executives simply because he was the only male in the group.)

Avoiding Clichés

Most of the photographic clichés have been around long enough to acquire names of their own: "grip and grin," "visiting fireman," and "giant check." As the wry humorist once said, "Avoid clichés like the plague!"

So, avoid pictures of two dignitaries shaking hands while they grin mindlessly at each other or, worse, directly at the camera. Instead, have them seated at a table having a discussion, perhaps reviewing a report. Your visiting "firefighter" (the name of the actual cliché is a bit sexist) can be shown participating in some activity that reflects the local ambiance. If your company builds cars, seat the subject behind the wheel of a model fresh off the assembly line. Or arrange for a demonstration of some sort. And, as for presenting a donation in the form of a giant check, don't do it, unless the check is really large (say, at least 10×20 feet) so that its sheer size becomes an interesting picture element. Otherwise, think up a more inventive visual way of showing money changing hands.

Arranging Your Subjects

All the rules for posing groups of humans described in the last chapter apply here. It's especially useful to get everyone grouped as close together as possible because the wider the photo is, the smaller everyone is going to appear. If you're featuring people, you'll want them to be large and recogniz-able. If it's a company product, you'll want that object large and visible, too.

If you know your target publication, study a few issues to see how they run photographs. Most papers run six columns wide, but the columns can vary in width. This is particularly true in view of the recent trend for newspapers to switch to a narrower 12.5-inch sheet, which looks positively slim alongside one of the old-time 15-inch-wide papers of yesteryear. Picture widths are described in columns—that is, a one-column, two-column, three-column, or four-column photo.

How you compose your photo can affect how large it appears in the newspa-per, although a good picture editor can crop a photo to fit just about any size. If you submit a vertically oriented photo that can't be easily cropped (that is, there is important information at both the top and bottom), you'll probably end up with, at most, a two-column photo in the paper. If you arrange your subjects so that the picture has a natural horizontal layout, you have a better chance of garnering a three- or four-column space, as shown in figure 8.5.

8.5 | This horizontal picture resulted in a three-column photo in a local newspaper.

Don't crop your picture too tightly; leave some space at the bottom that can be trimmed to make it fit the vertical space on the page. Cropping at the sides is less critical. The picture will likely be enlarged or reduced to fit the intended column width, then cropped at the bottom as appropriate.

If you need to break a large group of people into two photos, resign yourself to having only one published. You can enhance your chances of having both picked up by making each photo different and giving each an interesting angle. For example, if you have two photos, each with four people who have received an award, you might have one picture show one group working on the project that earned the award, and the other picture show the second group consulting with their manager about the project.

Lighting

Don't get fancy with lighting, especially if you're trying to create a picture that will reproduce well on cheap newsprint. Use even lighting and avoid shadows. If you're using your camera's built-in flash, make sure you're at eye level, or perhaps slightly higher, so the shadows will fall behind your subjects. Don't get too high (say, more than 1 foot above your subjects at a distance of 10 or 12 feet), or you'll capture the tops of everyone's heads. Too low, and you'll grab the undersides of their chins.

Moving everyone at least 4 or 5 feet from the wall or other background will reduce the chance that the shadows from a flash will fall on the wall. Watch for windows in the background, too! Step a foot or two to one side so that the flash won't be reflected directly back into the camera lens.

Case Study of a Successful Photo

To give you a better idea of what I'm talking about, let's look at how a particular PR photo was taken. In this case, an art teacher was having her classes prepare centerpieces for a local charity that served hot meals to needy people in our area. It was a good opportunity to get some publicity for the charity and the school.

The first set of centerpieces was of trees assembled from construction paper. I selected two cute kids who had made two of the nicest centerpieces, thus avoiding the problem of trying to get the entire art class in one photo. I posed them as you see in figure 8.6, with all the centerpieces in the foreground.

8.6 | This was a first attempt at a publicity photo.

This picture contains several problems. The cropping isn't very good, with lots of extra space at the top of the frame, but the newspaper's photo editor would probably take care of that. More important, the centerpieces in the foreground make a terrible clutter and aren't likely to be recognizable as anything other than a confetti collection. That's particularly true because this vertical composition would likely be run as a smallish two-column picture. The kids' faces would be too small, too.

Moving to a higher angle and composing a horizontal shot, I ended up with the picture shown in figure 8.7.

8.7 | Is this a better angle? Probably not.

The kids are larger, but the foreground is still ugly, and now we can clearly see a desk, trash basket, and a lot of clutter in the background. It's time to try again, as you can see in figure 8.8.

8.8 | A tighter composition improves the photo.

We're making some progress, but we're not quite there yet. The kids are larger, and they are the center of attention for the photograph. You can clearly see that the object the girl is holding appears to be a construction paper tree, so the foreground makes a little more sense. The boy is wielding the scissors he used to assemble his tree. Yet, a few problems still exist.

The big one is that the two kids are too far apart. The background is still quite cluttered. Figure 8.9 is the final picture I took, and the one the newspaper published.

8.9 | The final picture has all the elements of a good PR photo in place.

Although it's not perfect, this photo is a vast improvement over the original picture. Nice, large, smiling faces. The kids are grouped tightly together. The foreground has become a minor element of the picture and can be cropped out entirely if desired. It makes a good two-column picture or, if cropped at the bottom and top, a nice three- or four-column shot. (It was, in fact, published as a three-column picture.) If I had the picture to reshoot, I'd probably overlap the tree the girl is holding a little more with the boy's shirt and have him move his hand so it doesn't merge with the tree. But, all in all, it's a good publicity picture.

Producing "Placeable" Photos for Newspapers

First, a reality check. Most big city newspapers will not publish average publicity-oriented photos submitted by readers. If your event is truly newsworthy, you can arrange to have one of the paper's own photographers cover it, perhaps even accompanied by a reporter. You may even be able to round up some pre-event photo coverage if you dream up a worthy angle. Getting local press coverage is not that hard (I used to do it for a living), but explaining all the nuances of schmoozing the press is beyond the scope of this book.

However, suburban newspapers are often delighted to receive photos and short news releases from readers for individual, school, or club events. Weekly papers may even accept photos from local businesses. My own hometown newspaper (circulation 20,000) prefers to send its own photographers to events, but they regularly publish the photos and news releases that I send them.

The reasons why daily newspapers are reluctant to publish reader photos are numerous and complex. Newspapers must maintain their journalistic integrity; that's why, in the event a photo from a corporation is published in the editorial section, it is clearly labeled as such. Reader photos are rarely of the quality newspapers require, and they are often submitted too long after the event to be newsworthy. Unless you grab an exclusive picture at a breaking news event (in which case the newspaper will pay you for the picture) odds are against your photo getting published in larger papers.

Once you've captured your photo, you'll want to take the following steps to getting it published.

Printing

A good-quality 5×7-inch print is a must. Color-correct your image and adjust the brightness and contrast, then make a print on glossy photo paper using your ink jet printer. If you feel your printer is not up to snuff, run down to your local pharmacy or other retailer equipped with a Kodak Picture Maker kiosk. I've used the unit at my town's megastore when I was in a hurry.

Most kiosks accept SmartMedia or CompactFlash cards, plus various picture CD formats and, sometimes, PC Cards. Check before you visit the store. My pharmacy has a Kodak kiosk that does not accept memory cards; I have to travel an extra few miles to a store that does accept them. If you've copied the images from the memory card (say, for editing), save them back to the card in JPEG format, using the highest quality/lowest compression setting. I've had problems printing TIFF files at these kiosks, but I have never encountered a glitch when printing JPEGs.

You can print a single 8×10-inch sheet with various combinations of picture sizes for about $6.99. Two 5×7-inch prints will fit on a sheet with a little extra border at one side. That's your best size for submission to newspapers.

I usually also submit a CD-R disk with the photo as a full-resolution TIFF file, in case the newspaper's picture editors want to save a step. Even if I knew the paper was working directly from my CD-R, I'd still submit the hard copy photo. That's what gets the editor's attention: You can't expect a busy editor who receives dozens or hundreds of submissions a day to load your CD-ROM image to see if the paper can use it.

Cutline

Every photo should include a cutline, or caption, printed double spaced (so there is room for editing) on plain white paper, taped lightly to the back of the photo, and folded over the front so that the caption can be read while the editor reviews the picture, as shown in figure 8.10. Taping the cutline and picture together keeps them from getting separated on a cluttered desk. The editor can detach them when the photo enters the editing process.

Cutlines should include the following minimum information:

- *Name and phone number of the person who submitted the photograph*—The contact information is usually included in a line like "For additional information contact: Nancy Smith, 555-2395." The editor might want to check facts, get additional information, or merely confirm that the submission is legit.

- *Names and titles of every person in the photograph, clearly labeled*—Be sure to use directional terms like "Front row, left to right, Back row, left to right." Avoid other arrangements, such as "clockwise, from left," unless there is no possibility of misinterpreting the instructions. If you find it difficult to identify each person in the photo, you probably didn't compose the picture properly.

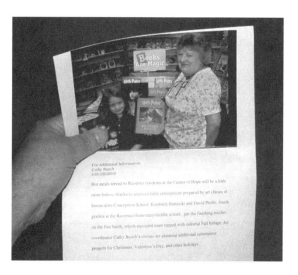

8.10 | Be sure to attach a caption to your photo.

- *All the basic "what, when, where, why" facts that accompany the "who" identification*—Don't worry about writing a polished news release; just put all the facts in there. Here's a caption I included with an actual photo submitted to our local paper (with some changes to protect the innocent):

> For Additional Information:
>
> Cathy Busch
>
> 999-555-2345
>
> Hot meals served to Smallville residents at the Center of Hope will be a little more festive, thanks to seasonal table centerpieces prepared by art classes at Smallville School. Kimberly Jones and Kevin Smith, fourth graders at the elementary school, put the finishing touches on the first batch, which represent trees topped with colorful fall foliage. Art coordinator Cathy Busch's classes are planning additional centerpiece projects for Christmas, Valentine's Day, and other holidays.

Note that I didn't include left/right instructions, because there were only two people in the photo, one clearly a girl and the other a boy, and the names were clearly gender specific (unlike, say, Pat or Robin). Under most circumstances, however, you'll need to specify the direction for the identification, to relieve the editor of the nagging doubt that, just this once, somebody has submitted a photo identified right to left.

Sending the Photo

Write the name of the editor who will receive the photo on the front of a sturdy envelope and place the picture and cutline inside. You may have to call the newspaper to determine the correct editor or reporter because most common beats, such as schools, city councils, clubs, general college news, and so on, are assigned to specific individuals. Getting the right name (and correct spelling) may make the difference between having your submission checked, or simply deposited in the circular file. At smaller papers, the clearinghouse may be a city editor who will pass your photo on to the right department or reporter.

I recommend dropping off the photo in person, if at all possible. You don't need to ask to speak to the reporter or editor directly. Just hand the envelope to the person at the front desk, or receptionist, and ask that it be delivered to the right person. Your photo will generally arrive sooner and won't be mixed up in the huge stack of mail every newspaper person receives (most of it junk news releases that the paper has not the slightest interest in). If you mention the content in a general way at the front desk, you might even prevent the photo from being misrouted and instead get it directed to an editor or reporter who is more interested in your material.

Keep in mind that this advice applies to smaller publications. The last thing a large newspaper needs is people walking in off the street with their priceless prose and photos. When in doubt, mail the photo instead.

Following Up

Don't let your photo fall into a black hole. A day or so after you submit the picture, follow up with the editor or reporter by phone, voice mail, or email, confirming that you delivered it and are hoping they find it useful. Don't ask for a reply. You want to nudge the recipient's memory, not become a pest. If they need more information, your phone number is right on the cutline.

If your photo is published, you might want to place a thank-you call to the editor or reporter, simply to show your appreciation and to determine if your submission was in the format they prefer. Henceforth, you probably won't need a lot of personal contact. (Unless you do want the reporter to consider doing a longer story.) You've established a relationship and have a better chance that your future submissions will receive the consideration they deserve.

Remember that reporters value contacts and sources for information they can call on when they need to. Don't flood the newspaper with submissions. I generally try to send in one item a month for my wife's art and Spanish programs at her school.

I recommend a book called *Taming the News Media* by J.W. Olsen for tips on preparing news releases, writing cover letters, and mounting low-budget PR campaigns. Although written for software authors looking for ink in the computer press, an amazing amount of the material applies to general-purpose newspaper PR. You can reach Olsen at his Web site, **http://www.jwolsen.com**. Readers who mention this book will receive a 50% discount off its list price.

Product Photography

If your company is a small one, it may not have a full-time photographer, and you may be called on to produce a quickie product photograph from time to time. Perhaps a product shot needs to go in the annual report, and there is no time to send the item out to a studio. Or perhaps you need a picture for a press kit. It's possible your club is selling entertainment coupon books and you'd like to put a photo of one in your club newsletter. Let your digital camera come to the rescue.

If your product is the size of a breadbox, or smaller, you'll find that the suggestions offered in Chapter 6 on close-up photography will tell you everything you need to know. As the product approaches people-size or elephantine dimensions, you're better off with the tips in Chapter 7 on photographing individuals and groups.

The chief things to remember when doing product photography follow:

- *The product has to look good*—Really good. You can mess up a portrait of your CEO, but you'd better not make your company's product look bad. I once had a client who insisted that his product, truck clutches, had to look glamorous. Fortunately, glamorous, to him, meant that I use a spotlight to provide sort of a halo effect around the clutch.

- *Correct color can be a crucial element of a product photograph, so do everything you can to get the colors right. (You can correct them using the techniques described in Chapter 11.)*—Colors of fabrics, metal surfaces, and other components, including parts that are part of a company's trade dress, such as official colors, logos, and so forth, must be exactly right.

- *Consider using a plain background that won't steal attention from the product*—A sports car might look best shot on a seaside cliff at sunset, but a truck clutch might best be pictured on a seamless backdrop. A porcelain figurine probably looks best on a plain background, too, as shown in figure 8.11.

8.11 | Most products look best on a plain background.

- *If the picture is intended for distribution to the press, you'll have to think up some way to make the picture more interesting than the product*—To show that a new component was dramatically lighter than previous versions, I once had a model pose with the item resting on a baby scale. It proved to be a popular picture because of the juxtaposition of human and baby scale with the industrial-strength component. However, although I liked this model's work enough to marry her, she's never forgiven me for getting her stuck with the title Miss Clutch.

- *Shoot the product from different angles*—Often, multiple angles will be needed to really show the product's features.

Next Up

Whether you're grabbing photos of the company softball game for your organization's newsletter, or immortalizing your family's exploits on the amateur soccer field, you'll find sports and action photography an exciting and rewarding avenue for exploring your digital camera's capabilities. You'll discover some valuable tips in the next chapter.

Digital
Photography
and Imaging
Color Studio

The gallery of images in this color section

showcases the kind of results you can

expect with your digital camera. You'll find

some of the best photos from the book,

plus four "bonus" pictures that didn't

appear in the text.

Horizontal layout.

Vertical composition.

Square arrangement.

Many scenes and objects lend themselves naturally to a particular type of composition (see Chapter 5). The landscape at top looks best with a horizontal layout. The figures at bottom left are naturally a vertical composition. Round objects, such as the inlaid gold plate (bottom right) often fit into a square arrangement.

Place important subjects in your photographs at the intersection of imaginary lines placed one third from the top, bottom, and sides of your frame (see Chapter 5).

Strong lines, like the diagonals of this shot of the Eiffel Tower, pull our gaze into a photograph.

Color Studio

Cropped too tight.

Balance better, but with distracting tree branch at right.

Final cropping with tree branch removed.

Cropping can improve a photo. The image at top is unbalanced and appears lopsided. The center version is more balanced, but includes a distracting tree at the right side of the frame. The bottom version is the best cropping for this picture, with all the elements balanced (see Chapter 5).

Using a wide lens opening can blur the background, which can make the foreground seem sharper in comparison, as you can tell by comparing the left and right versions of this flower photograph (see Chapter 4).

This restless feline rests peacefully in the arms of her owner, but focusing on the whiskers puts all the attention on the cat itself (see Chapter 4).

Close-up photography lets you explore worlds of your own creation through still life arrangements like this one (see Chapter 6).

A scanner was used to create this close-up "photograph." Simply place the object on the scanner's glass, cover it with a background, if you like, and scan (see Chapter 6).

Because inanimate objects stay put, you can use close-up photography to explore various lighting effects, such as the portrait-style lighting used for this photo (see Chapter 7).

Backlighting emphasized the edges of this porcelain figurine. There was enough existing light in the room to illuminate the front surface with no additional light fixtures required (see Chapter 7).

Color Studio

You can get by with one or two lights for portraits, but a full lighting setup will include a main light, fill light, background light, and hair light (see Chapter 7).

Avoid arranging all the faces in a group shot at the same level. In this photograph, the heads are arranged at slightly different positions (see Chapter 7).

This photo has a more interesting arrangement of the figures and faces, forming a good composition even if cropped more tightly than shown here (see Chapter 7).

Short lighting places the main light on the side of the face turned away from the camera (see Chapter 7).

Broad lighting, a less common lighting technique, places the main light on the side of the face turned towards the camera (see Chapter 7).

Rembrandt lighting is a flattering lighting technique that places the main light high and favoring the side of the face turned away from the camera. You can use this technique without any fill at all for a dramatic effect, or soften the shadows with a fill light or reflector (see Chapter 7).

Side lighting is an excellent technique for profiles (see Chapter 7).

Cluttered backgrounds aren't a good idea, but in this case all those books showcase the school's upcoming book fair.

Improve your chances of getting your publicity photos published by using a tight composition, with the people pictured close together, smiling, and doing something interesting (see Chapter 8).

A little blur can add excitement to an action photograph. Pan in the direction of the movement, and you can capture sports photos even with relatively slow shutter speeds (see Chapter 9).

High shutter speeds can freeze the action, but if the movement is towards you rather than crossing the camera's field of view, a shutter speed as slow as 1/250th of a second may do the job (see Chapter 9).

Compositing techniques let you combine several digital photographs to create one new image in your image editor (see Chapter 11).

Six or seven different special effects filters were used to create this image of a stork rising phoenix-like in front of the London bell tower that holds Big Ben (see Chapter 12).

Special effects filters, such as the pixelation filter used to create this abstract painting, can change an ordinary photo into an old masters' piece of art (see Chapter 12).

A Kai's Power Tools filter called Vortex Tiling created this fractal-like effect, repeating the image of a bee on a flower into a descending whirlpool (see Chapter 12).

The color effect shown here required little more than using an image editor's Unsharp Mask filter, applied to the model's hair only (see Chapter 12).

Sharpening filters can turn an ordinary close-up photo into an abstract composition (see Chapters 6 and 12).

Color Studio

Illuminated only by window light, this nook had a rustic appearance. Then I applied a filter called Neon Glow to change it into an eerie night-time shot with what looks like moonlight streaming through the window.

Chapter 9

Sports and Action Photography

There's only one thing more exhilarating than watching a well-played sports contest: capturing the skirmish with your digital camera and reliving the excitement afterwards. This chapter shows you some of the secrets to grabbing action shots you'll be proud of, even with inexpensive equipment.

Action Photography Is Not a Spectator Sport

I'm not much of a spectator. Even at my advanced age, I'd rather take to the basketball court and mix it up in a pick-up game with some decrepit friends than watch one of those boring NBA contests in which only the last two minutes actually count. Unfortunately, however, I'm not much of a jock, either. I learned early in life that getting down on the front lines with a camera at a sports event is a lot more fun that resting your fanny in a cushy seat in the grandstand.

So it was no surprise that my first full-time job was as a sports photographer for a daily newspaper. I didn't officially become a writer until the paper's sports editor began publishing the two- and three-page cutlines I was turning in with each photo, written in inverted pyramid style, complete with quotes from the coaches. Maybe you don't yearn to join the National Press Photographers' Association or pack a Nikon DX1 at major events as *Sports Illustrated*'s David Bergman does, but you can still have fun documenting everything from your kids' soccer games to your home-town major or minor league team with your digital camera. This chapter will show you the ropes of action photography.

The Decisive Moment

The heart of sports photography lies in getting the right subject, at the right moment. Incorporating both elements into your pictures takes some practice. My first lesson as a fledging professional came when the newspaper's picture editor rejected the shot I'd tentatively circled on my contact sheet. "It's a great action picture," Danny admitted, "but you've captured one of the scrubs making a meaningless play after the game was already in the bag. Even a so-so shot of a key player at the turning point in the third quarter would have been better."

Tip from the pros: If you're looking to produce a newsworthy shot, learn something about the teams you'll be photographing. Who are the star players, and what are their numbers? What are their strengths and weaknesses? You don't have to work up a scouting report, but your job will be easier if you know particulars, such as that a certain quarterback likes to throw deep to a particular receiver, for example, or that when a particular "enforcer" takes to the ice, you can expect that some hard body checking may be in the offing.

Hand in hand with choosing the right subject goes choosing the right moment. Photojournalists Henri Cartier-Bresson and Robert Capa are known for compelling photos taken at a crucial instant in time. Cartier-Bresson's enduring 1952 book *The Decisive Moment* popularized the important photographic concept that timing is essential, but it was Capa's chilling photograph of a Spanish Loyalist militiaman at the moment of his death in 1936 that embodied the concept for all future generations of photographers. Capa's tip for capturing the decisive moment? "If your pictures aren't good enough, you're not close enough."

Getting close and grabbing the decisive moment is excellent advice for the sports photographer, too. It's true that some action shots aren't particularly dependent on the precise moment when the picture is made, give or take a second or two. You need little more than a good eye and presence of mind—not hair-trigger timing—to capture a poignant photo of a jubilant field goal kicker who has just booted the ball between the uprights or to grab a shot of a pitcher watching what he thought was a high strike sail over his head and the outfield fence. In these cases, you need to know the sport, understand which events are important, and have the alertness to actually take the photo.

For many other photos, however, deciding when to take the picture is just as important as choosing what to include in the frame. Snap just a fraction of a second too soon or too late, and you may miss the most exciting moment. That may be when a kicked soccer ball leaves the foot, a hand stretches out to block a shot at the hoop, or a puck slithers past an astonished goalie. Some of the greatest sports photos of all time were taken precisely at a decisive moment, as in the game-winning field goal shown in figure 9.1.

Can you do the same thing? Most assuredly, if you know a few techniques that I outline for you in this chapter. But first, there's a serious issue with digital cameras that needs to be addressed.

Digital Cameras and Latency

For digital photography purposes, latency is the time between when you press the shutter release button and when the camera actually takes the picture. Ideally, that interval should be a tiny fraction of a second. In practice, however, the delay may be a large fraction of a second, or even much longer, depending on your digital camera. That means that when you see an exciting bit of

9.1 | The decisive moment may be a game-winning shot.

action that you want to capture and press the release button, nothing may happen until the moment has passed.

It's very frustrating to miss a great shot simply because your digital camera takes too long to start the exposure. There's no way to sidestep the problem entirely, but you can minimize the damage to a certain extent. Consider this checklist:

- *Let your camera set its exposure and focus prior to the decisive moment*— When you press the shutter release, a lot happens before your camera can take the picture. If it's set for autoexposure and autofocus, the camera will calculate the shutter speed and f-stop and focus the image before making the exposure. Most digital cameras have a mode that locks in both settings as soon as you press the shutter release partway. Learn to do this when the subject you may be photographing is in your viewfinder, even if a second or two elapses before you actually take the picture. Then, press the release down all the way when you want to snap a shot. Many cameras will respond much more quickly in this mode.

- *Set your camera to lock in the autofocus setting only when you press the shutter release*—Some cameras let you switch from continuous autofocus to autofocus only when you press the shutter release. Using the latter mode can improve response time significantly.

- *Use manual exposure, manual focus, or both*—It's usually more practical to set the exposure yourself in manual mode (the correct exposure settings may not change over a brief period of time) and leave the camera in autofocus mode. However, if you prefocus on a spot where you expect the action to take place, you can eliminate both these automatic functions to speed your camera's response.

- *Do your best to anticipate the decisive moment*—If you understand the sport fairly well, you can often predict when something exciting will happen, follow the action with the camera, and press the release just before the big event.

- *Be prepared to erase a significant number of exposures*—I use lulls in sporting events to view my LCD display to evaluate the shots I've already taken. Doing so lets me know how I am doing, so I can correct some errors I'm making on the spot, plus provides the opportunity to erase really bad pictures. Banishing the bad ones lets me stretch my memory cards that much further during a single event.

- *Explore your digital camera's multishot mode*—It's the digital camera equivalent of the Nikon motor drive I used back in the Dark Ages. This mode lets you start taking a series of pictures just before the decisive moment. With a bit of luck, one of them will be the exact picture you want. I'll discuss multishot mode in more detail later in this chapter.

Once you've followed all this advice, the only thing that remains is to take lots and lots of photos. You'll increase your chances that one of them will be really great—while you improve your skills.

Choose Your Weapons

You don't really need a lot of fancy equipment to take good action photos, certainly nothing on the order of the gear required for the close-up pictures we explored in Chapter 6. However, there are some minimum requirements and a few add-on accessories that can make your sports photography that much more fun and rewarding. The following sections include some tips for choosing your weapons.

Your Camera

Almost any digital camera can be used effectively for sports photography; I once wrote an article for a photography magazine that was illustrated with sports photos taken with both a point-and-shoot camera and a professional camera. Given a little care in taking the pictures, once the photos were subjected to the rigors of the halftone screening process, it was difficult to tell the difference between them. Figure 9.2 shows a sports photo taken with a very inexpensive camera. I used electronic flash to stop the action, then added motion blur to mask the low-resolution nature of the original picture. (Bisher University in this mock-up is fictitious; don't try buying tickets this season.)

9.2 | Even inexpensive cameras can be coaxed into action.

If you know the tricks I describe in the "Stopping Action" section later in this chapter, you can take great action photos with the digital camera you already own, regardless of its capabilities. If you have a fixed-focus model without a zoom lens and the ability to set shutter speed manually, you'll have to work around some limitations, but you'll be able to take photos nevertheless.

Lenses

For the most flexibility, you'll definitely want a camera with a zoom lens that will let you adjust your field of view as the action moves around the playing field. A lens with a 3:1 zoom ratio or better is best. Compare the effective focal length with that of a 35mm camera: A lens with a maximum length corresponding to 135mm to 150mm (or longer) with a 35mm camera will let you capture action on a football or soccer field if you're patrolling the sidelines. You'll also need shorter focal length, wide-angle capabilities for sports such as basketball or volleyball, where you may be right on top of the action.

Really long lenses are useful for football, baseball, and other sports where you may be some distance from the play. You'll find the longest true telephotos on only the most expensive digital cameras, particularly those with interchangeable lenses. As I mentioned earlier in this book, the sensors of 35mm film cameras converted to digital photography are generally smaller than a 35mm film frame, so interchangeable telephoto lenses gain a bit of reach. For example, a 200mm telephoto lens has the same field of view as a 320mm long lens, when used with one brand of digital camera.

Fortunately, you can get add-on magnifying attachments that provide telephoto and wide-angle effects for most digital cameras. Although not as sharp as true telephoto and wide-angles, they can provide a field of view you won't get with your unadorned camera. You may need to use a generic tele/wide accessory, but if you have a popular camera model, you'll find that your camera's manufacturer, as well as third-party vendors, build these accessories. For example, you can get an ultrasharp 3X tele converter made by Nikon for its CoolPix line for about $250, or choose 6X to 8X converters from third parties for $100 to $150 less. These can double as long-distance macro lenses, too. One model focuses down to less than 1 foot, letting you fill the frame with an image measuring 1cm×1.5cm (0.4 inches×0.6 inches). Figure 9.3 shows the view through a telephoto attachment from nosebleed territory in the upper deck at a major league baseball game. Although I was nearly 600 feet from home plate, I could zoom in on the action (such as it was during the pitcher's duel I chose to grab some illustrations for this chapter).

9.3 | A telephoto attachment can take you right down to the action.

Exposure and Focus Controls

Some cameras have autoprogram settings for sports, which tell the camera to use the highest shutter speed possible, with a few limitations. You can achieve almost the same effect by using your camera's shutter priority mode, which allows you to manually choose the shutter speed, with the camera selecting the appropriate f-stop.

Manual focusing is handy when you know in advance where the action will be taking place (for example, around the hoop), and you can help your camera operate more quickly than in autofocus mode.

Digital Film

Unless you're using one of those Sony cameras with the tiny recordable CDs capable of storing hundreds of pictures, running out of storage is a definite possibility at a sports event. That's particularly true if you use your camera's multishot mode to grab pictures in spurts.

I find that one or two 64MB CompactFlash cards are suitable for casual shooting sessions with a 3-megapixel camera, but for action photography it's best to have three or four such cards handy, or the equivalent in larger capacity cards. Even 256MB memory cards, which can store about 160 full-resolution, 3-megapixel photos using modest JPEG (Joint Photographic Experts Group) compression, are affordable these days. Some cameras accept tiny hard disk drives in capacities up to a full gigabyte. We've certainly come a long way since the early digital cameras that, in their professional incarnations, came equipped with paltry external 340MB hard disk drives that had to be worn on the belt and linked to the camera through a tether!

In using digital film, it's important to realize that some time is required to write the data from your image onto the memory card and that some memory devices are slower than others. If speed is important to you, then you should check out how quickly your camera can write images to your storage media. The camera's internal circuitry can make a difference, and not all memory cards are exactly the same internally.

That's why you'll see, for example, some CompactFlash cards rated as 4X cards and others as 12X or higher, with transfer speeds of 2MB or more per second, depending on how the vendor measures the card's speed. As you might expect, the faster cards are more expensive. In practice, the speed of your memory card doesn't make that much difference if you're shooting single pictures and saving in JPEG format. If you happen to be storing photos in TIFF (tagged image file) format, which uses much less image compression than JPEG, or shooting sequences of photos in rapid succession, faster cards can be 25 percent to 100 percent faster than older memory cards (or more: technology marches on). Your best bet, if speed is important, is to stick with well-known brand name products from vendors who are eager to keep their offerings on the leading edge of memory technology.

Tiny CompactFlash-sized hard disk drives, such as IBM's MicroDrive, have about the same speed as CompactFlash cards, higher capacities, and stiffer purchase prices. Your camera must have a CompactFlash II (CF/2) slot to use these tiny hard drives, plus enough internal juice to power them. You'll want to check with your camera manufacturer, although what your vendor says may not be the final word. For example, at this writing Nikon does not officially support IBM MicroDrives for its CoolPix line, but many photographers have reported that they work just fine.

Electronic Flash

Electronic flash can be helpful for indoor or nighttime sports events to provide the illumination you need for a good picture. Moreover, the relatively brief duration of an electronic flash serves to stop action. The downside is that flash pictures often look like flash pictures, with very bright foregrounds and pitch-black backgrounds. A digital camera's built-in flash is rarely powerful enough to illuminate anything farther away than 10 to 15 feet, either, which is OK for many basketball photos but not so useful for sports such as football. Figure 9.4 is an example of the traditional "basketball instead of a head" shot that every sports photographer strives for, made to seem as if it were taken outdoors at night thanks to the overpowering glare of an electronic flash.

9.4 | Electronic flash freezes the action but can make the background appear dark.

If you do need to use flash, consider getting a more powerful external flash unit that's compatible with your digital camera. Don't bother with multiple flash units. Pros used them more extensively before today's fast color films and more sensitive digital cameras became prevalent, sometimes spending hours suspending radio-controlled strobes from the rafters of sports arenas before an important event. You can probably get by with no flash or a single flash.

Tripod

A tripod will slow you down and rob you of mobility, but it is a necessity for using longer lenses, particularly at shutter speeds slower than 1/500 second. You may find that camera shake, magnified by the power of the tele lens, causes more blurring than the movement of your subjects, so a good tripod can lock down even a lightweight digital camera to improve sharpness for action shots.

Tip from the pros: Because a tripod is used to steady the camera for a relatively short exposure (as opposed to a long exposure of 1/30 second or more), many pros find a single-legged tripod called a unipod will do the job. A unipod is lighter and faster to move. You can also use devices called chestpods that brace against your chest. These can steady the camera, but they transmit more of the movement of your chest and body to the camera than a unipod or tripod does.

Choose Your Positions

An important part of sports photography is choosing where to stand. I realize that at professional sporting events you won't have much choice about where you position yourself unless you have press credentials. You may even run into restrictions at college games. However, at second-tier professional sports events, many smaller colleges and universities, and most other amateur outings, you'll be able to take pictures anywhere common sense and common courtesy allows. And the photos you take will be great training for when you do get your press credentials.

Tip from the pros: Show up early, find the right person, and ask for permission to take pictures up close and intimate. You just might get a temporary press pass. Don't expect this treatment at the Super Bowl or World Series; however, you might talk yourself into a choice spot at a minor league game. Look professional to enhance your chances. I shamefully admit to gaining admittance to several contests where I had no rightful place by the simple expedient of stringing three battered Nikon cameras around my neck and looking like I belonged. (The black ones with the paint worn off to reveal the brass underneath worked great in the days before even pro cameras turned to nonmetallic parts.)

The following sections include some sports-specific tips.

Baseball

Right behind home plate may be the best place to watch a game, but it's not the best place to take pictures, unless you're intent on showing the facial expressions of a pitcher uncorking a two-seam fastball. The netting typically used as a backstop can diffuse your photos a bit, too, although with a long lens the barrier will largely be out of focus.

Pro sports photographers often position themselves in the niche at the ends of the dugouts. The position closest to first base is often the best because you can swivel quickly to grab a shot of a runner sliding home, show the pitcher winding up (or eyeing the runner on first), or snap a picture of a steal at second base. You'll have a good vantage point of right field, too. However, for the best shots of pitchers, you'll want to spend some time on the third base side, too. Depending on their windup and delivery, right-handers and southpaws may look best from one side of the field or the other.

However, even if you're banished to the upper stands at a professional baseball game, you can still get acceptable photos if you're willing to look at the big picture, as shown in figure 9.5, which shows a runner being held at first base.

9.5 | **You can get good pictures at professional baseball games if you don't mind looking at the big picture.**

Basketball

Basketball is one sport in which all the action focuses around a single spot, the basket, so you'll find that one prime location is behind the backboards. The only problem with this position is that you end up with a lot of photos of guys and gals with their arms up in the air. Don't be afraid to move to the sidelines to capture some of the action from a different angle. Although low angles are not the best for a sport with so many tall players, and high angles tend to make your photos resemble screen shots from an NBA-themed video game, you may be able to get good pictures while seated in the first or second row. Figure 9.6 shows a picture taken from under the basket.

9.6 | If you shoot from under the basket, be prepared to get lots of photos of players with their arms in the air.

Football

I've always found football games problematic because there are always so many people in attendance who are eager to beat you up if you obscure their view. Below the college level, the sidelines are usually so close to the stands that an additional person pacing up and down the field will invariably outrage someone who puts up with the folks who wield the yardline markers only grudgingly. Standing behind the goalposts is no better because spectators usually mill around there, too.

You could try crouching down to lower your profile, a position that sometimes provides interesting angles. The big problem with crouching is that the position severely reduces your mobility. You can't jump out of the way as easily when a 200-pound receiver heads for the sideline to stop the clock, and you certainly can't reposition yourself to follow fast-moving action.

Your best bet is to stick to the sidelines and keep moving as much as possible, thereby outraging a different spectator on each play. Move to the end zones when appropriate, to catch the fullback bulling over from the 1-yard line or to capture the kicker lining up for a field goal.

Soccer

From a photographic perspective, soccer is a lot like football, in many ways, except with less belligerent fans, unless we're talking about elementary or middle school soccer or matches that take place in Europe. Follow the action up and down the sidelines. If one team is severely overmatched, you can probably hang around their goal a great deal because that's where most of the action will be taking place, as shown in figure 9.7.

Of course, orienting on the goals means you'll be concentrating on one team's fullbacks and goalie and the other team's wings and strikers. Alternate ends of the field, or do as I do and select which end is the best photographically from the physical, background, and lighting standpoints, and then photograph each team in turn. (Remember, they trade ends of the field after the half.)

9.7 | Hang around the goal at a soccer game, and you're bound to see some action.

Other Sports

You can use the same rules and a little common sense to position yourself for other sports. Tennis and auto racing often can be photographed from the spectator stands using a long lens; the participants twist themselves around enough during the action to give you many different angles from a single vantage point.

You can follow the gallery around during a golf tournament, but if you're allowed to use your camera, for heaven's sake, don't distract the players during their shots! I've never figured out why professional golfers demand absolute silence, whereas brain surgeons on TV work just fine with loud rock music playing, but that's the way it is.

Many digital cameras are totally silent if you disable the phony shutter click that's provided for your reassurance. Watch out for the autofocus and autoexposure confirmation beeps, too. A quiet camera is an unobtrusive camera. A digital camera with a swiveling lens, such as my Nikon, is handy for "stealth" photography because you can point the camera at the action from waist level and glance down at the LCD display to compose your picture.

Hockey is one sport that benefits from a higher-than-normal angle because an elevated view lets you shoot over the glass, and the action contrasts well with the ice. The same is true of professional wrestling, unless you have a ringside seat and can dodge the flying chairs. (Yes, pro wrestling is most certainly a professional sport, on the order of figure skating. Incredible athletic skill, intense training, and exhaustive practice are required for both, but the outcomes are preplanned.)

Track and field events present a world of possibilities in their own right. You may want to be under the bar at the pole vault, right in the path of a long jumper (but a few yards behind the sand pit and out of the jumper's field of vision), next to the starting blocks of the 100-meter dash, and not even in the same zip code as a discus hurler. Exactly how close you can be and where you will be allowed to stand will depend on the nature of the event and the level of the competition. (For example, at middle school events you may be able to get quite close to the action as long as you assure the officials that you're not a parent.)

No matter where you are at a sports event, don't forget to look around you for some human interest pictures. Sometimes, the best way to capture the spirit of a contest is to show the fans, mascots, or even the vendors. Figure 9.8 shows such a human interest photo.

Just Before Taking Your First Action Photo

Now that you're armed and dangerous, you're ready to grab your first digital action shot. This section will take you through the steps you need to follow. Before the game/match/bout/melee, you'll want to run down the following checklist:

- *Make sure your camera battery is freshly charged*—Have a spare battery if you think you might be taking more pictures than your original set will handle. Remember that flash pictures take more juice.

- *Check your supplies*—Do you have enough digital film, and have the memory cards been formatted or erased?

9.8 | Team mascots make great subjects during lulls in the action.

Tip from the pros: If a particular shoot is very important, you'll want to do as the pros do and have at least two of every essential component, from batteries to film to flash units. In practice, a professional is likely to have three or more of each tool, including cameras, and probably will have a half-dozen or more. Six of anything means you have two to use, two as backup, and two to send off for repair. Digital cameras are generally more reliable than even the mechanical/electronic hybrids that film cameras have become, so amateur digital photographers can probably get by with fewer backups for nonessential shooting sessions. But for once-in-a-lifetime sporting events (or weddings), you'll want plenty of spare equipment. Perhaps you and a friend can loan each other cameras when one of you needs a backup.

- *Refamiliarize yourself with the controls your camera uses to set aperture priority mode, focus, multiple-exposure mode, and any other setting you'll be using during the contest*—If necessary, write everything down on an index card and keep it in your pocket.

- *Activate your basic camera settings*—One task that's often overlooked is setting the ISO (International Standards Organization) speed of your camera. The task is a lot like choosing a film, and although your camera's default speed may be fine for ordinary photos, you'll want to customize it for many sports/action pictures, as described in the following section.

- *Check your camera's lens to make sure it's clean*—If you'll be shooting outdoors in inclement weather, you may want to put a neutral filter, such as a skylight filter, over the lens. You can wipe off these filters quickly without worrying about scratching your lens. If the filter becomes scratched, throw it away and use a new one.

- *Scout your position to see where you want to stand, if you have that flexibility*.

Setting ISO Speed

Your camera's sensor may have a provision for adjusting its sensitivity called ISO speed, which is similar to the various ISO film ratings. The lowest ISO speed your camera offers will usually provide the best quality. As you boost the sensitivity, your pictures will gain random picture information, called noise, just as faster films add grain to snapshots. Although digital ISO ratings don't exactly correspond to film ISO speeds, they are close enough that you can use them to determine which setting to use. The following sections include a couple rules of thumb you can use when setting ISO speed.

In Daylight

The next section, "During the Event," has a discussion about stopping action that will help you select the correct shutter speed. But how do you know which shutter speeds are available to you? Here's how you can calculate the likely range of speeds you'll have at your disposal.

In bright sunlight, the reciprocal of an ISO rating will equal the shutter speed you can use with an f-stop of f16, usually rounded to the nearest traditional speed for easy calculation. So, you can use f16 and a shutter speed of 1/100

Sports and Action Photography

to 1/125 second with an ISO rating of 100; 1/200 to 1/250 second with an ISO rating of 200; 1/400 to 1/500 second at ISO 400; and perhaps up to 1/1,000 second at ISO 800.

These are guidelines only. In practice, bright sunlight is not always exactly the same (for example, on the beach or on snow it may be twice as bright), and your digital camera's electronic shutter need not use the exact equivalents of traditional shutter speeds, nor will you typically be using f16.

Instead, use this rule of thumb to estimate how much action-stopping power you have in a particular situation. For example, if the sun is truly bright, you might want to set your camera's shutter speed to 1/2,000 second (if it's available), either manually or through the camera's shutter priority mode, and let the autoexposure system choose the correct aperture. The faster the shutter speed you want to use, the higher the ISO rating you'll need to use, as shown in the following table.

Table 9.1 ISO/Shutter speeds under bright sunlight.				
Shutter	f-stop (ISO 100)	f-stop (ISO 200)	f-stop (ISO 400)	f-stop (ISO 800)
1/2,000 sec	f4	f5.6	f8	f11
1/1,000 sec	f5.6	f8	f11	f16
1/500 sec	f8	f11	f16	f22

You can choose the f-stop and shutter speed from the table and see what ISO setting you should use, keeping in mind the following factors:

- You'll need a smaller f-stop (the larger numbers) with longer lenses/greater zoom settings to provide adequate depth of field.

- Digital cameras offer more depth of field at a given magnification, so you don't have to be afraid of what is considered a wide lens opening in the film camera world: f5.6 may be entirely usable even at a telephoto setting.

- Digital camera images can get dramatically noisy at higher ISO ratings, such as ISO 800, so you might want to choose the highest rating only when you want to use the fastest shutter speeds and the smallest possible lens opening.

- Bright sunlight can change significantly when a cloud moves in front of the sun. You can quickly lose half of your available light. Your camera's autoexposure system can compensate, of course, but you may not like the

results. You can end up with a lens opening that's too wide, or your camera may refuse to take a picture at all. When that happens, choose a slower shutter speed or, as a last resort, bump your camera's ISO rating up a notch.

When you're using manual settings or shutter priority mode, it's easy to forget that you may be pushing your camera to its limits. I've sometimes puzzled over an unfamiliar double-beep sound my camera emits during sports photography, finally realizing that it's telling me that there is no longer enough light to take a picture at 1/2,000 second, even at the widest aperture, using the ISO setting I've selected.

Indoors or at Night

Rules of thumb are more difficult to come by when indoors or when outdoors at night because the illumination in sports arenas can vary widely. Over the years, I've discovered you can usually expect enough light to shoot at 1/125 second at f2.8 with an ISO setting of 400 and 1/250 second at f2.8 with an ISO setting of 800. In modern facilities, you'll probably encounter quite a bit more light than that, but even twice as much illumination is no picnic when you can use only 1/500 second at an f-stop such as f2.8 with a noisy ISO rating such as 800. Figure 9.9 shows a murky, noisy shot in which technology was stretched to its limit to capture an image at a football game.

My advice is to see what you can do at ISO 400 before using a higher rating. You can still get acceptable sports photos with existing light. Your alternative, of course, is to use electronic flash. You'll learn more about getting the most from your shutter speeds and f-stops later in this chapter.

During the Event

It's show time! This section provides some advice for taking your best shot. I'll assume your camera is set up properly and the basic settings are in place and now all you need is some advice on how to use them.

Calling Your Shot

Watch the action and try to anticipate, as well as you can, where something will happen that you want to immortalize in pixels. It may be a serve, a shot on goal, some sideline action, an impending dunk, or some other bit of sports

9.9 | Higher ISO ratings produce noisy, grainy photos.

business. Rather than try to constantly reframe your picture as the event unfolds around you, it's often best to point your lens at the approximate point where the action you hope for will take place. Until you have a lot of experience, you won't want to be constantly zooming in and out and jerking your viewfinder all over the playing field.

Instead, plan ahead for a particular kind of shot and prepare for that. At a football game, it doesn't take a sports genius to know that in a third and long yardage situation odds are very good that a pass play may be coming up. Choose a receiver who may pass near you and follow him on his route. If you're lucky enough to guess correctly, you're in line for a great shot. Should you be using a digital camera that's slow to respond, remember to press the shutter release a bit before the crucial moment. Prefocus, if necessary, on the position where you expect to take the photo.

Stopping Action

First, even before you decide exactly how you want to stop the action, consider whether freezing your subjects in time is even what you want to do. Many sports photos can be improved simply by introducing a little motion blur into the mix. A slight amount of blur adds to the feeling of movement and can make

9.10 | A little blur can add drama to an action shot.

your image even more exciting. Figure 9.10 shows an image in which the blurriness of the softball player's arm and back leg help convey the action.

The following sections include some techniques for stopping (or not stopping) action completely.

Panning with the Motion

Two kinds of motion can cause blurring in your photo: camera motion and subject motion. The first takes place when your camera moves during the exposure. The second happens because your subject is moving faster than the shutter speed you've selected can stop. Both kinds of motion are not necessarily bad if they contribute to the image. You can even use camera motion to minimize subject motion, by moving the camera in the direction the subject is moving as you shoot.

Visualize a soccer halfback or a wide receiver racing across your field of view. If they are close enough and moving fast enough, even your highest shutter speed may not be able to stop the action. However, if you follow their movement with your camera and take a picture while panning, their apparent speed is much less, at least to your camera's sensor, so that even a relatively slow shutter speed may freeze the action. The nonmoving background will blur, of course, but that can be a good thing. Your relatively sharp subject will be isolated against a blurry background, making for a dramatic picture, as shown in figure 9.11. Consider the following rules of thumb when taking this kind of action picture:

9.11 | Panning in the direction of the motion can stop the action and put emphasis on your main subjects.

- *If you match your panning speed closely with the subject's actual speed, shutter speeds as low as 1/60 to 1/125 second can produce surprisingly sharp images*—Experiment with different shutter speeds, even speeds that are much slower than you think you'd need.

- *The slower your shutter speed, the more blurry the background will appear.*

- *If your pan isn't precisely parallel (for example, you pan up or down a bit or your subject is moving up or down), you'll get more blur than you anticipated*—Pan smoothly in the direction your subject is moving.

- *Even if you pan correctly, the parts of your subject that are not moving exactly in the direction of the pan will still be blurry*—Again, this is not necessarily a bad thing. You might find that the body and head of a running back are sharp, but his legs, which are pumping back and forth as he runs, blur in an interesting way.

- *The closer a subject is to your camera, the blurrier it will appear, even if you're panning.*

Stopping Action Head-On

Action that crosses your field of view blurs more easily than action that's coming toward you. It's a bit like looking down the railroad tracks and seeing a train approaching head-on. It doesn't seem to be going very fast until it gets very close and passes you. You can take advantage of this effect to stop action even when using a relatively slow shutter speed.

Instead of waiting for a player to run past you, take a picture as he or she runs toward the camera. You'll find that 1/500 or 1/250 second can stop action very well when it's approaching, or retreating, instead of zipping across your field of view, as shown in figure 9.12.

9.12 | **When the action is headed your way, even a relatively slow shutter speed can freeze the action.**

Watch Out for Camera Shake

In most cases, you don't want blur caused by a shaky camera and not directly associated with the movement of your subject. Use a higher shutter speed or a tripod, unipod, or chestpod to steady your camera, if necessary. Longer lenses, especially longer true telephotos and those front-heavy, screw-in tele converters available for some digital cameras, promote camera shake on two counts. First, their sheer weight can change the center of gravity of your camera enough to cause camera shake. In addition, their magnification emphasizes any shakiness that does exist.

Tip from the pros: *Can't tell whether the blurriness in your pictures is caused by camera motion or subject motion, or maybe just poor focus? Look at nonmoving objects in the background, particularly round point sources of light. If a nonmoving object that's supposed to be round is oval shaped and you didn't pan the camera, the shape distortion was caused by unwanted camera motion. If it's round, as it should be, but still blurry, it's simply out of focus.*

Stopping Action with Your Shutter

A fast shutter speed will stop action, and a good part of taking excellent sports photos is deciding just how fast a shutter speed to use. As you gain experience, you'll want to compromise between a shutter speed that absolutely freezes action, like the shot shown in figure 9.13, and one that stops most of the action but allows enough blur to make the picture realistic and exciting. I can't offer any rules of thumb here that you haven't gathered from the discussion so far. You've learned that the perfect shutter speed varies by how fast the subject is going, the direction in which the subject is moving, the distance between the subject and the camera, your zoom setting, and whether you're panning or not.

Stopping Action with Your Electronic Flash

Electronic flash units are sometimes called strobes or speedlights with good reason. One of the earliest applications of electronic flash was by Dr. Harold Edgerton at the Massachusetts Institute of Technology (MIT), who perfected the use of stroboscopic lights in both ultra-high-speed motion and still (stop-motion) photography, capable of revealing bullets in flight, light bulbs shattering, and other phenomena.

9.13 | Very fast shutter speeds, such as the 1/2,000 second used for this action picture, can produce pictures that are comical or that resemble statues rather than fast-moving athletes.

Electronic flash freezes action by virtue of its extremely brief duration (1/50,000 second, or less with some flash units). Some automatic flash units actually control the amount of light emitted by varying the duration, so a subject that is very close (or very bright) will be illuminated for only a tiny fraction of a second. The problem with electronic flash is that it has a lot of contrast and obeys that pesky inverse-square law I talked about in Chapter 6. If you properly expose an action subject that's 12 feet from your camera, anything in the background 24 feet away will receive only one-quarter as much light and will appear very dark in comparison, as you saw earlier in figure 9.4.

In addition, the flash units built into digital cameras are not very powerful and are not well suited for objects that are more than about 15 feet from the camera. They can work well at, for example, a basketball game, but not so well at a football game, where the distances are much greater. Electronic flash sports photos may look a little dated, too, smacking of the 1960s or 1970s, before film and digital camera sensors became as sensitive as they are today.

Shooting Sequences

Early in this chapter, I described the latency problems you'll encounter with digital cameras that are slow to respond to your feverish pressure on the shutter release. Using your camera's multishot mode is one way to increase your chances of getting a good picture. Depending on your camera, you may have one or more of the following options:

- *Continuous picture-taking*—In this mode, the camera continues to take pictures, at a rate of perhaps 1.5 to 3.0 shots per second, as long as you hold down the shutter release, until the camera's memory buffer is full. At that point, you'll have to wait until some of the picture information is written to your removable memory card before you can take another shot. With my camera, I find I can snap off three shots in about 2 seconds, then wait a second or two, and take one or two more. The advantage of this mode is that you can usually use the camera's full resolution; the downside is that this mode will take fewer shots in a given time interval than other modes.

- *Ultra-high-speed*—Some cameras can take pictures at a faster clip in a quasi-ultra-high-speed mode, using reduced resolution. If you're willing to accept photos with, for example, 640×480-pixel resolution, you may be able to grab them at a rate of two or three per second.

- *Multishot*—A few cameras can produce a quick blast of 16 tiny pictures on a single frame. Such images might be fine for analyzing your golf stroke, but they may be too small for other applications.

- *Minimovie*—Most digital cameras have the ability to shoot short video clips (typically 20 to 30 seconds in length) at 320×200 resolution and up to 30 frames per second. You can use the movies as is, or you can capture individual frames.

I prefer the continuous mode, and I frequently trigger the sequence just before I expect some action to take place, as shown in figure 9.14. This technique is still a hit-or-miss procedure because a lot can happen between frames. It's very likely that you'll still miss the decisive moment, but I had that happen to me when I

9.14 | Taking sequences of shots can improve your chances of capturing the action you want.

was using a six-frames-per-second motor drive with a conventional film camera, too. As with all sports photography, the more pictures you take, the more you increase your odds of getting some great ones.

Next Up

In Part III, we'll look at some ways to enhance your photos and put them to work. Next up, a discussion of digital presentations, including key ways to keep your audience awake long enough to appreciate your work.

Achieving a
Professional Look

Chapter 10

Digital Presentations

Family vacations or sales presentations can all be highlighted in a well-designed digital slide show. This chapter covers special requirements for digital photographs that will be used in presentations, with tips on creating digital slide shows for home or business.

Requirements for Digital Presentations

Whether you call them slide shows, filmstrips, or audiovisual presentations, graphical productions given before groups have been a time-honored way of educating, entertaining, training, or persuading. However, not all presentations are equally educational, persuasive, or entertaining. Some are even boring. If you have suffered through a filmstrip titled *Our Friend the Esophagus* in health class, have dozed off during your neighbor's vacation slide show, or have become distracted while enduring swarms of bullet points during a business meeting, you know what I mean.

Good digital photographs and scans can help keep your presentations from becoming dull to the point that your viewers start feigning serious illness or look with hope to their pagers every few minutes as an excuse to escape the torture. However, pictures alone won't do the job. You'll still need to use some creativity to build a presentation that captures your viewers' attention, keeps them interested, and conveys the information that you want to get across. Images are just one tool for transferring information.

Other tools you can use are sound, animation, interesting transitions between slides, and informative text that's kept brief and to the point. Your own narration, which can become an interactive dialogue as you respond to viewer questions, is another important part of the formula. The important thing to remember is that presentations don't have to be a chore. Digital cameras and scanners make capturing appropriate images easy, and presentation software like Microsoft PowerPoint can free you from the tedium that often results in tedious productions. (If you were bored making the slide show, odds are your audience will be bored viewing it.)

The following sections discuss some of the things you should think about when creating a digital presentation.

Number of Images

Oddly enough, in many slide shows, you probably won't want to have pictures on every slide. As they say, a picture is worth a thousand words, but there are many times when *you don't want a thousand words*. That's particularly true when you're using a picture to convey a message, but your image is open to interpretation. An ambiguous photo is worse than no image at all, as I'll demonstrate shortly. In such cases, you're better off with a simple text slide that states the information you want to transmit. That's why bullet points were invented!

Think about the message you want to leave with your viewers. If your presentation has specific facts, figures, or trends to convey, you'll want to rely on words, charts, or graphs. If you want to express emotions, show differences of scale between objects, or present an accurate picture of what something looks like, images will do the job.

Business presentations often need a few well-placed images to break up the endless flow of text or to illustrate a specific point. Personal slide shows—your vacation pictures, family histories, those shots of your kids that you and a few select relatives will think are cute—are usually best when they rely mostly on images accompanied by informal narration as you give the show. Capturing the right mix of pictures and nonimage material is one of the most important steps in planning and creating your presentation.

Expressing Thoughts through Pictures

Figure 10.1 is an example of a poorly conceived, ambiguous image as I mentioned earlier. This shot might be hopelessly confusing in several different contexts. Perhaps you meant it to be a humorous conclusion to a presentation about your company's future, or you wanted to use it to wind up a travelogue. You might *think* you were implying that the road ahead is a long one, but we'll travel it together, but your viewers were probably thinking something else.

Some will wonder if you're implying that the people of the organization are mindless sheep. Others will squint and try to figure out which direction the sheep are headed. A few may be thinking, "Oh, dear! I'm staring at the hind ends of a bunch of sheep!" The more imaginative in your audience may be picturing what would happen if a large truck suddenly appeared from the side street. None of these thoughts are likely to be what you intended.

You need to think carefully about what each image in a presentation will say and discard those that require a lot of explanation. Unless a lot of narration accompanies a slide, most images won't appear on the screen for more than 15 to 20 seconds (if that long), so your image should be sweet and succinct. In most cases, rich imagery that draws the viewer in is best left for photos in books or for prints that are framed and displayed on a wall.

10.1 | Your photos can't be too ambiguous.

Image Orientation

In Chapter 5, I encouraged you to look at your subject matter and frame your pictures to suit, with some images composed horizontally and some vertically. With slide presentations (both the digital and film kind), there are some significant restrictions on exactly how you orient your images.

We've become accustomed to watching movies, television shows, and those health class filmstrips in a horizontal format, and most computer monitors are also oriented in a wide, or landscape, position. So, even material that itself is vertically oriented, such as word processing documents or Web pages, is most often viewed on a screen that is wider than it is tall. So, in practice, all the slides in a presentation must be shown in a horizontal format, and all should have the same size image area (the screen size, obviously, can't change). Changing orientations or relative sizes can be very disorienting because the show moves from one image to another. Figure 10.2 shows a series of slides that would be disconcerting to watch.

That doesn't mean you can't include both horizontal and vertical pictures in your slide shows; you simply cannot mix both orientations as full frame images. To use a vertical image in a presentation, you should compose it with a horizontal slide with other elements to balance it. Figure 10.3 shows a series of slides in which this was done.

10.2 | Mixing vertical and horizontal orientations in a slide show can be unnerving.

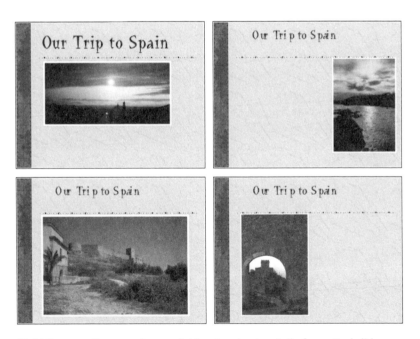

10.3 | Here are the same images laid out on horizontally formatted slides.

Your presentation software, such as PowerPoint, may let you compose your slides in a vertical format in the Page Setup menu. However, all slides in the presentation will be vertical, and if they are shown on a landscape-oriented monitor or projection screen, there will be dark, blank space at each side of every slide. Use this option only for special effect.

Resolution/Size

Keep the resolution of the display device in mind when creating pictures for a digital presentation. An image that looks good on your 17-inch monitor might not be quite so compelling on a projection screen with a 35-inch to 52-inch diagonal or larger. Fine details that you think can be seen can be pixilated and become indistinct when enlarged to mammoth proportions.

In contrast to Web pages, slide presentations lend themselves to higher resolution images. The presentation software will automatically resize your high-resolution image to fit the space you've assigned to it on a slide, making the best use of your available resolution. The chief drawbacks of using more detailed digital images in a presentation are that slower computers may take longer to load and display such pictures, and very large images make a presentation that much bigger in file size.

In practice, though, you'll find the resolution/size limitations apply only to older computers—particularly if you are lugging around your presentation on an old laptop with a slow processor and limited hard disk space. In these days when 800 GHz CPUs are practically the bare minimum found in any new computer (in both Windows and Mac realms), and 100 GB hard disks are selling for a few hundred dollars, you should worry about having not enough resolution rather than too much.

Composition

You'll recall my advice earlier in this chapter about not wanting your pictures to be worth a thousand words. Your slides will appear on the screen for only a limited amount of time, perhaps half a minute or less. (If you're going to be narrating for two or three minutes while displaying just one slide, you probably should consider adding another slide or two.) In addition, there are other things that will be going on while your image is visible. Text may accompany the picture, or you may have a few things to say about what the audience is seeing. So, it's very likely that even in the brief time the image is in view, your audience won't be concentrating on it in earnest.

From a composition viewpoint, this means your picture should be as simple and as effective as possible. Viewers should know at a glance what it "says" and be able to derive most of the important information in a few seconds. Here are a few tips for composing effective slide images, most of which will be familiar (or are variations) from the discussion in Chapter 5.

- Have only one center of interest. Conventional photos can include other interesting things in a scene, but in a slide presentation such complexity is merely confusing.

- Make the most important object in the picture the largest, brightest, and sharpest object. This is even more important than it is for a conventional digital image that will be viewed on screen or in a print.

- Use lines, curves, or repeating objects to create patterns or to draw the eye. Doing so actually simplifies the image, making it easier for the viewer to concentrate on the main subject.

- Use large objects or shapes, rather than small ones. If you can fill half or more of your image with a single object, so much the better.

- Watch for fusion/merger of objects in your images. Be especially careful about objects at the borders.

- Note the colors in your image and make certain they don't clash with the slide template or images that immediately precede or follow the current one. For example, if you jump back and forth between pictures that are predominantly yellow and red, you're likely to give your audience a headache.

- When previewing your slide show, be conscious of how well the images flow and complement those before and after.

Composition for slide shows follows much the same guidelines as for conventional digital images, with the few exceptions noted here. Figure 10.4 shows how image and text compositional elements can come together.

NEW KITCHEN TABLE
CD-RW-R-DVD

• *Really Fast*
• *Looks Good*
• *Less Filling*

10.4 | Large images and simple, easy-to-read text make an effective slide.

Creating Digital Slide Shows

Creating a digital slide show involves several steps. This next section will provide an outline summarizing what you need to do to create a successful presentation.

Planning Your Show

The most important step is, of course, to prepare a script or storyboard (or both). You'll want to plan your show before you start assembling slides. Make a list of the topics you want to cover, collect all the images you want to include, and then arrange them in an outline.

You may be able to get by with a script alone. The script will consist of text that makes up the narration and a description of the images that accompany the text. Your text narration may be sketchy if you plan to "wing it" (perhaps just a few notes of what you want to cover), or it may be as detailed as a speech. Your image descriptions need to be complete enough that you or anyone else working from the script can glance at the display screen and confirm that the right image is being displayed. Include cues to change to the next slide.

If your presentation includes a large number of visuals, you may want to create a storyboard that shows all the images in the order you want to display them. You'll find that presentation packages (discussed in the next section) include a storyboard or thumbnail mode that allows viewing or printing groups of slides, in order, on a single page. Figure 10.5 shows PowerPoint's Slide Sorter mode, which can be used for arranging slides in storyboard fashion.

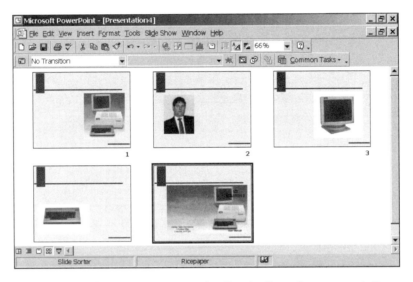

10.5 | Storyboards are a great way to visualize the flow of your presentation.

Simply create a quick-and-dirty slide show with images only and use that as your storyboard. If some of the images require a bit of setup and preparation (for example, you want to include photos of your board of directors, key managers, that new facility your company is building, or a product that hasn't even been finalized yet), you can use your digital camera to snap some dummy shots to use in the planning stages. Grab a few volunteers, arrange them as if they were the board of directors, company bigwigs, and so forth, and grab the simulated photos you need. Take a photo of the outside of any building to represent your new facility or use an existing product to stand in for one being prototyped.

You might even be able to use these dummy shots (sorry, gang!) to get approval of your script/storyboard, if necessary. Then, when your planning is finished, get your digital camera out again and take the actual photos you'll use. Working in this way can be a huge time saver because you often can avoid taking shots that you'll never need. If the picture of the new factory gets scratched, or that promising product is delayed, you can dump the dummy picture and move on with little effort wasted.

Getting Started with Presentation Software

Once you have planned your show and have taken the images needed, it's time to get to work with your presentation package. The software you use to create a digital slide show is up to you. There are packages designed specifically for presentations, such as Astound, Corel Presentations, Kai's Power Show, Harvard Graphics, or Microsoft PowerPoint. These all have sophisticated tools for creating slides, building reusable templates, and incorporating special effects and animations.

You don't have to pay a lot for advanced presentation software, either. I've found that StarImpress, a component of Sun Microsystem's StarOffice suite, has virtually all the features of PowerPoint, is easier to learn, and can be downloaded at a cost of $0 from **www.staroffice.com**. You read that right: Sun offers a downloadable version of StarOffice for free. You also can purchase a CD-ROM with documentation for a reasonable price. StarImpress even includes the equivalent of PowerPoint's Pack and Go feature. In both PowerPoint and StarImpress, there's a slick component that bundles up your presentation into a file that you can transport to another computer to play the slide show on systems that don't have the host software.

StarOffice is available for both Windows computers and those running the Linux operating system (whereas PowerPoint is available for Windows and Mac systems). If Mac compatibility isn't important to you (or Linux compatibility is), you'll want to check out StarOffice.

If you're looking for something simpler, many image management/albuming packages like ULead PhotoImpact Album have a slide show mode that lets you select images on the fly to create an ad hoc slide show. PhotoImpact Album even allows you to specify the types of transitions between slides (dissolves, wipes, and so forth).With PhotoImpact you also can decide whether to display the next slide after a self-selected interval or by tapping the mouse button or keyboard, and you can save a particular show to reuse at any time.

Tips for Enhancing and Delivering a Polished Presentation

Scripting and creating slides for a presentation are only half the work (and half the fun). The following sections provide some tips for enhancing your show and delivering a polished presentation to a captivated audience.

Before the Presentation

You should consider the following points when you're finalizing your presentation.

Don't Overdo It

Have you ever been in a presentation where the lighting of the room kept you from seeing the screen easily? Or the speaker used so many animation effects that your colleagues were placing bets on the next animation instead of concentrating on the content of the speaker's talk? Then you have at least an idea or two about what *not* to do in a presentation. Don't overdo the enhancements. You might have a tasteful animation on every slide (say, revealing the title or the bullet points in a consistent way), but you wouldn't want to have half a dozen animations, some sound effects, and a flashing marquee more often than once (if ever).

When applying slide transitions and animation effects, adhere to the old adage that "less is more." Use one or two transitions between slides and use animation effects to emphasize your most important points or your audience may be distracted from the content of your presentation.

Practice, Practice, Practice

That goes without saying (even though I've said it anyway). But you also must time yourself when you run through your presentation, so you'll know how long the show will take and will be able to pace yourself. If you don't allow yourself enough time when rehearsing, the slide show that is set to automatically advance will move ahead to the next bullet point or slide—whether you're ready or not. Also consider whether to allow audience questions during the presentation.

Consider a Critique

You might want to ask a presentation-savvy colleague to proofread or critique your presentation and ask for constructive feedback. This will help you present the best overall presentation package.

Pretend You're Delivering Your Inaugural Address

Basic guidelines of public speaking can help you plan the content of your presentation. Consider your audience. Who are they? What are their needs? Planning your presentation with the audience in mind can save you editing time later.

Limit Slide Word Counts

Use your slides as a jumping off point for your speaker notes, limiting slides to only key words or phrases.

At the Presentation

When it's presentation time, it's not too late to make sure everything goes right.

Research Available Equipment

Ask questions of the facilities coordinator about items such as the sound system and the display or projector. Will you be using a lapel microphone or a podium microphone? What type of projector will be used? If you will be using a projector that you're unfamiliar with, plan to arrive at your meeting room early enough to have a dry run through of your presentation. Become familiar with the equipment.

Check the Lighting

The lighting of the room in which your presentation will take place can affect the visual quality of your presentation. Is it very bright with few lighting options or is there more flexibility? If you are able to plan ahead, consider using a slide with a light background and darker text in a room that's very bright. It can be difficult to see text if the background is obscuring it. If the room is very dark, with few dimming options, consider using a dark background and brighter color text. Save your audience from the horrendously blinding white-screen effect we all encountered during family vacation slide shows!

Be Prepared When Traveling

If your presentation is to take place on the road or on a laptop that does not have PowerPoint installed, make sure you use the Pack and Go option (or your presentation software's equivalent) when saving a presentation on disk. Pack and Go includes everything you need to give a presentation, including the display software required, on a disk. This will ensure that you will be able to give your presentation, regardless of whether your hosts have PowerPoint or your other software or not. PowerPoint's Pack and Go Wizard will walk you through the steps.

Be Ready for Queries

If allowing questions, pausing a PowerPoint presentation that uses automatic timings can be accomplished by right-clicking in the slide show and choosing Screen, Pause from the shortcut menus. To resume the slide show, right-click and choose Screen, Resume from the shortcut menus.

After the Presentation

Your job isn't over when the lights come back on.

Follow Up with Your Audience

Distribute your handouts (presentation packages can generate them for you automatically).

Be Alert for Feedback

Accept accolades and praise (especially those directed at your digital photography), but encourage the kind of feedback that will help you do an even better job next time.

Relax

Time to come down from the stratosphere and bask in a job well done.

Next Up

I promised I'd keep the chapters on image editing to the essentials, so I have just two slated for you. The next chapter looks at techniques for editing and retouching images, and the chapter that follows that will show you how to create some cool special effects.

Chapter 11

Editing and Retouching Images

This chapter shows you how easy digital color correcting and retouching can be and reveals the few simple tools you need to master to transform sound, but imperfect, images into prize winners.

Images, Hues, and Tones

Every picture tells a story, but even the best stories can benefit from a little editing. One of the many differences between very good amateur pictures and most of the professional photographs you see published is that the professional image probably had some retouching done sometime during the production process. Often, something as simple as correcting the colors of an image can make dramatic improvements.

What's Color Balance?

Color balance is the relationship between the three colors used to produce your image; with a digital camera or scanner, they are the red, green, and blue hues captured by the sensor. Adjusting the relative amount of each of these primary colors isn't enough—you'll need to be concerned with the following three factors:

- *Color intensity*—If you have too much red, the image will appear too red. If you have too much green, it will look too green. Extra blue will make an image look as if it were created under a full moon at midnight at the North Pole. Other color casts are produced by too much of two of the primary colors, when compared to the remaining hue. That is, too much red and green produce a yellowish cast; red and blue tilt things toward magenta; and blue and green create a cyan bias.

- *Color saturation or richness*—Saturation is how much of the hue is composed of the pure color itself and how much is diluted by a neutral color, such as white or black. Think of a can of red paint and white paint. Pure red paint is fully saturated. As you add white paint, the color becomes less saturated, until you reach various shades of pink. Color can also become desaturated by adding black paint, making it darker. Your image editor can help you adjust the saturation of a color by removing these neutral white or black components.

- *Brightness and contrast*—These values refer to the relative lightness or darkness of each color and the number of different tones available. If, say, there are only 12 different red tones in an image, ranging from very light to very dark, with only a few tones in between, then the red portion of the image can be said to have a high contrast. If you had 60 or 100 different red tones, the reds might appear to be relatively low in contrast. The

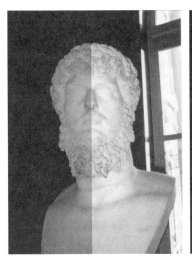

11.1 | The left bust is a high-contrast image; the right bust is a low-contrast image. The left side of each bust is dark, the right side light.

brightness is determined by whether these available tones are clustered at the denser or lighter areas of the image. If 80 percent of your red tones are dark, the reds in your image will be dark, regardless of whether there are 12 of them (high contrast) or 100 of them (low contrast). Figure 11.1 shows high-contrast/low-contrast, bright/dark images for comparison.

Causes of Bad Color

Bad color balance can crop up for several reasons. If your image was captured with a digital camera, you sometimes can place the blame on the camera itself or the light source used. If your image was created with conventional film and then scanned to create your digital version, there may be other culprits. The major sources of bad color include the following:

• *Wrong light source*—Your camera's sensor, like color films, is balanced for a particular color of light. Daylight at noon is significantly bluer than daylight at dusk. Indoor lighting has a reddish balance. The white balance control of your digital camera should automatically compensate for these variations. If not, you need to reset your white balance or, if using a film camera, add a filter designed to correct for incorrect light sources. It's always best to correct for this kind of color error before you take the picture.

- *Fluorescent light source*—The chief difference between tungsten and daylight sources is the proportion of red and blue light. That's not the case with fluorescent lights. Some types produce illumination that has a severe deficit only in certain colors, such as just particular shades of red. If you looked at the spectrum or rainbow of colors encompassed by such a light source, it would have black bands in it, representing particular wavelengths of light. Many digital cameras have a fluorescent light setting. If not, your camera retailer can provide you with color filters recommended for particular kinds of fluorescent lamps. Because it's difficult to correct for fluorescent lights digitally, you'll want to investigate this option if you shoot many pictures under fluorescents and are getting greenish results.

- *Incorrect photofinishing*—Here's another advantage that digital cameras have over their film counterparts. If you use a scanner to capture print images, you may encounter this problem. Equipment that makes prints from color negatives is highly automated but sometimes makes incorrect guesses, producing images that have bad color or are too light or too dark. Change finishers if this happens often. Ask that your prints be reprinted. If you'd rather not bother, you can often make corrections digitally after you've scanned the prints.

- *Mistreatment of film*—Chalk up another one for digital imaging. Film spoils even before it is processed. If you regularly store a film camera in the hot glove compartment of your car, or take a year or more to finish a roll of film, you can end up with color prints that are off-color—sometimes by quite a bit. If your prints have a nasty purple cast, or even some rainbow-hued flares in them, your negatives probably suffered this indignity. Unfortunately, film that has been fogged or given a nasty color cast cannot be corrected.

- *Mixed light sources*—Using light sources with different color balances can give your images the same motley appearance. Perhaps you bounced your flash off a surface such as a colored wall or ceiling, and the pictures picked up the color of that surface. Or perhaps you took an indoor picture with plenty of tungsten light, but the subject was near a window and was partially illuminated by daylight. Quickest fix? Don't do that. If some of your image is illuminated by the colored bounce flash or daylight streaming in through a window, and other portions by another light source, you'll find it very difficult to make corrections. Investigate turning that picture into an arty shot.

- *Faded colors*—The dyes in color prints and slides are not stable and will change when exposed to strong light or heat for long periods, or with no further impetus even if kept in the dark for much longer periods (say, 5 to 20 years or more). In the case of color prints, you can sometimes make a new print from the original negative if you can find the negative and if it was kept in a cool, dark place. Faded color prints and original slides can often be corrected digitally after scanning because the color changes tend to take place faster in one color layer than another. You may be able to add missing colors by reducing the amount of the other colors in the photograph.

Color Correction Made Easy

Color correction can be quite complex, and I promised you at the beginning of this book not to burn up pages describing image editing techniques when you purchased this volume to learn about digital photography. I figure that if you want a Photoshop book, you'll go out and buy a Photoshop book. So, I'll keep things simple and easy in this section, providing you with just enough information to get you started.

Keep in mind that no correction techniques can add detail or color that isn't there. All techniques work well with photographs that have, say, all the colors somewhere, but with too much of one hue or another. The extra color can be removed, leaving a well-balanced picture behind. Or you can beef up the other colors, so they are in balance once again. Your image editing program does that by changing some pixels that are relatively close to the color you want to increase to that exact color.

Removing one color, or changing some colors to another color, doesn't add any color to your image: Either way, you're taking color out. So, if you have a photograph that is hopelessly and overpoweringly green, you're out of luck. When you remove all the green, there may be no color left behind. Or you can add magenta until your subject's face turns blue (well, it won't happen that way), and all you'll end up with is a darker photo. You must start with a reasonable image; color correction is better suited for fine-tuning than for major overhaul.

Using Color Balance Controls

The first way to color correct an image is using the color balance controls that virtually every image editing program has. Depending on your particular

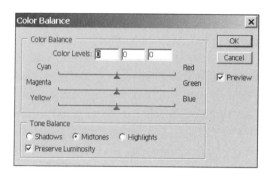

11.2 | Most image editors have sliders or a similar control that you can use to directly modify the balance of colors.

software, you may have to hunt to find a set of sliders, which can be used to adjust all colors for an entire image. No matter what program you're using, the dialog box will look more or less like figure 11.2, with a few differences.

These let you adjust the proportions of a particular color, from 0 percent to 100 percent, or, in some cases, you can either add one color or subtract its two component colors. For example, moving the Cyan/Red slider to the right toward the red end adds red and subtracts cyan, and it has the exact same effect as moving the Magenta/Green and Yellow/Blue sliders both the same amount to the left. This is easy to master if your image editor shows a preview in realtime of your image as you move the sliders. The biggest challenge is deciding in exactly which direction you need to add or subtract color. Magenta may look a lot like red, and it's difficult to tell cyan from green.

Adobe Photoshop Elements, which should eventually replace Photo Deluxe and the Photoshop LE software supplied with many scanners and digital cameras, takes a different approach. With Elements, you're prompted to click with an eyedropper tool in an area of your image that is supposed to be black, white, or gray. The software then adds or subtracts color to make that area a neutral color, with no slider manipulation required on your part.

Using Hue/Saturation Controls

You also can color correct an image using the Hue/Saturation/Lightness (Brightness) controls found in most image editors. The advantage of correcting color this way is that you can change the saturation (or richness) of individual colors or of all the colors in an image, without modifying the hue or lightness/

darkness of those colors. The Color Balance method changes only the relationships between the colors and leaves the saturation alone.

These dialog boxes, like the one shown in figure 11.3, have three main controls. They let you change the saturation alone, modify the overall hue (making all the colors more reddish, greenish, bluish, and so forth), or change the overall brightness/darkness of the image while leaving the saturation and hue unchanged.

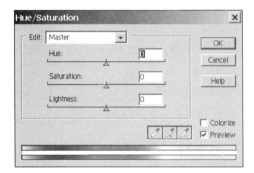

11.3 | The Hue/Saturation sliders from Adobe Photoshop Elements are typical controls found in most image editors.

For example, you might have a holiday picture that needs to have its reds and greens enriched, but with muted blues. Perhaps the green grass and foliage in another color have picked up an undesirable color cast, and you want to shift all the green values one way or another to improve the color. Or perhaps you may want to darken or lighten just one color in an image.

Using Color Ring Arounds and Variations

Most image editors offer a color ring around or variations mode, in which the software generates several versions of an image, arranged in a circle or other array so you can view a small copy of each one and compare them. Photoshop Elements' Variations mode is an example of this method. You can see the dialog box in figure 11.4.

In the upper-left corner, you'll find thumbnail images of your original image paired with a preview with the changes you've made applied. As you apply corrections, the Current Pick thumbnail will change. Immediately underneath is another panel with the current pick surrounded by six different versions,

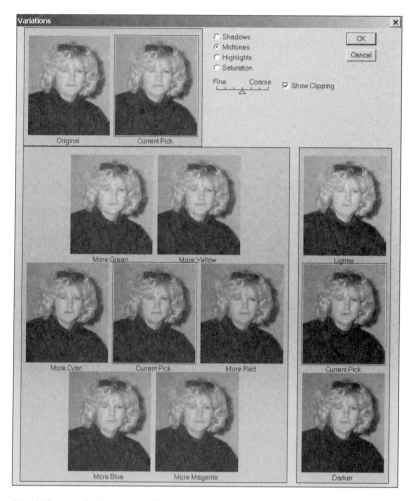

11.4 | Choose the best color from a set of samples with Variations.

each biased toward a different color: green, yellow, red, magenta, blue, and cyan. These show what your current pick would look like with that type of correction added. You can click on any of them to apply that correction to the current pick. To the right of this ring around is a panel with three sample images: the current pick in the center with a lighter version above and a darker version below.

Your Tools for Retouching

Photography has always been part craft, part science, and part fine art, with a little alchemy and magic mixed in. Early photographers were often skilled artisans who built their own cameras, amateur chemists who sensitized photographic plates, as well as artists. Digital imaging cranks up the science component several notches, giving the artist in all of us more powerful brushes and an infinite palette of colors, tools, and effects.

The goal of simple retouching is often to remove defects from a photograph. Of course, a defect is often in the eye of the beholder (if not in the bags underneath). A high school senior portrait (male or female) showing less than silky-smooth skin is sometimes viewed as a disaster by those who have just traversed the rocky roads of puberty. On the other hand, removing the character lines from the face of a 60-year-old corporate chief executive would provoke outrage. Emphasizing that steely glint in the eye may be much more important. In advertising photography, the product must be presented just so, and 20 hours of retouching can be a lot less expensive than reshooting a photo when locations, props, models, and well-paid photographers are involved.

You never really believe a picture is worth 1,000 words until somebody starts critiquing one of your beloved photos. Then, the words really seem to flow! Your problems may involve dust spots on a scanned image, defects in your original subject (such as skin blemishes or bags under the eyes), or simply something that appears in a photo that you wish wasn't there.

I'm not going to tell you how to use each of these tools (there are whole books dedicated to doing that), but I will outline the basic weapons in your image editing arsenal.

Rubber Stamp/Clone Tools

The Clone tool, usually represented by a Rubber Stamp icon, duplicates part of an image, pixel by pixel, in a location of your choice. The stamp analogy isn't very good, however, because you're actually drawing with a brush, which you can size and control in other ways allowed by your image editor (for example, transparency of the image laid down or some other behavior).

Cloning can be used to copy portions of an image to another location in the same or a different image. If your desert scene is too sparse for you, a single cactus can be multiplied several times or even copied from a different desert altogether. You may add a window to the side of a building by painting one from another building using the clone tool.

Some image editors clone portions of an image as they were when you started the process: If you try to copy an area that has been modified by cloning, you'll apply the original pixels, not the changed ones. That helps you avoid repeating patterns that result when you clone a clone. If your program doesn't operate in this way, create a duplicate of your original image and clone from that to avoid the problem.

If you're simply retouching a photo with no intent to add or subtract anything other than the defects, the clone tool is useful for copying portions of an image over the parts you want to replace. Or you can combine several images to create visions you might not encounter in nature, as shown in figure 11.5.

11.5 | Use cloning and compositing to combine several images into one.

Dodging/Burning Tools

When color or black-and-white prints are made by exposing photosensitive paper under an enlarger, the darkroom worker can modify how the image appears. That's done by giving extra exposure to some areas of the print (burning) and holding back other areas so they don't receive as long of an exposure (dodging).

You can use dodging and burning to lighten some shadows under and above the eyes of a subject, or you can use burning to darken a highlight that is too light. These tools are a good choice for selectively brightening and darkening only parts of an image, rather than the entire photo. To create the image at right in figure 11.6, I used dodging, burning, and cloning, as well as blur/sharpen and orientation tools described next.

11.6 | Can you find six differences between these two photos? How about 60?

Blur/Sharpen Tools

Image editors have plug-ins called filters (which we'll explore in the next chapter) that process all of an image, or just a selection, to provide a particular special effect, such as blurring or sharpening. Most also have special brush tools that can apply blurring or sharpening effects to a section of your image as you paint.

Sharpening isn't difficult to understand. Blurry is bad, so sharper must be good, right? Not necessarily. You should use sharpen tools carefully to avoid making your image look too sharp. When an image or portion has been sharpened too much the defects in the picture become more readily apparent, whether those defects are dust spots, scratches on a scanned print, or the pixels themselves in a digital photograph.

And blurring isn't always bad. In fact, selective blurring of unimportant areas of your image can make the rest of the picture look sharper in comparison. Blurring is also valuable for minimizing defects, including those dust spots or scratches. Figure 11.7 shows an image that has been sharpened by blurring the background!

11.7 | Blurring the background makes the foreground look that much sharper.

Image Sizing Tools

Image editors let you resize an entire digital image or rescale portions of the image while leaving the rest of the picture untouched. Go ahead, make that soccer ball huge. Enlarge that tree in your front yard to see what it will look like in 15 years. Make your company's products larger in comparison to your competitors'.

Image scaling tools can be used to resize a picture or object proportionately (that is, the same amount in all directions) or in only one direction. I've used sizing to make myself look taller and thinner, to stretch out a wall, or make a patch of sky I was pasting into an image wider to fill a larger area.

Cropping Tools

Cropping tools let you strip excess image area from your photos, providing a better composed image or one that better fits the hole you have for it in a desktop publication or picture frame.

Orientation Tools

Use orientation tools to flip an image left to right or vertically, to suit a composition or just to provide a new view. Image editors also allow you to rotate images around an axis of your choice, so you can, for example, appear to be climbing a steep slope when, in the original picture, you were walking on flat ground and merely leaning forward.

Compositing Tools

The term compositing tools applies to a broad array of image editing features that let you remove parts of pictures and paste them down elsewhere in the same photo or in an entirely new image. Compositing aids include selection tools that let you extract parts of an image and feathering or combining features that blend the composited images together. Once mastered, these tools can help you with the following:

- *Photo restorations*—Pictures from 20 to 150 years old may have been damaged by the ravages of time, and you'll need to remove scratches, replace missing sections of the photo, and perhaps reconstruct facial features from the fragments that remain.

- *Photo travesties*—These are snapshots with major digressions from desired content. That is, there's a tree growing from someone's head, an unwanted bystander gawking at the main subject, or other pictorial clutter. Your job will be to remove these elements.

- *Major facial surgery*—Your subject is wearing glasses in the photo but switched to contacts years ago. An unfortunate accident of lighting accentuated slightly protuberant ears, transforming them from an interesting characteristic to features that would make Dumbo blush. Bad shadows have given someone a double chin. They don't really look like this photo—can you improve it?

Next Up

Retouching is only half the image manipulation picture. Sometimes you want to do more than just fix a photo. At times, you'll want to enhance it dramatically using special effects like those built into all image editors. In the next chapter, I'll show you some of the things you can do.

Chapter 12

Special Effects

Image editors can transform a dull image into an old masters' painting with delicate brush strokes or create stunning, vivid color variations in a mundane photograph. This chapter introduces you to the magic you can perform with these features.

Special Effects with Filters

Whether you want to blast apart your images into a cascade of sparkling pixels or simply add some subtle sharpness or contrast to dull or blurred areas, the special effects modules called filters have the power to effect a complete makeover on all or parts of a digital photo or scanned image. You also can use these add-ons to produce undetectable changes that make a good image even better.

Filters are actually miniature programs in their own right, designed to manipulate the pixels of your image. For example, the Invert filter found in all image editors looks at each pixel in turn and simply flips it to the exact opposite value. A pure white or light gray pixel will be changed to pure black or dark gray, and the color value of the pixel will be changed to the opposite color (a dark blue pixel will become light yellow, and so forth).

Other filters may remove pixels entirely, or shift them around in an image in relation to others that remain in place. The miniprograms that make up filters can be very simple and require no user input, or they may be extremely complex and bristle with dialog boxes, slider controls, buttons, and preview windows.

Filters fall into several different categories, which include the following:

- *Image enhancement filters*—These filters improve the appearance of images, without making basic changes in the content of the images. Sharpen, unsharp masking, blurring filters, and others in this category can be applied to an entire image or to just the portion that you have selected.

- *Attenuating filters*—I borrowed this word from the photographic world to describe filters that act like a piece of glass or other substance placed between the image and your eye, superimposing the texture or surface of the object on your picture. Think of a piece of frosted glass, translucent scrap of canvas fabric, or a grainy sheet of photographic film. These, or any of dozens of other filters, including most noise and texturizing filters, can add a texture or distort your image in predictable ways. Attenuating filters may be applied to a whole image or to just a select portion.

- *Distortion filters*—These filters actually move pixels from one place in an image to another, providing mild to severe distortion of the photo. Filters that map your image to a sphere, immerse it in a whirlpool, or pinch, ripple, twirl, or shear bits here and there can provide distortion to some or all of an image.

- *Pixelation filters*—This group of filters adds texture or surface changes, much like attenuating filters, but they also take into account the size, color, contrast, or other characteristic of the pixels underneath. These include crystallize, mezzotint, and most brush-type filters. Such filters don't simply overlay a particular texture—the appearance of each altered pixel incorporates the underlying image. Figure 12.1 shows the same image processed with a distortion filter (Photoshop Element's Diffuse Glow) on the left and a pixelation filter (Facet) on the right.

**12.1 | The same image, processed with a Diffuse Glow filter (left) and
Facet filter (right).**

- *Rendering filters*—These filters create something out of nothing, in the way that a three-dimensional rendering program creates a shaded model of an object from a wire frame skeleton. These filters may or may not use part of the underlying image in working their magic: Adobe's Clouds filter, found in Photoshop Elements and other image editors, creates random puffy clouds in the selected area, whereas Difference Clouds inverts part of the image to produce a similar effect. Lens flare and lighting effects filters generate illumination out of thin air, whereas chrome filters produces shiny surface effects.

- *Contrast-enhancing filters*—These filters operate on the differences in contrast that exist at the boundary of two colors in an image. By increasing the brightness of the lighter color, and decreasing the brightness of the darker color, the contrast is enhanced. Because these boundaries mark an edge in the image, contrast-enhancing filters tend to make the edges sharper. The effect is different from pure sharpening filters, which also use contrast enhancement. Filters in this category include all varieties of filters, including Find Edges, Glowing Edges, Accented Edges, Poster Edges, Ink Outlines, and even most Emboss and Bas Relief filters. Figure 12.2 shows our test image with rendering filter (Lighting Effects) applied at left and a contrast-enhancing filter (Poster Edges) applied at right.

 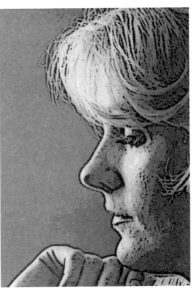

12.2 | Rendering filters, such as Lighting Effects (left), create interesting special looks, whereas contrast-enhancing filters, such as Poster Edges (right), emphasize the borders between tones.

Using Filters

Some general tips apply to nearly all filters that we'll be working with. To apply a filter, keep these steps in mind:

1. Choose the portion of the image that the filter will be applied to, using your image editor's selection tools, including the marquee, lasso, or magic wand. If you don't select a portion of an image, the filter will be applied to the

12.3 | Filters are often most effective when applied to only a portion of an image.

entire image. Because it can take anywhere from a few seconds to several minutes to apply a filter, you may want to work with a representative section of the image first before applying the filter to the whole thing. Figure 12.3 shows an image with a filter applied only to part of the photo (in this case, the sky).

2. Select your filter from your image editor's filter menu. Some filters, called single-step filters, operate immediately with no additional input required from you (Elements' Sharpen and Blur filters are examples of this type). Others prompt a dialog box with controls you'll need to set.

3. When using a filter that incorporates a dialog box, you'll usually see a Preview window that provides an idea of what your filter will do when applied to a selected portion of an image.

4. Apply the filter by clicking on the OK or Apply button.

5. When the filter is finished, be careful not to do anything else (such as move the selection) until you've decided whether or not the effect is the one you want. That way, you can quickly undo the filter and apply another rendition.

Sharpening and Blurring Photos

In the last chapter, I mentioned how sharpening—and even blurring—can be used to enhance a digital image. Sharpening and blurring work in the same basic way, by increasing or decreasing the contrast between adjoining pixels.

When applying sharpening, this has the effect of making details stand out more and making edges appear sharper. With blurring, the reverse is true.

When you use the plain sharpen or blur filters of most image editors, the effects are applied everywhere in an image or selection. You'll also find variations on this theme, such as sharpen edges filters, which emphasize the edges in images; unsharp masking filters, which do the same thing but with more user control; and Gaussian blur filters, which let you apply the same controls to blurring. Here are some tips for using sharpening and blurring filters:

- Remember that sharpen filters increase contrast, whereas blur filters decrease contrast. If your image is low in contrast, experiment with applying sharpening first, then adjusting the brightness/contrast of your sharpened image. Reverse the order of the steps and you may end up with an image that has too much contrast for your taste.

- Sharpen edges and unsharp masking filters can avoid the grainy effect you get with overall sharpening.

- Buildings and other heavily textured objects, which contain many fine details, can benefit from overall sharpening, as you can see in figure 12.4.

12.4 | Structures and other subjects with much detail can withstand a great deal of sharpening without looking processed.

- People and faces often look better with only the edges enhanced. With most portraits, the outlines of eyes and other features should look sharp, but you don't want every flaw in the skin to be accentuated.

- Try using one of the blur filters to smoothly blend a selection you've pasted into an image. The effect can provide a smoother transition if the area being pasted has more noise, grain, or sharpness than the area it is pasted into.

Unsharp masking is a technique that was first applied to images made on sheet film. To produce the effect conventionally, a film positive is made from the original film negative (a negative of the negative, so to speak). The positive is slightly blurred, which spreads the image slightly. When the positive and negative are sandwiched together and used to expose a new image, light areas of the positive correspond very closely to the dark areas of the negative, and vice versa, canceling each other out to a certain extent. However, at the edges in the image, the blurring in the positive produces areas that don't cancel out, resulting in lighter and darker lines on either side of the edges. This extra emphasis on the edges of the image adds the appearance of sharpness. It's fairly easy for a computer to simulate the blurry positive mask and then mate it with a negative image of the original picture—with the added advantage of realtime control over the effects.

Eliminating Dust, Scratches, and Artifacts

If you're working from a scanned image, you may need your image editor's dust/scratches filter, which selectively blurs areas of your image that contain dots, spots, scratches, and other defects. When the filter is applied, the image editor typically examines each pixel in the image, moving outward radially to look for abrupt transitions in tone that might indicate a dust spot on the image. If a spot is found, the area is blurred to minimize the appearance of the defect.

Despeckle filters are in some ways similar to edge sharpening filters. Instead of increasing the contrast in the edges and leaving the rest of the image or selection alone, despeckle filters decrease the contrast in all of the selection except for the edges. In both cases, the edges end up with relatively more detail than the rest of the image. Don't confuse this filter with dust and scratches remedies. It can remove dust spots in an image through its blurring effect, but that's a bonus—despeckle filters are much "dumber" add-ons that don't specifically search for spots.

You can tell which image-enhancing filter to use by following these guidelines:

- If your image has dust spots in random locations and you don't need edge enhancement, use dust and scratches filters.

- If your image is already relatively sharp, to the point where there is objectionable detail or noise in the image areas, use a despeckle filter to provide a blurring effect that doesn't mask edge detail.

- If your image doesn't contain excessive noise, use sharpen edges to sharpen it up a bit without introducing an undesirable texture.

- If you need a lot of control over how an image is sharpened, use your image editor's unsharp masking filter.

Noise Filters

Noise filters blur images in their own way, by adding random pixels to an image or selection, thereby replacing details that are there with noise. Adding noise blurs an image without reducing the contrast. In addition, standard blur filters obscure details in an image by smoothing everything out and reducing contrast. You may not want that effect if you end up with a smooth surface that looks fake because it should contain some texture.

Noise filters instead add texture to areas that have been made too smooth by other effects or filters, or which have been painted in from scratch using a nontextured brush. Adding noise can actually help these smooth areas blend into other parts of the image that already have texture. In other cases, a bit of noise can mask very fine scratches or dust spots in an image.

If you find a blended, gradient-type area of one of your photographs (for example, a sky image that has a smooth transition from light blue to dark blue), adding a little noise can make the gradient reproduce more easily, without banding.

Adding Special Effects

Many good image editors exist that you can use to add special effects to your digital photographs. You also can find many interesting third-party effects sets that extend the capabilities of even the most filter-rich image editor. Among my favorites are the venerable Kai's Power Tools (now called KPT because Kai Krause is out of the picture) from Corel, the wildly innovative Eye Candy 4000 and Xenofex from those freaky folks at Alien Skin Software, as well as Andromeda's rich lineup of filters for reproducing the effects of many popular photographic effects. A promising newcomer is DreamSuite, from Auto FX Software, a full-fledged, stand-alone program that also can be used within your favorite Photoshop plug-in-compatible image editor.

Kai's Power Tools

The KPT plug-ins come in three different versions, all with different filters. The most widely used set is KPT 3, which is the last version of Kai's Power Tools that anyone really understood how to use. Despite the unusual interface, which some have described as a dashboard from a Martian station wagon, KPT 3 includes some easy to use and useful filters, including glass lens tools, fractal effects, and my personal favorite, the Vortex Tiling tool which can turn a simple photo of a bee exploring a flower into a kaleidoscope of amazing beauty, as you can see in figure 12.5.

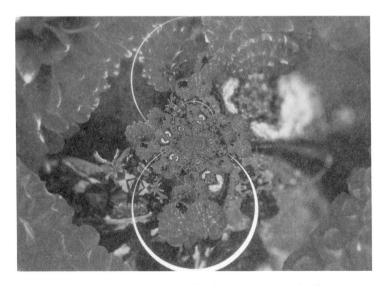

12.5 | KPT's Vortex Tiling produces this bee's-eye view of a flower.

KPT 5 and KPT 6 went a bit off the deep end, with tools such as Frax 4D, which works with "2D slices of 4D space" (I'm not making this up) to generate eye-popping three-dimensional images that may or may not have anything to do with your original photograph. Graphics professionals who work with these plug-ins every day love them because they can achieve looks with KPT that are impossible to reproduce with any other tools. Figure 12.6 shows the KPT Blurrrr tool, one of the more comprehensible plug-ins in the set, in action.

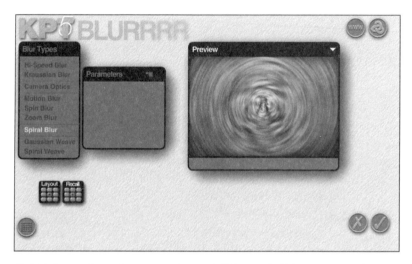

12.6 | Advanced—*really* advanced—capabilities are built into KPT 5 and KPT 6.

Alien Skin

You know Alien Skin Software is a company with attitude when you see their corporate motto ("We will never wear suits.") and the titles on their business cards (Minister of Propaganda, Interplanetary Trouble Maker, and The Secret Weapon). Their two key products, Eye Candy (EC) 4000 and Xenofex, are just as innovative.

EC 4000 includes the absolute best fire- and water-effects filters on the market, including some very cool water drop and drip modules, and you'll find them both indispensable when you want to set fire to things in your images or drench them with liquid, as I did in the Phoenix-themed image in figure 12.7.

Eye Candy makes it easy to create interesting textures—such as fur, glass, wood, and basket weaves—and performs all this magic with an interface that is simple and intuitive, as you can see in figure 12.8.

Special Effects

12.7 | Use Eye Candy 4000 when you want to add fire and brimstone to
your pictures.

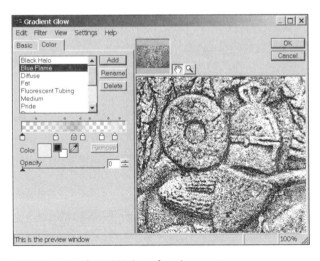

12.8 | Eye Candy 4000's interface is easy to use.

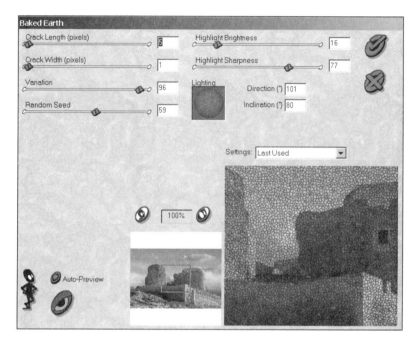

12.9 | Alien Skin's Xenofex provides its own set of special effects tools that are easy to apply with a few slider controls.

Xenofex is a laudable earlier effort by the Alien Skin folks, with its own completely different set of effects, including unique Baked Earth, Electrify, and Flag filters. Its interface, shown in figure 12.9, is a little different from Eye Candy's but is equally simple to master.

Auto FX DreamSuite

DreamSuite is a brand-new effects package that you can use in stand-alone mode or run within your favorite image editor. It includes more than a dozen powerful effects workshops that let you create cubistic looks, liquid metal, photo borders and frames, ripple effects, and other interesting enhancements. Like the Alien Skin programmers, the imaging gurus at Auto FX really put some thought into creating effects that you can't get anywhere else. DreamSuite is shown in figure 12.10.

12.10 | DreamSuite is a new effects package with some novel capabilities.

A Special Effects Sampler

If you count the special effects built into some image editors (which number around 100), and the dozens more available from third-party software houses, the possibilities for enhancing your photos is mind-boggling. Explaining exactly how to perform specific effects with all of these tools is beyond the scope of this book. However, to get the ideas flowing, I'm going to provide a gallery of enhanced photos with some brief descriptions of what was involved in creating them. You wouldn't want to duplicate my images exactly, in any case, but you might get some ideas for your own pictures from the sections that follow. You can view any of these images that don't make it into the color section of this book at my Web site **www.dbusch.com**.

Zoom, Zoom, Zoom

Our stork returns, Phoenix-like, for an encore in this photomanipulation that combines images from three different digital pictures. I started with a sunset shot of the sky, which I gave a Van Gogh-like texture using Eye Candy 4000's Twirl filter, then emphasized with an application of an unsharp masking filter. Then, I lifted the tower that houses Big Ben (which is itself actually a bell) from a mundane shot of London, and dropped it on top of the sky background. The eerie silhouette effect required nothing more than fiddling with the brightness/contrast controls of my image editor.

12.11 | Credit Alien Skin's Eye Candy for most of the effects in this photo.

Next, I placed an image of a stork on top and applied Eye Candy's Motion Trail filter and a few other supersecret mods to achieve the look shown in figure 12.11.

Joust the Facts

Because of an iron fence that barred access, I couldn't get close to a stone carving on the walls of a cathedral in Europe, so the finished picture had a distinct distant quality. Enlarging the image enlarged the pixels, so I used various edge-enhancing and sharpening filters (to excess, perhaps) to produce an image in which the jousting knights really stand out. Figure 12.12 shows the final result.

Painterly Effects

DreamSuite has some incredible tools for turning rejects into old masters' paintings, as shown in figure 12.13. I really liked this photo of an arbor in a European urban park because it makes such strong use of converging lines to draw your attention into the photo. There are a series of repeating vertical lines of the poles of the arbor, the converging horizontal lines pointing toward

12.12 | You can almost feel the sandstone texture of this stone carving after extra sharpening was applied to the original photograph.

12.13 | An ordinary photo can be transformed into an impressionist painting using special effects filters, such as DreamSuite.

the "horizon" at the end of the row, and the repeating line of benches. Topping it all is a repeating line of arches.

Although the "center" of the photo is a little too close to the physical center of the picture for my taste, I thought the original looked like an impressionist painting. So I applied DreamSuite's Cubism filter using hexagonal brush tips. The pastel blues and greens really unify the image, too.

Text Effects

After more than a dozen trips to Spain in the last two decades, we tend to wander off the beaten paths, visiting abandoned castles and monuments that even most locals haven't seen. So when I wanted to create a Visit Spain poster, I used this old castle and added some text, as you can see in figure 12.14.

12.14 | Add text effects to your photographs using common plug-ins designed to add bevels, ridges, or edges to a selection.

I used the text itself as a selection, so the text was filled with the sky background image. Then, I applied Ulead's Buttonizer filter to create a ridged appearance. Add a drop shadow (which is built into most image editors, or you can just duplicate the text, fill it with black, and offset slightly), and you're finished. Finding this dramatic setting was the hard part.

3-D Effects

If you want to make your images leap off the page, you can use various three-dimensional effects available as filter plug-ins. Here's a quickie example of what you can do.

In another life, I spent most weekends working on portfolios for nascent models, and after a time the stacks of 8- x 10-inch prints began to look a little like the surreal landscape shown in figure 12.15. It was an easy image to create, though, using KPT's Planar Tiling plug-in. The filter puts the tiled image in the lower half of the document, leaving the upper half available for your own components. I elected to use the original photograph.

12.15 | KPT's Planar Tiling filter generates surreal landscapes with ease.

Next Up

In this chapter and the one before, I've tried to provide you with some what-to-do tips, rather than step-by-step how-to-do-it examples. You can find many good books on image editing (head for **www.amazon.com** and type my name into a search box if you'd like to see a couple). If you believe, as I do, that image creation just begins with the click of the shutter, you'll want to explore graphics manipulation further. And if you're looking for ways to share your photos with a wide audience, you'll want to move on to the next chapter on creating images for the Web.

Chapter 13

Digital Images for the Web

Digital cameras and scanners are perfect

tools for creating images for the Internet.

This chapter explains some of the things

you must keep in mind when creating

images for the Web or email.

Special Requirements for Web Graphics

Digital cameras and scanners and the Web were made for each other. They both have the speed, fast turnaround, and image quality that's perfectly suited for Web graphics. Was there an addition to your family over the weekend? Did a dissident group on your company's board of directors stage a coup de société at the last meeting? Don't panic! You can post Web photos of your new child or your organization's incoming corporate junta within minutes of the blessed events thanks to your digital camera.

Or, do you suddenly need to convert a printed chart for use in an online report? Or perhaps you need to add pictures of a long-departed relative to your Internet-based family tree. Slap the relevant artwork down onto your scanner and minutes later you can have the image you need ready for uploading.

Digital cameras and scanners give you the ability to capture a huge variety of images quickly in digital form. Even the least expensive digital camera has more than enough resolution to capture images that are perfect for Web pages. Indeed, a 640×480-pixel photograph is at least four times too large for most typical Web page applications. Scanners can grab images of tiny postage stamps or an 8x10 portrait print as fast as you can position the originals for capture.

Web images have some special requirements that may take some getting used to if you're accustomed to the non-Web digital world, in which bigger is better and more resolution means only that you have to find enough disk space to store a big, fat image. On the Web, the priorities are sharply different as the following list shows (the list is in no particular order; we'll cover these priorities in more detail later in this chapter):

- An image must be small enough that it fits comfortably on a page at various sizes without overwhelming the rest of the content of the page. Some visitors to a Web page may be using a browser with a 600×400-pixel window or smaller; others may have 1,000×700 or even larger views of your page, as shown in figures 13.1 and 13.2. Images should be sized to look good at any screen resolution.

- An image must be small enough (in terms of file size) to download quickly. Although cable modems and other broadband access has become more

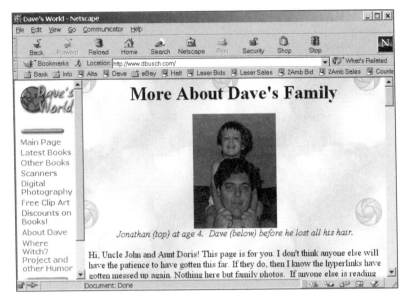

13.1 | Size your images so that they look good in small browser windows . . .

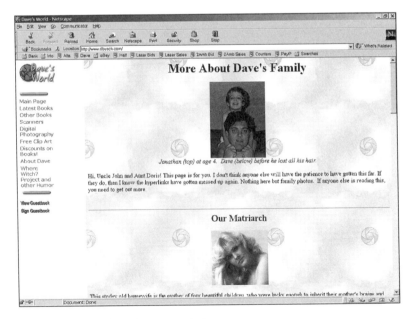

13.2 | . . . Or very large browser windows.

common, millions of folks may be watching your graphics download at 33Kbps—or slower. If your image takes a long time to load, they may just hit their Back button or go elsewhere.

- An image should be just sharp enough to convey the information you want to pass along, yet without noticeable blur that will be distracting. It's possible for a Web graphic to be too sharp (if the sharpness makes it too big to download quickly) as well as too fuzzy.

- Web graphics need to have colors that are compatible with your viewers' screen displays. Fortunately, working with browser-safe palettes is less important these days because the vast majority of those cruising the Internet are using a full-color display. I'm not going to pad out this chapter with a discussion of choosing a Web palette; any good image editing book contains that information, if you feel you need it.

If you read this list carefully, you'll see that much of what is important about Web graphics involves the physical screen size and file size of the image. The two are closely related, but they don't necessarily move in lockstep. They are affected by the factors described in the next two sections on screen size and file size.

Screen Size

The screen size is determined by the dimensions of your image and the screen resolution of your viewers' displays, plus the size of their monitors. A 256×256-pixel image will be twice as large in each dimension as a 128×128-pixel image, but it will occupy comparatively less screen real estate when your visitor's screen resolution is set to 1,280×1,024-pixels, rather than 800-x600-pixels. To complicate things, some may be using a 19- or 21-inch monitor, whereas others are happy with a 17-inch or smaller monitor. At a resolution of, say, 1,280×1,024 on each of these, your 128×128-pixel image will vary sharply in size on these different monitors. Figure 13.3 shows what I am talking about.

You need to keep this in mind when designing Web graphics. Your company's logo may look good at a particular size on your monitor, but it may appear to be a bloated graphic or tiny button at a different resolution on a different monitor. If possible, try to view images at different resolutions to see what screen size suits them best.

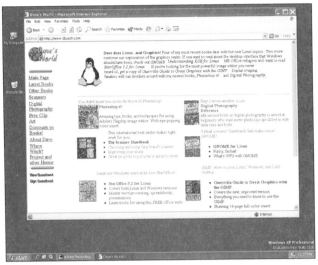

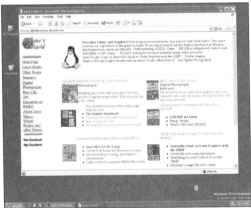

13.3 | Both images show display screens at 1,280×1,024 resolution. At top, the view is what you'd see on a 22-inch monitor; at bottom, the comparative size of the same view on a 17-inch display.

Also remember that a visitor's browser window also can vary in size independently of the screen resolution. I usually view my 19-inch monitor at 1,280×1,024 resolution, but I frequently keep several small browser windows tiled on the screen. Images should be sized so they look good at different resolutions and within differently sized browser windows.

File Size

An image's file size determines how quickly it can be downloaded and is loosely related to the physical dimensions of the image. That is, a 512×512-pixel graphic is likely to be quite a bit larger, and take longer to download, than a 64×64-pixel image. However, the file format you choose for your image can have a dramatic effect on the file size. It's entirely possible for a larger image to have a smaller file size and faster downloading time than a relatively small image.

The culprits in this case are the two most common Web image formats: GIF (Graphics Interchange Format) and JPEG (named after the Joint Photographic Experts Group that designed it). All image editors you'll use to work with your digital camera and scanned images can save in these two formats. Each has its own set of advantages and disadvantages.

GIF

GIF supports only 256 or fewer colors, but it makes for excellent display of certain types of images on all Web browsers, regardless of the color capabilities of the visitor's monitor (that is, even if a visitor is using an older computer set to display only 256 colors). GIFs also produce fairly small file sizes.

However, GIF is often a poor choice for photographic images that contain many more than 256 hues. Such graphics will look posterlike with noticeable bands of color where similar tones have all been converted to the same color, as you can see in figure 13.4.

13.4 | Obvious banding occurs when a full-color image is converted to 256 colors for the GIF format.

GIF's lossless compression scheme doesn't discard any image information, other than colors, as it squeezes files down in size, so it retains all the sharpness of the original. That makes GIF the best format for images, such as charts and graphs, that contain hard edges. In addition, GIFs can be made transparent, so they can float on a background; interleaved, so they can be progressively revealed as files download; and animated to add action to your Web page.

The only way to make a GIF file smaller is to reduce the number of colors it contains from, say, 256 colors to 128, 64, 32, or even fewer hues. So the size of your GIF image is likely to be determined by the number of colors you really need. The file size of a chart, graph, or logo with only a dozen or so colors can be made really small with a GIF. For photographs, you'll almost always get a better image and smaller file size with JPEG.

JPEG

JPEG compresses images in a different way. Rather than discarding colors wholesale, JPEG instead divides an image into blocks and examines all the pixels within a particular block. Pixels that are similar enough in color are converted to one common color, reducing the amount of information that must be retained to reconstruct that particular block.

JPEG can reproduce the whole 24-bit range of 16.8 million colors without breaking stride (although any given JPEG image is likely to contain far fewer different colors than that), so it's a good choice for reproducing full-color images. JPEGs potentially offer even smaller file sizes than GIF, although the resulting images may not be as sharp because JPEG discards some resolution-oriented image information to squeeze the file size down.

Fortunately, all image editors let you trade off sharpness against file size to produce the best compromise. You can save a particular image at a desired quality level, which is measured in different ways by different image editors. Some use word descriptions such as Low, Medium, or High quality. Others use a numeric scale from 1 (low quality/high compression) to 10 (high quality/low compression) or even percentages (from 0% to 100% on a quality scale). Figure 13.5 shows a JPEG image with the typical "blocky" look that occurs when the file has been squeezed too much.

13.5 | At left, the image has been saved as a JPEG, using a high compression/low quality setting; at right, the same image has been saved at a low compression/high quality setting.

As an experiment, I took a very large 1,400×1,000-pixel 24-bit color file and saved it in the TIFF (tagged image file format) format using the lossless LZW compression scheme Photoshop uses. The file in that form was about 3.3MB in size. Then, I saved it as a JPEG file using the maximum quality setting of 10. The file was squeezed down by almost 67 percent to 1.3MB. Finally, saving the file using the minimum quality/maximum compression setting of 0, I was able to produce an 82KB file—more than 40 times smaller than the original. Yet, the image was still acceptable for Web use.

Your challenge in using JPEG is to discover a quality level that's high enough to avoid making your image look blocky but not so high that the image takes a long time to download. I recommend saving several different versions of an image, then reloading each of them for comparison.

Avoid loading and resaving JPEG images; each time you save an image in JPEG format, additional image information may be lost.

What's the Ideal File Size for Web Graphics?

The ideal size varies with the subject matter and its importance to your Web's message. Some simple rules of thumb you can use when determining file size include the following:

- Try to keep each Web graphic no *larger* than 25 to 50KB, especially if you plan to include a lot of them on a page. Things like rules and buttons can often be trimmed to 7KB or smaller. Cropping or squeezing images with a bit more compression may be all you need.

- Limit each page to a total of 200KB or less in graphics.

- If you're featuring your digital photography, the 200KB limit may be hard to adhere to. Instead, confine the heavy-duty images to certain pages and provide your visitors with a warning before they enter them.

- Include only enough graphics on your main page to entice visitors into your gallery of larger scale digital images.

- A small thumbnail image can be placed on a page and used as a preview of a larger graphic image. You can place the full-size image on another page or have it displayed when the visitor clicks on the thumbnail. That way, a visual clue is provided that helps the user decide whether to proceed with the full download. It's also a good idea to show the file size of the full image so downloaders can anticipate the time involved. Figure 13.6 shows a Web page with thumbnails linked to a larger image.

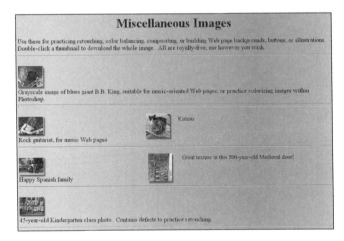

13.6 | Improve download times for your pages by linking large images to thumbnails.

Working with Transparent GIFs

Whether it's a viewfinder on a digital camera, a picture frame on the wall, or an image on the Internet, humans try to squeeze all visuals into a square or rectangular format. Although dropping every inline image into a box makes a browser's job easier, it complicates things for anyone who wants a round button, an irregularly shaped rule, or even something as basic as fancy text to pop out of a page's background.

Transparent GIFs help you out by making all the pixels surrounding a nonsquare object that you want to highlight invisible, making triangles, other polygons, ellipses, and irregularly shaped objects valid fodder for your Web page graphics. Figure 13.7 shows a Web page with three different floating objects created with transparent GIFs.

13.7 | You can float photographic images, text, or other objects on your Web pages using transparent GIFs.

The secret is in the GIF89a format specification, which includes a provision for allowing a single color (and only one) to be designated as invisible, or transparent. When a program such as a browser displays such an image, it ignores that particular color anywhere it finds it and, instead, substitutes pixels representing the underlying background for the pixels of that color.

The background can be a background color, or, alternatively, a background image that is tiled, if necessary, to cover a page's window in the browser. So, although transparent GIFs are actually rectangular in shape (meaning that no text or other images can intrude on the area they cover), the actual GIF image merges smoothly into the background. Figure 13.8 shows the same Web page with the outlines of the GIF files clearly marked.

13.8 | Transparent GIFs are actually rectangular images with see-through areas surrounding the object.

Explore your image editor's tools for creating transparent GIFs. Usually, you'll need to extract the object you want to float and paste it on a layer of a solid color, or on a transparent layer, and then designate that color or transparency

13.9 | The stork, photographed against a plain blue sky, was easy to extract for use with a transparent GIF.

to become the transparent portion of the GIF when saving the file. If you think ahead as you take a picture, you can sometimes photograph a subject against a plain sky, blank wall, or other background that makes it easy to extract the object, as shown in figure 13.9.

Animated GIFs

You've probably seen graphics that move in an animated way on Web pages. You may have been looking at video files, Shockwave animations, Java applets, or Dynamic HTML, but it's more likely that what you saw were simple animated GIF files. These easy-to-create graphics can spin your logo, point visitors to your favorite link or ad banner, or simply add a little motion to flat pages. You can create the individual images for an animated GIF and then use a special tool, such as GIFConstruction Set or Adobe ImageReady, to combine them into a graphic that Web pages will display with motion.

Whether you're more familiar with flip-books than Homer Simpson, you probably know how animation works: The eye is presented with a series of slightly different, progressive images, which the brain blends into smooth motion. Although the average feature-length cartoon (before the age of computers) reportedly required a googol of separate hand-painted cels requiring the equivalent of 10,000 person-years of effort, one person can easily create GIFs with a few frames for fast, effective Web display.

Animated GIFs are GIF files that contain multiple images and the instructions that tell a Web browser how to display them. Although you could theoretically embed a minimovie inside an animated GIF, given the speed of Web transfers in most cases, you'll be doing your visitors a kindness if you stick to slim, trim animations. A two-image GIF can flash a message, attract attention to a link, or provide any simple kind of repetitive movement. With three or four images in your GIF, you can create a crawling marquee or produce the illusion of motion. An animation can display one time, or cycle repeatedly. For the smoothest repeating effect, your animations should be created in *loops*, where the last image in the series flows right into the first one.

To reduce download times, animated GIFs shouldn't cover much space on your Web page, either. A 36×36-pixel multilayered GIF will download four times faster than a 72×72-pixel version, which can make the difference between a tolerable 15-second wait and a painful 1-minute delay. Nor should you overuse animations. In most cases, you'll want just one or possibly two moving objects on your page. Any more than that and each animation will be competing with the others for your visitors' attention. You don't want to induce bouts of seasickness, either, with a roiling Web site. Keep 'em small, fast, and relevant, and everybody will be happy.

You can easily create animated GIFs from your digital photos. Shoot an image from several different angles or positions or use your digital camera's minimovie capability to create successive frames. Each frame should differ slightly from the last in a way that simulates motion. That might be as simple as moving the image slightly to one side. With many image editors, you can use the cursor arrow keys to nudge a selection left, right, up, or down, one pixel at a time, creating a simple animation. Figure 13.10 shows three successive frames that can be combined into an animated GIF.

13.10 | Capture three frames with your digital camera's minimovie capability and create an animated GIF for your Web page.

Sending Graphics in Email

Don't forget that the Internet isn't limited to the Web. Once you've collected some great digital images, you'll want to share them with friends. You can always post them to semipublic Web pages, such as Kodak's PhotoNet, but I think you'll want to explore a more personalized approach of emailing your best shots directly to family members, friends, and colleagues.

Most email software allows you to attach photos directly to email messages, so sending an image or two is easy. However, you need to mind the same file size precautions mentioned earlier in the section "Special Requirements for Web Graphics." Unless you know your recipient has a fast broadband connection, you'll want to save your image as a space-saving JPEG file, or as a GIF for non-photographic images. You probably don't have to adhere strictly to the Web-size guidelines; your friend will probably be patient enough to wait for a download of a minute or two for a larger picture (say, 100KB to 200KB, but definitely not a megabyte or two!).

Another thing to keep in mind is that your recipient may have a limit on their mailbox size. They may be able to accept, for example, mail totaling only 5MB or 10MB. Normally that isn't a problem because it would take hundreds of text messages to fill an ordinary mailbox. However, if you start sending dozens of pictures to acquaintances, you may end up filling up their box allocation. When that happens, their other email may start bouncing back to the sender. So, if you plan to email lots of pictures, spread them out, or check with your recipient to see if they have any mailbox limitations.

Next Up

The last chapter of this book deals with another way of distributing your images: through hard-copy prints you create with your printer. You may have more options open to you in the printer arena than you imagine. I think you'll find the short, final chapter interesting.

Chapter 14

Printing Your Digital Images

This chapter explains everything you need to know to choose a printer to print sparkling hard copies of your most vivid images.

Making Your Prints Charming

Prints have long been the favored end result of photography, in both digital and conventional realms. Indeed, early daguerreotypes could be considered the first "hard copies" (they were produced on hard silver-plated sheets of copper), except that none of them were copies. Every daguerreotype was an original: If you wanted three portraits from a sitting, the photographer took three separate pictures. It was possible to make daguerreotype duplicates of daguerreotype originals, of course, but it was easier to simply take another shot.

A competing process for making rather soft-looking paper prints from negatives was developed, so to speak, by Englishman William Fox Talbot and spurred the invention of glass and, later, the film negatives in common use today. Most of us who have used film cameras use negative films and make hard-copy prints. Even color transparencies, favored by professional photographers for their superior quality when reproduced, usually end up as paper prints or published in magazines or books.

Digital photography has changed the way we work with our images. Unlike photos captured on film, every digital picture you take isn't routinely converted into a print by a photofinisher. In fact, thanks to the "quick erase" buttons on many digital image grabbers, some pictures are deleted from your solid state "film" before they even make it out of the camera. Anyone who has shot an entire roll of film just to get a shot or two that was worth printing will appreciate the film-saving economy of a digital camera.

The digital camera makes even more sense when you realize that a huge number of electronic images are never intended for hard copies that you can pass around and show to friends. You may take a picture for a Web page, drop a shot into your PowerPoint presentation, or place an image in a desktop publication without the slightest need for a print.

That said, it should be obvious that the burgeoning non-hard-copy outlets for images haven't eliminated the need to make prints. If anything, the availability of inexpensive photo quality printers encourages digital photographers to make bigger and better prints of their efforts, where before they might have been satisfied with puny 4×6-inch prints from the photolab. Computer technology lets you make prints of just the pictures you want, much more simply than previously possible.

Your Output Options

The surest sign that hard-copy prints are alive and well are the number of options available to you for creating them. Vendors are jumping all over themselves developing better printers. (Although, as we'll see, the motive for that is often to make big bucks from the consumables such as paper and ink.) You can visit your local discount store and pop a memory disk in a kiosk that lets you crop, enlarge, rotate, and print your favorite pictures. Your photofinisher will be happy to accept digital images over the Internet and deliver your pictures to you as prints or on a CD-ROM. With so many choices, your biggest problem may be in selecting the one that's right for you.

The short answer is that, depending on your needs, all of them may be suitable at one time or another. This next section provides a summary of what you should consider.

Laser Printers

You may already have a black-and-white laser printer (or its cousin, the LED printer), particularly if a lot of your output is text. If you work in a business that needs color text and graphics, you may even have a color laser printer. Both are best suited for text and line art but may be acceptable for certain types of digital photographic output. Some color lasers, in fact, do an excellent job with photographic images.

For example, if you need a quick black-and-white copy of a black-and-white or color digital image, even an inexpensive monochrome laser printer can churn one out for you in a few seconds. Perhaps you need the quick-and-dirty copy to paste into a layout or to distribute for approval in cases where the color and resolution aren't important to the approval process. If you need a lot of copies quickly and cheaply (for example, you'd like 200 "Have You Seen Our Missing Kitten?" posters,) a black-and-white laser printer is great.

Color page printers work in much the same way as their black-and-white cousins. However, each image is run through the exposure, image writing, and toning steps four times, once each for cyan, magenta, yellow, and black portions of the image. Obviously, separate toning stations must be provided inside the printer for each color, making for a large, bulky device. Once all four colors of toner are transferred to the electrically charged drum or belt, they are transferred to the paper and permanently heat-fused to the paper.

Because of their complexity, color page printers are often considerably more expensive (priced at $3,000 or more) than any of the technologies described next. Laser-type color printers typically don't provide quality that is as good as other types of printers for photographic output, but they do much better on fine lines and text. These printers are best suited for spot color—images with specific elements that must be represented in cyan, magenta, yellow, red, green, blue, or some other shade. The consumables cost for ordinary paper and the color toners is likely to be less than it would be for an ink jet printer, so if you have many images to print, a color laser can reduce your incremental per-print costs.

Ink Jet Printers

I knew the computer age had reached my small town (population 10,000) when I turned down an unfamiliar aisle of our new grocery supercenter and was confronted with an eye-opening shelf display. It was amazing to realize that if I ever had a printing emergency at 3 A.M. on a holiday, I could trot down to our all-night grocery and purchase a backup ink jet printer for $50. These ubiquitous peripherals were located in the school supplies section between the CD-Rs and the packaging tape.

Ink jet printers have come to dominate the low-cost printer market, chiefly because they are low in cost (surprise!), and probably more important for digital photographers, they can produce hard copies that look very much like conventional glossy or matte photographs. A $100 printer that can produce vivid 8.5×11-inch photos is hard to beat.

If you've owned an ink jet model, however, you know there is a darker side to these devices. The consumables costs can eat you alive. Start with the paper or plastic substrate onto which prints are made. Most ink jet printers can make decent looking prints on ordinary paper that costs only a few cents a sheet. However, in practice, their output really doesn't shine until you use special "photo" papers (I'll explain why shortly) that cost $.50 to $1 a sheet or more. A buck per print isn't cheap, especially if you like to experiment or if you make many mistakes.

But wait, there's more. Color ink cartridges can cost $25 to $35 each, and generally they must be used in conjunction with a black-and-white ink cartridge, priced at $20 and up. Some printers use two-color cartridges (a "strong" color cart and a "weak" color cart) to provide additional tones. Although you may get hundreds of pages printed if you're outputting only text, once you start printing photographs, your ink consumption rises dramatically. Achieving only 20 to 30 full-page, full-color images from a $35 ink cartridge isn't uncommon, raising your cost to $1 per print for ink alone.

If your particular printer's ink cartridge includes all three colors in a single module, you may find that one color runs out more quickly than the other colors (because, say, you're printing images that contain scads of yellow). In this case, you must throw away a cartridge, even when plenty of the other hues remain in the tanks.

Many people have been happy using ink jet refill kits, which come with bottles of ink and one or more syringes and can provide several refills at less cost than a single new cartridge. If you like to tinker and really want to save money, you can try one of these. They work better with some kinds of ink cartridges than others. If your printer has a nozzle built into the printer itself, rather than into the ink cartridge, refills might work OK. If your printer has precision nozzles built into the cartridge instead, those nozzles may wear out after a few refills. It's always better to reuse a cartridge only a few times rather than press your luck, in any case.

My own experience with refills has been horrible. I've managed to coat my fingers, arms, and previously pristine portions of my office with ink. I've encountered cartridges that seemed to dry up after one use. I've gotten sick of cleaning syringes with distilled water between applications, and I've gone to the extra expense of getting disposable syringes. However, lots of people swear by ink jet refilling, even while I am swearing at it.

When you compare the cost of ink jet prints to those created by your photolab, you'll see that your personal, custom-tailored hard copies often don't cost that much more.

Ink jet printers offer good resolution—1440 dpi and up—and the ability to produce color at reasonable prices. Unless you need prints larger than 8.5×14 inches, it's hard to spend more than $300 on an ink jet these days.

How Ink Jets Work

Ink jet printers work exactly as you might think—by spraying a jet of ink onto a piece of paper, under precision computer control. Images are formed one dot at a time with a fine stream of ink, either water based or solid (which is melted just before application) in disposable or (sometimes) refillable ink cartridges. With one common technology, piezoelectric crystals in the print head vibrate as electric current flows through them, issuing carefully timed streams of ink from a tiny nozzle, generating a precisely positioned dot.

Liquid inks tend to soak into the paper. This spreading enlarges the size of the dots, so your 720 dpi printer may produce output that looks no better than 300 dpi when the page dries. Liquid inks can also smear when wet. You may need to use a special paper stock for optimal results with this kind of printer.

The very first ink jet color printers used just three ink tanks—cyan, magenta, and yellow—and simulated black by combining equal quantities of all three colors. Several problems came with that approach. So-called composite blacks tended to be brown and muddy, rather than true black. In addition, black ink is a lot cheaper than colored ink, so it made little sense to use three times as much expensive ink to create black tones. Three-color printers are particularly wasteful when generating black-and-white-only pages, such as pages of text. So, most color ink jet printers today use four tanks, adding black. Some use a total of six color tanks, a "strong" cyan, magenta, and yellow ink plus a diluted "weak" cyan, magenta, and yellow to allow creating many more color combinations.

Dye Sublimation Printers

The third type of color printer uses a thermal process to transfer dye to the printed page. The advantage of thermal dye sublimation is that the heat used to transfer the dye can be varied continuously over a range of 0 to 255, so many different shades of a given color can be printed. The resolution lost through converting images to half-tone dots isn't a factor, allowing these devices to reproduce with photographic quality. If you want the absolute best quality reproduction of your images, a dye sublimation printer is the only way to go.

However, most of the dye sub printers available to consumers at reasonable prices produce only snapshot-size prints. You can't use them for enlargements, and you can't use them to print documents or anything else. If you want to make lots of snapshots, a low-cost printer in this category can be a good choice.

Unlike ink jet printers, the typical dye sub model doesn't complete each line in all four colors before moving on to the next. Instead, each page is printed three or four times, depending on whether a three-color or four-color process is being used. As you might guess, such printers must maintain rigid registration standards to ensure that the dots of each color are positioned properly in relation to those of other colors.

The print head is a component with tiny heating elements, which turn on and off to melt dots of dye coated on a wide roll of plastic film. The roll contains alternating panels of cyan, magenta, yellow (and often black), each the size of the full page. The print head applies all the dots for one color at a time as the page moves past. Then the roll advances to the next color (each panel is used only once), and those dots are printed. After three or four passes, the full-color page is finished.

Because this type of dye sub printer always uses all three or four panels in a set, some capacity is wasted if your image only requires one or two of those colors, or if it applies color only in a small area of a page. On the other hand, it costs no more to produce pages that have heavy color demands (such as overhead transparencies), so, if you do much of this type of work, you may come out ahead of ink jet printers in cost as well as image quality. In addition, the capacity of each roll is precisely predictable: A roll capable of 100 images will produce 100 images—no more, no less.

The dye sub printer's image quality comes from its print head. However, these heaters aren't just switched on and off—their temperature can be precisely controlled to transfer as much or as little dye as required to produce a particular color. The dye sublimates—turns from a solid into a gas, without becoming liquid—and then is absorbed by the polyester substrate of the receiver sheet. However, a special receiver paper with a substrate and coating that accepts the dye transfer is required for this type of printer. Media costs can run to several dollars per page.

Because they don't need dithering to reproduce colors, dye sublimation printers can offer photographic quality without needing as high a linear resolution as other printers. The dots diffuse smoothly into the receiver sheet, producing a smooth blending of colors. However, though you'd never notice that a dye sub printer uses many fewer dots per inch to generate dazzling full-color images, text printed in small sizes and finely detailed line art printed at that resolution definitely suffer from this diffusion. These printers are great for 24-bit images but are less stunning when your bit maps are combined with text or lines.

You might find such output useful for preparing special reports and other photo-intensive material in small quantities. Thermal sublimation printers are expensive (both to buy and to operate), and they are slow. Because these printers are entirely practical for use as color-proofing devices, make sure you get and use a color matching system to calibrate your printer to the final output device.

Other Printer Types

You'll find a variety of other lesser used printer types, each with a particular set of advantages.

For example, thermal wax printers, which use wax instead of ink or dye, aren't as inexpensive as some ink jet models, but they are capable of producing amazing quality at somewhat higher speeds. These printers no longer necessarily require special ultrasmooth paper, and many can now use ordinary paper.

Like an ink-jet printer, solid-ink printers use a block of ink, either wax or resin, which is sprayed directly onto a page. Some apply ink to a drum that rolls against a piece of paper, like an offset printing press.

These *phase change printers* are less finicky about paper quality because any tendency to absorb ink can be ignored. On the other hand, solid inks can produce washed-out overheads when you print on transparency material, so your choice between these two technologies should include that factor as well as the extra ink costs of phase change printers.

Going Professional

Sometimes your best choice for getting the hard copies you need is to let a professional service handle it. Hundreds of eager picture services are ready to create prints for you. They'll print your images directly from your camera's film card or allow you to upload them over the Internet for printing at a remote site.

The easiest way to use a service is to stop in at your local department store and look for one of those stand-alone kiosks, such as the Kodak Picture Maker. This versatile device accepts images in many formats, including memory cards from your camera, plus CDs, diskettes, or even original prints, slides, or negatives. You can fix bad color, remove red eyes, add borders and text, crop, enlarge, or reduce, and then make a print in any of several different sizes.

Search online and you'll find many different services, such as Kodak PhotoNet, which let you upload your images, display them on Web pages, or order prints.

Tips for Getting the Best Digital Prints

If you make prints from your digital images yourself, you'll want to keep these tips in mind to get the best quality and best economy.

- Use your image editor's provision for calibrating your monitor, if available, and any procedures offered for calibrating your scanner to your printer. This will help ensure that what you see (on your monitor) is what you get (in your prints). If you're an advanced worker, learn to use the color matching software provided with your printer.

- If quality is important to you, get the best glossy photographic paper for printing out your images. Experiment with several different stocks to see which you like best. You'll probably find that the paper offered by your printer manufacturer will be fine-tuned for your particular printer.

- Remember to clean your ink jet's print heads periodically and keep the printer's rollers and paper path clean, using the techniques recommended by your printer's manufacturer. (It's easy to damage a printer if you don't know what you're doing.) You'll avoid blurry or spotted prints and un-wanted artifacts, such as visible lines.

- Don't touch your prints after they've emerged from the printer. Give them a chance to dry before you handle them.

- Experiment with special paper stocks that let you get even more use from your digital prints. You'll find paper designed especially for making T-shirt transfers, fabric printing, greeting cards, or overhead transparencies.

- Don't risk ruining one of those expensive sheets in a paper jam. If you're making prints one at a time, load your printer with one sheet of photo paper each time. Load multiple sheets only if you want to print many pages unattended, and even then make sure that only photo paper is loaded.

- Avoid disappointment by not blowing up your digital images more than the resolution of your camera allows. Use these guidelines as a rule of thumb:

Resolution guidelines.	
Camera Resolution	Recommended Maximum Print Size
640×480 pixels	3.5×5 inches
1024×768 pixels	5×7 inches
1,280×960 pixels	8×10 inches
1,600×1,200 pixels	11×14 inches
2,400×3,600 pixels	20×30 inches

Next Up

This chapter concludes the tutorial portion of our program. The next steps are all yours: to take what you've learned and apply that knowledge to creating your own digital masterpieces. If the last months are any indication, we can look forward to cheaper, sharper, more fully featured, and easier-to-use digital cameras and printers in the near future, so your skills and capabilities can only grow with the technology. Good luck!

Appendix

Image Editing Software

You've taken the best picture ever captured
on silicon, except for that unfortunate
poster in the background with the
television puppet scowling over your
subject's left shoulder. Here's a list of image
editing software that will let you make
everything picture-perfect.

Choosing Image Editing Software

Fully featured or fully usable? Do you have to make a choice? Certainly, you don't want to spend the rest of your life learning to use a professional-quality graphics editor, unless you are a professional, in which case learning Photoshop will, indeed, become your life's work. Everyone else, on the other hand, wants a combination of ease of use with features that will actually remove red-eye, disguise facial blemishes, remove unwanted objects, or fix bad color. Fortunately, many vendors with a broad range of image editing software packages are vying for your dollars. Some packages are no-brain picture fixers for those who really don't want to get involved. Others have tools you can easily master to gain real domination over the most stubbornly imperfect image. Then there are the high-end applications that may cost more than your digital camera. Here's a list of some of the leading contenders. These all work well with a variety of file formats, from JPEG (Joint Photo-graphic Experts Group) to TIFF (tagged image file format), and most of them also support Photoshop-style plug-ins, so you can use them with Eye Candy and other third-party filters described in Chapter 11.

Adobe Photoshop Elements

This is the newest offering in the Adobe line, intended to replace the "lite" versions of Photoshop that are provided with many scanners and digital cameras. Available for both Windows and Mac OS, Photoshop Elements looks and works much like Photoshop itself, with full access to creating images on layers, all the popular Photoshop filters, and other tools. The best news is that at $99 it's priced less than one-sixth of Photoshop's suggested retail price. I recommend this package for those who are willing to learn a fully featured application but can't afford or don't need Photoshop.

Adobe Photoshop

The latest Version 7.0 introduced early in 2002 cemented Photoshop's position as the number one graphics professional's tool. If you get paid for your pictures, you need to understand Photoshop. Not knowing Photoshop puts a professional photographer at a disadvantage, whereas understanding its finer points can mean gainful employment for life. Photoshop has all the tools for correcting, retouching, and compositing images, as well as features that let you output images in formats for commercial reproduction. Be prepared to spend a lot of time learning Photoshop and set aside some money for buying

Photoshop tutorial books. In the last decade, I've made a decent part of my living writing a dozen or so Photoshop books that help perplexed users avoid duplicating the mistakes I made.

Adobe PhotoDeluxe

This is one of those no-brainer programs, filled with wizards (called Guided Activities) that take you step-by-step through the most common photo-editing tasks. You can remove red-eye, touch up images, correct color, share photos via email, or create calendars and postcards using the built-in templates. I recommend this package for only those who will do light-duty image manipulation. Like Photoshop and Elements, PhotoDeluxe is available for both Windows and Mac OS.

ArcSoft Imaging Software

The last six or seven scanners I've reviewed (and my Nikon digital camera) came with ArcSoft's product, so the company has to be attracting a lot of attention. It includes four easy-to-use components: Photo Studio for image editing; Photo Printer for creating multi-image layouts; Photo Montage, which creates those interesting photos assembled out of a zillion microscopic images; and Photo Fantasy, which produces creative background effects. If you want only the Photo Studio component, it's available separately for both Windows and Mac OS for about $40.

Corel Photo-Paint

Corel Photo-Paint, available in a Digital Camera Edition furnished with some cameras, is virtually the equal of Photoshop in many respects, and there are plenty of professionals who prefer it. The Windows and Mac OS versions are priced roughly the same as Photoshop, too, but you can usually find a competitive upgrade offer for a tiny fraction of the list price. Photo-Paint's strengths include its library of textures, varied brush types, and ability to import and edit multilayered Photoshop PSD files. If becoming a Photoshop expert isn't an important career move, you may prefer Photo-Paint's simpler interface.

Corel Custom Photo

This is Corel's consumer image editing package, along the lines of Adobe PhotoDeluxe, complete with T-shirt transfer, postcards, calendar, and other projects. One plus is 10,000 stock photo and line art images you can add to your own pictures. If you like a lot of hand holding and step-by-step wizardry, this Windows/Mac OS program may appeal to you. Its $25 list price is also appealing.

JASC Paint Shop Pro

One of the all-time top shareware programs graduated to a full commercial product a few years ago, and the reason for its success is an incredible range of tools and features at a price of around $100. It has multiple layers, sophisticated selection tools, retouching capabilities, and a ton of special effects (more than 75 at last count). You can work with an amazing 40 different file formats, use pressure sensitive tablets to draw with a stylus, and create optimized Web graphics. As befits its shareware origins, a 30-day trial version is available for download at the company's Web site (**http:// www.jasc.com**). Paint Shop Pro is available only in a Windows edition.

MGI PhotoSuite

MGI's product is especially good for those who want to create pictures for Web sites. It includes templates for building photo-oriented Web pages and sites without exploring the intricacies of HTML. PhotoSuite also excels at creating animations and panoramas and includes all of the expected image editing tools. Unfortunately, Mac owners are left out in the cold with this Windows-only product.

Microsoft PictureIt!

The PictureIt! line is a family of products that include the capabilities of Microsoft's old PictureIt! software with those of the discontinued PhotoDraw. Many different versions are available, all priced under $60, and with an Adobe PhotoDeluxe wannabe flavor. PictureIt! Photo has a modest complement of stock photos and a very simple interface, whereas its sibling, PictureIt! Publishing (itself available in Silver, Gold, and Platinum versions), is oriented toward projects such as greeting cards and newsletters. The top-of-the-line PictureIt! Photo Premium has more advanced tools for correcting red-eye, improving brightness, sharpness, and color and has image management features in the form of a gallery. This product is available only for Windows.

Ulead Systems Photo Impact

Photo Impact has long been a favorite image editor of mine, both for its ease of use and extensive options as well as its interesting palette of features. I'm still using a 1996 version of Photo Impact's album program (because later versions removed some features that were vital to me), despite some minor incompatibilities with Windows 2000. The latest edition has no such drawbacks and boasts a nice set of capabilities, including the ability to generate complete Web pages, including your images. This Windows-only application has great batch processing capabilities that let you perform the same tasks on a series of images automatically. Chalk this one up as a powerful, but easily learned, image editor.

Ulead Systems Photo Express

If you can tolerate banner ads running through your application, you can download and use this simple image editor for free. Without the ads, it costs just $30. It does little more than adjust your photos with simple features such as rotation, color correction, resizing, brightness/contrast controls, and minor fix-ups. It also creates and displays slide shows and prints your images for you, either in full size or in easy-to-review contact sheets. This is another Windows-only product.

Glossary

This glossary includes definitions of the important digital camera and photography words used in this book, plus many that aren't which you might encounter as you produce and work with images.

additive primary colors—Red, green, and blue, which are used to create all other colors when direct, or transmitted, light is used (for example, on a computer monitor).

airbrush—An artist's tool that sprays a fine mist of paint. You'll find a version of this tool in most image editing software.

ambient lighting—The overall nondirectional lighting that fills an area. That is, light that doesn't come from a specific light source but, instead bounces off walls, ceilings, and other objects to provide soft illumination. See also *backlighting*.

animated GIF—A GIF (graphics interchange format) file that contains the multiple images of an animation; these images are displayed one after another by a Web browser to produce the illusion of movement.

antialias—A process in image editors that smoothes the rough edges in images.

aperture preferred—A camera setting that allows you to specify the lens opening that will be used; the camera selects the appropriate shutter speed automatically. See also *shutter preferred*.

artifact—An unintentional image element produced in error by a digital camera or scanner or inaccurate software. Dirty optics are one common reason for artifacts.

aspect ratio—The proportions of an image, for example, an 8×10-inch or 4×5-inch photo each have a 4:5 aspect ratio.

autoexposure—A camera setting that allows the camera to determine automatically the f-stop and shutter speed.

autofocus—A camera setting that allows the camera to choose automatically the correct focus.

automatic document feeder (ADF)—A device attached to a scanner that automatically feeds one page at a time, allowing the scanning of multiple pages.

background—In photography, the area behind your main subject of interest. On a Web page, the color or pattern of a Web page on which text and images are displayed. Also, a background can be the bottom layer of an image or the area behind layers in an image editor.

backlighting—A lighting effect produced when the main light source is located behind the subject. If no front lighting, fill lighting, or ambient lighting is used with backlighting, the effect is a silhouette. See also *front lighting; fill lighting; ambient lighting.*

balance—In composition, having equal elements on all sides of an image so it doesn't appear lopsided.

bandwidth—The amount of information that a communications link can carry at one time.

bilevel—An image that stores only black-and-white information, with no gray tones; Photoshop calls such images bitmaps.

bit—A binary digit—either a 1 or a 0. Scanners typically use multiple bits to represent information about each pixel of an image. A 1-bit scan can store only black or white information about a pixel. A 2-bit scan can include four different gray levels. Other values include 15- and 16-bit images (with 32,767 and 65,535 colors, respectively) and 24-bit images (with 16.8 million colors).

bitmap—An image that represents each pixel as a cell in a row and column format.

black—The color formed by the absence of reflected or transmitted light, for example, the combination of 100 percent values of cyan, magenta, and yellow ink (in the subtractive color system) or 0 values of red, green, and blue light (in the additive color system).

bleed—A printed image that extends to the edge of a page, often accomplished by trimming a larger image to a finished size.

blend—To create a more realistic transition between image areas. Image editing software, such as Photoshop, allows you to merge overlapping sections of images to blend the boundary between them.

blur—To reduce the contrast between pixels that form edges in an image, thus softening it.

brightness—The amount of light and dark shades in an image. The relative lightness or darkness of the color, usually measured as a percentage from 0 percent (black) to 100 percent (white).

burn—In photography, to expose part of a print for a longer period, making it darker than it would be with a straight exposure.

calibration—A process used to correct for the variation in the output of a device such as a printer or monitor when compared to the original image and the data received from the scanner.

camera ready—Artwork already laid out as a hard copy in a form usable for producing negatives or plates for printing.

capture modes—Settings that dictate the rate at which images are captured. You may be able to take several photos per second, multiple images on the same frame, or minimovies using various capture modes.

cast—A tinge of color in an image, usually an undesired color.

CCD (charge-coupled device)—A type of solid-state sensor used in scanners and digital cameras.

center of interest—The main area of a photo that you want the viewer to focus on.

chroma—Color or hue.

chromatic color—A color with at least one hue available, with a visible level of color saturation.

chrome—Photographer-talk for a color transparency, such as Kodachrome, Ektachrome, or Fujichrome.

CIE (Commission Internationale de l'Eclairage)—An international organization of scientists who work with matters relating to color and lighting. The organization is also called the International Commission on Illumination.

close-up lens—A lens add-on that allows you to take pictures a distance that is less than the closest-focusing distance of the lens alone.

CMYK color model—A way of defining all possible colors in percentages of cyan, magenta, yellow, and black, commonly used for reproducing images in print.

color correction—Changing the color balance of an image to produce a desired effect, usually a more accurate representation of the colors in an image. It is used to compensate for the deficiencies of process color inks, inaccuracies in a color separation, or an undesired color balance in the original image. Color correction is done using one of several available color models, including RGB and CMYK.

comp—A layout that combines type, graphics, and photographic material, also called a composite or comprehensive.

CompactFlash—A type of memory card storage for digital cameras and other computer devices.

compression—Reducing the size of a file by encoding using smaller sets of numbers that don't include redundant information. Some kinds of compression, such as JPEG (Joint Photographic Experts Group), can degrade images, whereas others, including GIF (graphics interchange format) and TIFF (tagged image file format), preserve all the detail in the original.

concept of thirds—In composition, arranging important objects in an image so that they fall at the intersections of imaginary lines located one third of the way from the top, bottom, and sides of the borders.

continuous tone—Images that contain tones from the darkest to the lightest, with an infinite range of variations in between.

contrast—The range between the lightest and darkest tones in an image. A high-contrast image is one in which the shades fall at the extremes of the range between white and black. In a low-contrast image, the tones are closer together.

crop—To trim an image or page by adjusting the boundaries.

density—The ability of an object to stop or absorb light. The less the light is reflected or transmitted by an object, the higher its density.

depth of field—The range in which portions of an image are acceptably sharp.

desaturate—To reduce the purity or vividness of a color. Desaturated colors appear washed out and diluted.

diffusion—The random distribution of gray tones in an area of an image.

digital zoom—A digital camera's capability of producing a zoom effect by using only a portion of the sensor image to fill a frame. See also *optical zoom*.

digitize—To convert information, usually analog information, such as that found in continuous tone images, to a numeric format that can be accepted by a computer.

dither—A method of distributing pixels to extend the visual range of color on screen, such as producing the effect of shades of gray on a black-and-white display or more colors on an 8-bit color display. By making adjacent pixels different colors, dithering gives the illusion of a third color.

dodging—A photographic term for blocking part of an image as it is exposed, lightening its tones.

dot—A unit used to represent a portion of an image. A dot can correspond to one of the pixels used to capture or show an image on the screen, or groups of pixels can be collected to produce larger printer dots of varying sizes to represent gray or colors.

dot gain—The tendency of a printing dot to grow from the original size when halftoned to its final printed size on paper. This effect is most pronounced on offset presses using poor quality papers, which allow ink to absorb and spread.

dots per inch (dpi)—The resolution of an image, expressed in the number of pixels or printer dots in an inch. Scanner resolution is also commonly expressed in dpi, but, technically, scanners use an optical technique that makes samples per inch a more accurate term.

dummy—A rough approximation of a publication, used to evaluate the layout.

dye sublimation—A printing technique in which solid inks are heated directly into a gas, which then diffuses into a polyester substrate to form an image. Because dye sublimation printers can reproduce 256 different hues for each color, they can print as many as 16.7 million different colors.

emulsion—The light-sensitive coating on a piece of film, paper, or printing plate.

existing light—Illumination that is already present in a scene.

export—To transfer text or images from a document to another format.

eyedropper—A tool used to sample color from one part of an image, so it can be used to paint or draw elsewhere.

file format—A way in which a particular application stores information on a disk.

fill—To cover a selected area with a tone or pattern. Fills can be solid, transparent, or have a gradient transition from one color or tone to another.

fill lighting—Lighting used to illuminate shadows. See also *backlighting*.

fill-in flash—Use of electronic flash, particularly in daylight, to provide additional illumination in the shadows.

FireWire—The IEEE-1394 specification for a high-speed serial interface, used to link scanners and (in the future) digital cameras and other devices to computers.

focal length—A measurement used to represent the magnification of a lens.

focus range—The range in which a camera can bring objects into sharp focus.

framing—In composition, using elements of an image to form a picture frame around an important subject.

front lighting—Illumination that comes from the direction of the camera. See also *backlighting*.

f-stop—The lens aperture, which helps determine both exposure and depth of field.

filter—In image editors, a feature that changes the pixels in an image to produce blurring, sharpening, and other special effects. In photography, a device that fits over the lens, changing the light in some way.

flat—A low-contrast image.

flatbed scanner—A type of scanner that reads an image one line at a time, recording it as a series of samples, or pixels, by bouncing light off the area it needs to digitize.

four-color printing—Another term for process color, in which cyan, magenta, yellow, and black inks are used to reproduce all the hues of the spectrum.

FPO (for position only)—Artwork deemed not good enough for reproduction, used to help evaluate a page layout.

frequency—The number of lines per inch in a halftone screen.

full-color image—An image that uses 24-bit color (16.8 million possible hues).

galley—A typeset copy of a publication used for proofreading and estimating length.

gamma—A numerical way of representing the contrast of an image, shown as the slope of a line showing tones from white to black. Gamma is a method of tonal correction that takes the human eye's perception of neighboring values into account. Gamma values range from 1.0 to about 2.5. The Macintosh has traditionally used a gamma of 1.8, which is relatively flat compared to television. Windows PCs use a 2.2 gamma value, which has more contrast and is more saturated.

gamma correction—A method for changing the brightness, contrast, or color balance of an image by assigning new values to the gray or color tones of an image. Gamma correction can be either linear or nonlinear. Linear correction applies the same amount of change to all the tones. Nonlinear correction varies the changes tone by tone or in highlight, midtone, and shadow areas separately to produce a more accurate or improved appearance.

gamut—The range of viewable and printable colors for a particular color model, such as RGB (used for monitors) or CMYK (used for printing).

gang scan—The process of scanning more than one picture at a time.

Gaussian blur—A method of diffusing an image by using a bell-shaped curve to calculate which pixels will be blurred, rather than blurring all pixels in the selected area uniformly.

GIF87a and GIF89a—The graphics interchange formats used for Web applications and for saving animations. GIF is a lossless-compression format that compresses the image through reduction of the available colors. GIF87a does not support transparency. GIF89a is used to make selected colors invisible on a Web browser.

grayscale image—An image represented using 256 shades of gray.

halftone—A method used to reproduce continuous-tone images, reducing the image to a series of dots.

highlight—The lightest part of an image.

HTML (Hypertext Markup Language)—One of the programming languages used to create Web pages.

hue—The color of light that is reflected from an opaque object or transmitted through a transparent one.

import—To load text or images from a particular format into a document.

indexed color image—An image with 256 different colors.

interlacing—A way of displaying an image, particularly interlaced GIF (graphics interchange format) or JPEG (Joint Photographic Experts Group) images, in multiple fields, for example, odd-numbered lines first, then even-numbered lines, thereby updating or refreshing half the image on the screen at a time, allowing visitors to view a rough version of an image even before the entire file has been downloaded from a Web page.

interpolation—A technique used to calculate the value of the new pixels required whenever you resize or change the resolution of an image, based on the values of surrounding pixels.

invert—To change an image into its negative—black becomes white, white becomes black, dark gray becomes light gray, and so forth. Colors are also changed to the complementary color; green becomes magenta, blue turns to yellow, and red is changed to cyan.

ISO (International Standards Organization or International Organization for Standardization)—A rating that measures the relative sensitivity of film or the equivalent sensitivity of a digital camera's sensor.

jaggies—Staircasing effect of lines that are not perfectly horizontal or vertical, caused by pixels that are too large to represent the line accurately.

JPEG (Joint Photographic Experts Group)—A file format that supports 24-bit color and reduces file sizes by selectively discarding image data.

landscape—The orientation of a page in which the longest dimension is horizontal, also called wide orientation.

latency—The time between when you press the shutter release button and when the camera actually takes the picture.

LCD (liquid crystal display)—In digital photography, the display screen used to provide a preview of the image as seen by the sensor. Often, the camera will have a second, monochrome LCD to show various status indicators, such as how many pictures remain.

lens aperture—The lens opening that admits light to the film or sensor. The size of the lens aperture is usually measured in f-stops.

lens flare—An effect produced by the reflection of light internally among elements of an optical lens. Bright light sources within or just outside the field of view cause lens flare. It can be reduced by the use of coatings on the lens elements or with the use of lens hoods. Photographers sometimes use the effect as a creative technique.

lens hood—A device that shades the lens, protecting it from extraneous light outside the actual picture area. Also called a lens shade.

lighten—An image editing function that is the equivalent to the photographic darkroom technique of dodging. Gray tones in a specific area of an image are gradually changed to lighter values.

line art—Usually, images that consist only of white pixels and one color, such as pen and ink illustrations.

line screen—The resolution or frequency of a halftone screen, expressed in lines per inch.

lithography—Another name for traditional offset printing.

lossless compression—An image-compression scheme that preserves image detail. When the image is decompressed, it is identical to the original version.

lossy compression—An image-compression scheme that creates smaller files but can affect image quality by dropping some of the image's details.

luminance—The brightness or intensity of an image. Determined by the amount of gray in a hue, luminance reflects the lightness or darkness of a color. See also *saturation*.

LZW compression—A method of compacting TIFF (tagged image file format) or certain other types of files using the Lempel-Ziv Welch compression algorithm.

macro photography—Close-up photography.

maximum aperture—The largest lens opening or f-stop available with a particular lens or with a zoom lens at a particular magnification.

mechanical—Camera-ready copy with text and art already in position for photographing.

midtones—Parts of an image with tones of an intermediate value, usually in the 25 to 75 percent range.

moiré—An objectionable pattern caused by the interference of halftone screens, frequently generated by rescanning an image that has already been halftoned.

monochrome—Having a single color.

negative—A representation of an image in which the tones are reversed. That is, blacks are shown as white, and vice versa, and colors are reversed to their complements.

neutral color—In RGB mode, a color in which red, green, and blue are present in equal amounts, producing a gray.

noise—In an image, pixels with randomly distributed color values. Noise in digital photographs tends to be the product of low-light conditions, particularly when you have set your camera to a higher ISO rating than normal.

optical zoom—The magnification produced by a lens by adjusting the elements in the lens. See also *digital zoom*.

parallax compensation—An adjustment made by the camera or photographer to account for the difference in views between the taking lens and the viewfinder.

Photo CD—A special type of CD-ROM developed by Eastman Kodak Company that can store high-quality photographic images, along with music and other data, in a special space-saving format.

pixel—A picture element of a screen image.

pixels per inch (ppi)—The number of pixels that can be displayed per inch, usually used to refer to pixel resolution from a scanned image or on a monitor.

plug-in—A module that can be accessed from within a program such as Photoshop to provide special functions. Many plug-ins are image-processing filters that offer special effects.

point—Approximately 1/72 of an inch outside the Macintosh world, exactly 1/72 of an inch within it.

portrait—The orientation of a page in which the longest dimension is vertical, also called tall orientation. In photography, a formal picture of an individual or, sometimes, a group.

prepress—The stages of the reproduction process that precede printing, when pages of text and images are laid out, and halftones, color separations, and printing plates are created.

process color—The four color pigments used in color printing: cyan, magenta, yellow, and black (CMYK).

red-eye—An effect from flash photography that appears to make a person or animal's eyes glow red. It's caused by light bouncing from the retina of the eye and is most pronounced in dim illumination (when the irises are wide open) and when the electronic flash is close to the lens and therefore prone to reflect directly back.

red-eye reduction—Any of several methods of reducing or eliminating the red-eye phenomenon. Simply placing the flash farther away from the taking lens works. Some cameras offer a red-eye reduction mode that uses a preflash that causes the irises of the subjects' eyes to decrease in size just prior to emission of a second, stronger flash that is used to take the picture.

reflection copy—Original artwork that is viewed by light reflected from its surface, rather than transmitted through it.

register—To align images, usually different versions of the same page or sheet.

registration mark—A mark that appears on a printed image, generally for color separations, to help in aligning the printing plates.

resample—To change the size or resolution of an image. Resampling down discards pixel information in an image; resampling up adds pixel information through interpolation.

resolution—In digital photography, the number of pixels a camera or scanner can capture.

retouch—To edit an image, most often to remove flaws or to create a new effect.

RGB color mode—A color mode that represents the three colors—red, green, and blue—used by devices such as scanners or monitors to represent color.

saturation—The purity of color; the amount by which a pure color is diluted with white or gray. See also *luminance*.

scale—To change the size of a piece of an image.

scanner—A device that captures an image of a piece of artwork and converts it to a bit-mapped image that the computer can handle.

seamless paper—Long rolls of wide paper used as backdrops for photography.

selection—An area of an image chosen for manipulation, usually surrounded by a moving series of dots called a selection border.

sensitivity—A measure of the degree of response of a film or sensor to light.

shadow—The darkest part of an image, represented on a digital image by pixels with low numeric values or on a halftone by the smallest or absence of dots.

sharpening—Increasing the apparent sharpness of an image by boosting the contrast between adjacent pixels that form an edge.

shutter preferred—An exposure mode in which you set the shutter speed, and the camera determines the appropriate f-stop. See also *aperture preferred*.

SLR (single lens reflex)—A camera in which the viewfinder sees the same image as the film or sensor.

SmartMedia—A type of memory card storage for digital cameras and other computer devices.

smoothing—To blur the boundaries between edges of an image, often to reduce a rough or jagged appearance.

solarization—In photography, an effect produced by exposing film to light partially through the developing process. Some of the tones are reversed, generating an interesting effect. In digital photography, the same effect is produced by combining some positive areas of the image with some negative areas.

spot color—Ink used in a print job in addition to black or the standard process colors.

step-up/step-down rings—Adapters that allow using filters and other lens accessories with lenses that have front diameters that are larger or smaller than the accessory was designed for.

subtractive primary colors—Cyan, magenta, and yellow, which are the printing inks that theoretically absorb all color and produce black.

telephoto—A lens or lens setting that magnifies an image.

thermal wax transfer—A printing technology in which dots of wax from a ribbon are applied to paper when heated by thousands of tiny elements in a printhead.

threshold—A predefined level used by the scanner to determine whether a pixel will be represented as black or white.

thumbnail—A miniature copy of a page or image that provides a preview of the original.

TIFF (tagged image file format)—A standard graphics file format that can be used to store grayscale and color images plus selection masks.

time exposure—A picture taken by leaving the lens open for a long period, usually more than 1 second. The camera is generally locked down with a tripod to prevent blur during the long exposure.

tint—A color with white added to it. In graphic arts, often refers to the percentage of one color added to another.

tolerance—The range of color or tonal values that will be selected, with a tool such as the Magic Wand, or filled with paint, when using a tool such as Paint Bucket.

transparency scanner—A type of scanner that captures color slides or negatives.

tripod—A three-legged device used to steady and support a camera during framing and exposure. Single-legged versions called unipods are also available.

unsharp masking—The process for increasing the contrast between adjacent pixels in an image, increasing sharpness.

USB (Universal Serial Bus)—A high-speed serial communication method commonly used to connect digital cameras and other devices to a computer.

viewfinder—The device in a camera used to frame the image. With an SLR (single lens reflex) camera, the viewfinder is also used to focus the image, if focusing manually. You can also focus an image with the LCD display of a digital camera, which is a type of viewfinder.

vignetting—Dark corners of an image, often produced by using a lens hood that is too small for the field of view but that also can be produced later within an image editor.

white balance—The adjustment of a digital camera to the color temperature of the light source. Interior illumination is relatively red; outdoors light is relatively blue. Digital cameras often set correct white balance automatically or let you do it through menus.

white point—The lightest pixel in the highlight area of an image.

zoom—To enlarge or reduce the size of an image using the magnification settings of a lens.

Index

overview, 117–118
portrait studio, 144
versus unipod, 199
Tripod socket, 11
Twirl filter, 259

U

Ulead PhotoImpact Album, 228
Ultra-high-speed mode, 215
Ultrafine resolution, 29
Umbrellas, 147–149
Unipod, 199, 213
Unity, 96
Unsharp masking filters, 248, 252
USB/serial port, 11, 50

V

Variations mode, 239–240
Velour cloths, 113, 120, 141
Vertical lines, 95
Vertical orientation, 92, 95, 222–224, 245
Vertical supports, 143
Viewfinder
    cropping photos, 132
    location on camera, 11
    options, 33–34
    parallax errors, 131–133
Viewing frames, 79, 193
Vignetting, 68
Voice message, 34
Vortex Tiling tool, 255

W

Washed-out photograph, 128
Web graphics
    animated GIFs, 276–278
    browsers, 266, 268–269, 270–271
    colors, 268, 270, 271
    download time, 266, 268, 270, 273, 277
    emailing, 279

file size, 270–273
GIF files, 270–271, 274–278, 279
guidelines for, 266–268
JPEG files, 271–272
main page graphics, 273
minimovies, 277
resolution, 28, 266, 268–269, 271
screen size, 266, 268–269
sharpness of, 268
thumbnail images, 273
transparent GIFs, 271, 274–276
White balance control, 78, 121, 235
White cardboard, 120
Wide-angle lens. *See also* Lenses.
    image emphasis, 90
    overview, 67–68, 69
    protraits, 165
Wrestling, 204

X

Xenofex, 258

Z

ZDNet, 46, 49
Zoom, digital, 25, 65
Zoom, optical, 25, 65
Zoom lens. *See also* Lenses.
    action photography, 195
    characteristics of, 64–65
    depth of field, 61–62, 63
    f-stops, 60
    focal length, 26
    location on camera, 11
    maximum aperture, 65
    overview, 25
    ranges, 65
Zoom ratio, 8, 195
Zooming
    composition, 84–85
    definition, 64
    and electronic flash, 128